Cheap Cabernet

A Friendship

CATHIE BECK

voice

HYPERION   NEW YORK

This is a work of nonfiction. I have changed some of the names and identifying characteristics of persons discussed in the book to protect their
identities. I have also, at times, combined certain characters to allow for
narrative sense. Memory can be a faulty device, but I have tried faith-
fully to recount the circumstances as best as I lived and remembered
them. —*C. B.*

Library of Congress Cataloging-in-Publication Data

Beck, Cathie.
Cheap cabernet : a friendship / Cathie Beck. — 1st ed.
p. cm.
ISBN 978-1-4013-4154-1
1. Beck, Cathie.   2. Journalists—United States—
Biography.   I. Title.
PN4874.B15A3 2010
070.92—dc22
[B]
2010008319

Hyperion books are available for special promotions, premiums,
or corporate training. For details contact the HarperCollins Special
Markets Department in the New York office at 212-207-7528,
fax 212-207-7222, or email spsales@harpercollins.com.

FIRST EDITION

10 9 8 7 6 5 4 3 2 1

To

J. L. and C. A.

CONTENTS

CONTENTS

ACKNOWLEDGMENTS

Get an agent you privately nickname "Stealth Bomber" because that's how she operates: cool, quietly, collected, and effective to make your heart stop. Make sure she's got the heart mine does, one larger than the New Orleans Superdome, with the combined literary sensibilities of Dorothy Parker and Frank McCourt.

Have the Stealth Bomber secure you an editor that is part Lisa Lampinelli, part Anna Wintour, and part Amanda Farrow. Make sure she kicks your ass on a (almost) daily basis into whipping long and winding copy into publishable shape. Make sure you tell her how much she means to you and how lucky you know you are.

A million thanks to "Stealth Bomber" Dorian Karchmar at William Morris Endeavor and "Amanda Farrow" Brenda Copeland at Hyperion/Voice for listening, for pushing back, and for gracefully allowing me to push back.

Then remember all the people who've helped to bring a notion, a thought of a book, to fruition, which is what I'll try to do here. I apologize to those I may have forgotten (for the moment). Trust me, I'll never forget you and your help and your unfailing support over the long haul. They include (but are not limited to):

Jennifer Breslin and Craig Cummings; Neil and Jane Beck; Pauline, Patrice, Margie, Tom, and Eddie Beck.

Pam Burrell and Liz Toomey, Andi Duitch, Deb Gerring, Deb Sperlak, Devron Campbell, Eddie Moore, Elle Newmark, Emerson Schwartzkopf, Freddy Page, *Glimmer Train* literary anthology, Heather Gallien, Herb Rubenstein, Jim and Kathy Hay, K. Schipper, Kevin Dorr, Lauren Woosley, Louisiana Tech University's Journalism School, Maia Tress, Annette Shope, Sara Wade, Teresa Sanders, Mary Bennett, Mike Duitch, Mrs. Anderson, Cathedral Catholic Grade School's 1963–64 third-grade teacher, Rebecca Anderson, Richard Duncan, Wendy Fopeano, Rick Evans, Rufus Wright, Sandi Gelles-Cole, Shelli Bennett, Susan Gatschet-Reese, Teah Bennett, the Denver Women's Press Club, Belinda Litchko, Laura Taylor, the *Louisiana Press* Women, Tom Hay, Esther and Mike Ableidinger, Al and Nancy Kelsey, Bob and Janice Brown, and Tracy Rogers. Desiree Nowaczyk, Sloan Dorr, Sean Prentiss, Kathryn, Winnie, Lydia, Aunt Verna, James Murray, Michelle Wallace, Christine, and all the other gems who read and then helped *Cheap Cabernet* get out there (and who also so lovingly offered feedback)—too many to mention here—you will never, ever be forgotten and words alone are not enough to even begin to express my appreciation and love.

"I wanted a perfect ending. Now I've learned, the hard way, that some poems don't rhyme, and some stories don't have a clear beginning, middle, and end. Life is about not knowing, having to change, taking the moment and making the best of it, without knowing what's going to happen next."

—Gilda Radner

"People think you're a twit if you twirl. It's a prejudice of the unknowing."

—Jane Martin, "Twirler"

Tommy Lee Jones's Ass
Summer 1997

We are hurtling north of Denver on Interstate 25 in Denise's death-trap, bottle-cap excuse of a car, at eighty-three miles per hour, with the plan to stalk Jerry Jeff Walker of "Mr. Bojangles" and "Up Against the Wall Redneck Mother" fame.

It's important to note the "Up Against the Wall Redneck Mother" fame because I know nothing of Jerry Jeff Walker or his music. I know he exists and I vaguely remember those two tunes, but that's about it—which mortifies Denise, who owns every single album he's ever produced and who's brought one along for him to autograph. As anyone can plainly see, I'm not the one who's obsessed. I'm also not the one who pretended to be a newspaper reporter, calling every hotel in Fort Collins, Colorado, to find out where he was staying so we could invite him out for a beer.

"Right!" I'd laughed at her earlier in the week when she spilled the plan. "You're just gonna sashay in, order the bell-man to retrieve him, and then the three of us will belly up to the bar?" I can't decide if she's obscenely arrogant or unbelievably naïve. It's hard to tell with her. One minute, she's all boss-lady and making decisions. The next, she's assuming that just because she wants to meet a celebrity, she will.

"Media gets press releases ahead of time," I tell her. "Even *then* they don't get a personal interview."

No, I am not the one who is obsessed; I am just the one along for the ride.

Jerry Jeff Walker is performing tonight at Mellancamp's, a mountain bar known for lime-crusted buffalo wings, bar fights, and the Harley-Davidsons that pack its parking lot. That Denise has never owned, has never even worn a pair of cowboy boots, that she doesn't smoke dope or ride Harleys or eat lime-crusted anything is beside the point.

"Jerry Jeff Walker is *perfect*," she yells above her open window, gunning the engine and then shifting the Geo into third gear. "I mean listen to him. Just shut up and listen." She pushes a cassette into the tape player.

"You don't know *PERFECT*!" I yell back, turning down the volume so she can hear me. "Know what's *really perfect*? Deb's Pizza is perfect. We didn't eat dinner."

"What's Deb's Pizza?" She looks at me like I'm nuts.

"Deb's is a joint from my old neighborhood in Indiana. When we were kids, we'd round up enough change to buy a sixteen-inch with everything on it. The O'Callahans would steal their dad's station wagon while he slept one off, and we'd go gorge ourselves. There's never been pizza built like that since."

The wind whips and thrashes around the car, and we both swipe our hair from our faces. We watch bighorn sheep move up a mountainside in one familial herd. They pause and, all at the same time, lift their heads to us as we rush by.

"No," Denise says and downshifts behind a semi. "You don't have a clue what perfect is." She grins to herself as she says this. "Elvis Presley. Now *that's* perfect. He was perfect to look at, and that voice. Oy, that voice."

"He was a drug addict, and he stole music from blacks who'd been trying to make it in the business for years." I lean toward her so she can hear me as she speeds us around the semi. Then the road's empty, nothing but us and the tarmac. I feel a rush of liberation and danger, winging in her little car along the highway like we're pioneers or something.

"Are we almost there?" I call out.

"The turnoff is right along here somewhere," she says. "It's on a side road, and it should be pretty close." She slows the car and strains to see a sign in the pine trees. "Mellancamp's is beautiful. It sits on the Big Thompson River, and there's a deck over the water. I want to get there early. Maybe we can find Jerry Jeff, say hello, get him to buy us a drink." She says this last part with a smirk, for my benefit.

"We've got another ten miles, according to the map," I tell her. "I'll watch for the turnoff."

Neither of us says anything for a while. We sit in silence and smell the evening air.

"So I had a perfect day one time," I announce, then sit back and feel the drone of the car cruising beneath us. "I ran away to the beach for the entire day. I pretended like I was a grown-up, single woman. I remember pretending I was French."

"What made it perfect?" She swigs on her water bottle and then offers it to me.

I take a swallow and shout back above the wind, "The aloneness. I loved that no one knew I was there, that no one knew me."

In spite of our speeding, an oversize pickup truck pulls alongside Denise's window but, instead of passing, slows to our pace so it's riding right next to us. Denise glances over, and I sit forward to look around her. Three big men lean forward from the front seat. The one closest to us rolls down the window and tips his hat, then turns to the other two and says something we can't hear. They all laugh, and the two guys not driving give us a wave as the truck speeds off.

"Now *that's* perfection," Denise says. She's a little jazzed by the flirtation. "I wonder if they're going to the concert."

"Okay," I say. "What's the most perfect experience you ever had? Just one. The first one that comes to mind, quick," I order. "Don't think about it."

She doesn't. She says right off, "I don't know what made it perfect, but there was this evening in the Bronx, in our apartment, near that diner where I took you for the egg creams. I was sitting at the kitchen table, maybe I was twelve or thirteen, I don't remember. My dad had been at the race-track, and when he got home, he'd won a lot of money. It was finally warm outside, so the windows were open and you could hear people down on the street. My mom had been walking or riding a bike or something. I don't know where my sisters were. It was just me sitting at the table looking out of the window and feeling so glad about everything. There was this brilliant red stripe across the sky. The streetlights were starting to come on. My mom was flushed from her exercise, and my dad thought he was something with that roll of cash in his pocket. He took my mom's hands, and they did a little spin in the living room. They were beautiful together."

I lean back in my seat and swim inside her memory like a dream. The car speeds north and the light shifts along the mountain range. It's hard to make out shapes, and I look toward Denise's side of the car for a turnoff but don't see any. Then a big, graceful bird climbs from a craggy rock outcropping, lifting high and slow, its silhouette slicing across the deep, rust-colored sky.

"An eagle!" I scream and watch it glide beyond the ridge and out of sight.

"Where?" she asks. She leans out the window, straining to find the eagle against the fading light.

"Tommy Lee Jones's ass in *Coal Miner's Daughter*," I say after a moment, tossing her the non sequitur for fun. We both love to ping-pong with each other. Snatch a thought and throw it into the mix. Let the other grab it.

"You're watching for the turnoff, right?" She drops back into the car and turns Jerry Jeff up a little.

"Yeah, I won't miss it." I turn the cassette player back down. "Tommy Lee Jones was Loretta Lynn's Kentucky husband in *Coal Miner's Daughter*," I say. "You should watch the movie just to see his perfect butt."

Denise slows to maneuver the road as it snakes around sage and ragged, red stone ridges. A luxurious, purple-coated fence blurs along the road's shoulder like a broad swash of deep plum-blue paint.

"That's creeping clitoris!" Denise yells. "That entire fence is covered in it!" I look back and see a thick blanket of clematis built of layers, literally years, of flowers.

When I turn back around, there's a road sign coming up. I lean forward, take off my sunglasses, and squint. "Slow down," I say. "Maybe this is it."

WELCOME TO WYOMING.

"*Wyoming?*" we yell together.

She smacks me on the shoulder. "You *missed* it!"

"*I* missed it? I've never been to the stupid place."

"We're forty-five miles too far north," she says and lets the car slow a little, her sense of urgency dissipating. "We'll never get there in time. All the good seats will be taken."

"This is just deserts for trying to trick everyone into letting you meet Jerry Jeff Walker in person," I call out to her over the wind. "Now you don't even get to hear him sing."

Denise laughs. She races the engine, shifts the gears, and speeds up. The next sign reads: CHEYENNE 23, CASPER 179. The next: NO FACILITIES NEXT 20 MILES.

"Where are you going?" I ask. For a moment I'm actually concerned, but then something inside me shifts and I smile. I turn Jerry Jeff Walker up loud and watch Wyoming, a vista of barrenness and lonely plains, open up in front of us.

"Pull out that album I brought," Denise says.

I reach behind her and pull up a record album from the backseat. It's wrapped in old plastic, and tucked inside the cellophane is a 1970s-era, faded, orangish snapshot. I study the girl and the cowboy-hat-wearing guy. He's got his arm around her shoulder, and he beams at the camera, full of himself and his rakish grin. His thumb is cocked through his front belt loop in a jaunty pose. I look closer. The girl is Denise, a barely-out-of-her-teens Denise, with hip-hugger Levi's, a bare midriff, and a shy-girl smile, but Denise nonetheless. I have to ask.

"Who is this?"

"Who do you *think*?"

"Is this you?"

She grins, and I study the picture. But I wouldn't know Jerry Jeff from a jackrabbit.

"I saw him in the restaurant of his hotel," she yells. "It was some performance . . ." Her voice trails off and she glances at the photograph in a way that tells me she's trying to recall when, exactly. "About a million years ago. I invited him to my table, and I bought him a coffee and a prune Danish."

"You couldn't offer him anything better than prune Danish? Why not some carrot cake or a cognac?"

"Did you hear me?" Denise drives easily. "*I* bought prune Danish and coffee for Jerry Jeff Walker." She laughs over at me to see if I'm getting it. "He didn't even offer to pay. Not that I expected him to. I invited *him.* Still."

The cassette tape cover reads: "The Very Best of Jerry Jeff Walker," and it doesn't have his picture on it. I pretend to study the snapshot.

"I don't know," I say and look at her. "I don't think this is him." I hold the picture toward her, to emphasize my point. "This is some cretin you picked up in Boulder. This ain't no Jerry Jeff Walker."

Jerry Jeff belts, and Denise sings along. I listen to her inability to come close to even one note, but she's acting like she's Patsy Cline. She knows every word, and she even inflects little nuances, as she and Jerry Jeff warble on together.

Oh, I like my women just a tad on the trashy side
When they wear their clothes too tight
*   and their hair is dyed*
Too much lipstick and too much rouge
Gets me excited, leaves me feeling confused
I like my women just a tad on the trashy side.

"*This* is perfect! Just fucking *PERFECT*!" she yells. "Woo-woo!" And she tap-a-taps her fingertips on the steering wheel to the beat of the song and dances her shoulders all around. She races us deeper into a state neither of us has ever been to before and, as it turns out, will never go to again. She races her death-defying car so fast I think we might flip and be killed.

And then something lets go in me and I relax.

I quit worrying about why she's heading us toward nowhere in particular, a place that looks like it could use about a week of steady rain, and I sit back and chill. Happiness washes over me, and I am content, glad to be done with the locate-the-turnoff chore, glad to be with my complicated and funny friend.

We don't go home for three days. We just drive and look and eat. We play the radio loud for hours and don't talk. We make friends with two old Indians who run a one-pump gas station in the middle of nowhere. We buy Walgreens toothbrushes and underwear so we can clean up. Then we visit Cheyenne, Casper, and Jackson Hole, sleeping in $39.99-a-night motel rooms.

And she is right. It is perfect.

CHAPTER ONE

Wanted: Women

The September 23, 1994, *Boulder Daily Camera*'s community events calendar ad read:

WOW (Women on the Way)—to an insane asylum, a bar, wherever. Smart, sassy women's group forming. Mutual support, networking, etc. Weds. 7 p.m.

My phone started ringing at 8:00 A.M. The old, the young, the stoned called all morning long wanting to join WOW. One woman called from a hospital bed.

"You're where? St. Joseph's? You're thinking the appendicitis incision won't be so tender next week?"

I was incredulous. Not just at the hospital patient but at the deluge. One dozen phone calls turned into two dozen. I had been hoping for eight.

I'd invented a women's group because I needed friends, preferably the instant kind. I'd just spent half a year living in Russia with Oliver, my eleven-years-my-junior boyfriend, but he'd dumped me the moment our toes touched American soil. My grown daughter and son were living their own lives in states far away. I'd raised them alone and wore my cloak of single-momdom with the martyrlike air of a Judi Dench–inspired queen, and now they were on their own, juggling friends, jobs, and college courses.

Besides, kids aren't friends. Kids fill you with love, melt your heart, make you laugh. But they aren't friends, and all my friends from graduate school had long ago left Colorado to return to their home states. I was completely alone in Boulder, a place so hip, so smug, so over-the-top cosmically *conscious* it made me want to put my finger down my throat, except that the place is also so spectacular, so boundlessly beautiful, I couldn't stay away.

The fall I launched WOW, University of Colorado coeds populated Boulder in tight, high-pitched droves, giddy with anticipation. Brilliant gold aspen leaves blew about the streets like fancy skirts. Everyone had somewhere to go, someone to be with. Everyone, that is, but me.

Suddenly, more than ever, I needed a group of women friends to mitigate what felt like my lifelong loneliness. I don't know why I thought placing an ad was the answer, except to say that for a great many quiet years I had looked for—yearned for—just one other person who was living the same life I was. I'd wanted to find someone else who was young and alone, someone who was raising two children and working two jobs and paying all the bills on a rented three-bedroom duplex. But everyone my age seemed to be sleeping on their parents' couches and scoring nickel bags.

At twenty-three, I could have been in college, traveling abroad, living in strange cities, and experiencing the exciting life of blossoming young adulthood. Instead, I'd been alone with my kids. I couldn't help it, but I was plagued by the feeling that if I had a friend, just one friend with whom I could share my experiences, it would all be better somehow. Now, at thirty-nine, I wasn't leaving friendship to chance.

MY LONELINESS HAD GROWN OUT OF POVERTY AND HER ugly sisters—shame and desperation. It was hard to shrug off. I had spent decades walking the world with my feet simultaneously planted in two distinct places. One was the normal place, the apparently steady ground where I earned a living and managed a so-called normal life. I got up, went to work, did not commit violent crimes or make money in a wet T-shirt or on a pole. My children were clean and safe and healthy.

Even those people who knew my crushing circumstances thought me noble, not desperate. All seemed well.

I had married my first boyfriend my senior year of high school. I was seventeen. He was eighteen. He had been the first boy ever to ask me out, the first male ever to tell me "I love you." I had two children by the time I was nineteen. I was twenty-two when he slunk off in the middle of the night, emptying our meager bank account and driving away in our only car. But everyone agreed that I was managing.

I was an expert at fooling the world and myself, an expert at keeping people away from that other place, the shifting ground where I walked each day. I worked to never let on how difficult it was to cope with the fallout, the grief, the striving to patch together three lives. I never let anyone see that you never completely relax in that state. You never fall into a deep sleep. You never answer the phone certain it's just a friend. You never rest assured the noise under the hood is normal, and you never, ever feel everything will work out okay. In fact, you know, absolutely, that it won't.

I was anxiety-ridden and on point for years, ready for the other shoe to drop, which it did, chronically, like migraines and asthma attacks. I managed all right, like countless other women in similar circumstances. I got along in a world full of regular, successful people even as my inner life routinely went to hell.

But I wept a lot in private, alone.

I HAVE ALWAYS BEEN INVENTIVE. AS A KID, I BABYSAT for fifty cents an hour and offered to clean houses for tips. At thirteen, I invented "coat-check girl" at a New Year's dance my parents attended. My sister and I met grown-ups walking into the dance, gave them cheesy smiles, and offered to hang up their coats. We went home that night with a bucket of dollar bills.

When I was fourteen I invented that I was sixteen years old to secure a Dairy Queen job. It was a good gig that lasted years and paid my high school tuition and not a few of my parents' light bills. I got busted when the owner demanded I get a city-issued work permit, but, when I admitted my fib, he didn't care and waved away the requirement. I was already trained, and built beautiful Dilly bars and photo-worthy banana splits with all the swirls and less ice cream than necessary.

It was income all the other fourteen-year-olds envied.

That's the flip side of poverty. You learn early on to make something from nothing, to build a house without supplies, swim the ocean without water. It becomes habitual, part of who you are. I'd been doing it for years.

I remember a particularly scorching morning in March 1981. I'd announced to the kids that they were going to play hooky. They'd just earned terrific report cards, and, I explained to them, we would celebrate by going to the New Orleans Funarama Fantasy Farm—a seedy cluster of amusement park rides of dubious cleanliness and safety standards. First we had to make one short stop.

We piled into the Pinto and drove to the New Orleans Parish Human Welfare Office.

Inside Human Welfare it was quiet. A large black woman with a Jackson-size Jheri curl and a tight navy blue suit sat at a small metal desk. Several feet away a man busied himself with paperwork. My children and I seemed to be the only other people in the office, a fact for which I was glad. I couldn't bear the thought of hordes of people watching me, watching us, so I'd made sure we got there early. I sat my five-year-old son on my lap. My seven-year-old daughter, whom

I had to grab twice to keep her away from the filthy wall, leaned against the desk and twirled her spectacular, buttery blond hair around her fingers.

"I'm here to apply for food stamps," I said, as if this were just another errand in an ordinary day.

The woman behind the desk gave me a look, which I registered to mean, "Girl, what are *you* doin' here?"

I smiled slightly and shifted in my chair. It felt wrong to be there with my kids, sitting on those grimy plastic chairs that were chained to the wall, a wall smeared with you didn't want to know what. What *was* I doing there? I had been the smart girl in school, the clever one. The one who read literature and studied film and knew to blend her foundation carefully around her chin, to check her teeth regularly for lipstick, and to go without underwear under panty hose to avoid panty lines. No one I'd ever known, including my own family, which often went without food or utilities, no one had ever even entertained welfare or food stamps or a charity box from the church.

I struggled to pay polite attention to her. I had to. I had driven an eleven-year-old car with 237,000 miles on it, a backseat window missing, and almost no brakes to Human Welfare because my crummy typing job no longer covered the $385-a-month rent on our half of a crumbling duplex. Neither I nor the legal aid lawyer I'd asked had a clue how to even begin to find a deadbeat ex-husband three years missing, let alone get him to pay anything toward his children's upkeep.

I did my best, hoped for better days, and, late at night, I escaped through books, a habit developed as a child. I loved it when the world went to sleep and my reading lamp turned on.

My escape had always been books because they showed me other experiences, other ways of being. Some were better and some were worse, but the lives I found in books were always different from my own, and that's what mattered.

My parents weren't readers, so I don't have a clue how I discovered libraries. I suspect the fact that libraries were free and accessible helped. By age eight, I'd won every summer reading club contest the library held, reading more books in a single summer than any other kid my age. So as a young adult, I read *The Thorn Birds* and Fran Lebowitz. I'd also read Alex Haley's *Roots* and Elie Wiesel's *Night*. Slavery and the Holocaust served as necessary gauges that I visited in my mind again and again, benchmarks against which I could measure our own despairing circumstances. At least we weren't black and in McComb, Mississippi, in 1925, I naïvely reasoned. At least we weren't Jewish and in Germany in 1940. Certain people—crazy, heroic individuals—lived horrors I could barely stand to read about. If they could suffer that, I told myself, I could do this. I could keep my head, not put on an office skirt, but instead dress down and drive to the Human Welfare office.

But nothing I read could help me shake the daily, claustrophobic cloak of shame and fear. Not being able to afford real beds, putting free mattresses on the floor and covering them with free sheets from Catholic Charities, trying to make the assembling of that sleeping mishmash festive and cozy for the kids left me wide awake, with hand tremors, chain-smoking Virginia Slims well into the night.

Knowing I desperately needed to find a way to get my daughter the eight-thousand-dollar series of corrective ear surgeries she needed, saying no twenty times to the new baseball glove my son hopelessly coveted, accepting the bags of free food at Thanksgiving and Christmas so I could assemble a holiday meal from boxed Rice-A-Roni and generic canned fruit—it all poured over my soul like so much solidifying, imprisoning cement.

Something had to give.

My son played baseball every day after school. His growing appetite had him often wolfing down two hot dogs those days, instead of one, and he washed them down with half a bag of potato chips and almost a quart of milk. My daughter was tall and filling out. She and my son both needed haircuts and outgrew shoes on what seemed like a monthly basis. I sent them to the parochial school, which required uniforms and tuition, instead of the free public one because Louisiana vied each year for the highest illiteracy rate in the nation. Besides, the public schools were frightening in ways reminiscent of the Indiana slums that had bordered my childhood neighborhood. Living next to those ravaged tenements, I'd heard about stabbings and drug dealings long before those events became daily headlines.

The New Orleans I was raising my own kids in—out east and built scary-cheap on the swamp—was not the "New Orleans: Magic in the Crescent City!" stuff of the tourist brochures. For one thing, we had Schwegmann's, a cavernous warehouse built beneath the rarely photographed New Orleans

Industrial Canal Bridge, where canned foods sold for ten for a dollar and day-old bread could be bought by the bagful and frozen for use during the rest of the month.

Schwegmann's shoppers were bottom-feeders, like us, welfare recipients, food stamp and Social Security check people, people like me who worked to make a twenty-dollar bag of groceries last two weeks. Elderly Schwegmann's shoppers regularly got their groceries ripped from their arms. Once a mother and her baby were found shot point-blank and left to die in their car at the back of the Schwegmann's parking lot.

Schwegmann's made the nightly news a lot.

The week before our Human Welfare visit, the hotel cocktail lounge where I tended bar from 10:00 P.M. to 2:00 A.M. had closed shop. It was good tip money, cold cash that bought our groceries. It was work I could do while the kids slept, so I could help them with homework, read to them, tuck them into bed, like regular families did. For fifty cents an hour, I could pay a teenager down the street to watch TV in our living room all night long, three nights a week, while I hustled Crown Royal and Harvey Wallbangers. Behind the bar, I'd always felt some measure of security, because I knew that a heavy hand landed a few extra dollars in the tip jar. When the place shut down, I lost a life-sustaining revenue stream.

I had never applied for charity before, and I had no idea if we'd qualify for anything in this office. I certainly didn't want to sit across from this woman, this social worker who held the key to our diet. I didn't want to register her pointed, "you *soooo* full of it" glances. I didn't want to take the day off, without pay, to fill out an application that asked the exact questions I'd years ago pushed so deep into my subconscious that they'd been rendered nonexistent. *Name of children's father:* Winston Coffin. *When last seen:* Three years, one month, and twenty-six days ago. *Last known address:* Unknown. Might try Texas.

I worked hard to pretend each and every day that it was okay to be alone in my early twenties with two young children. I did so in part because I had to. The other part was that I needed to prove to myself, to my children, and to the world that our lives weren't throwaway lives. We were still worth something. We were just as good as the people who lived in houses they owned and who drove cars without rusted floorboards.

We were just as good as those with dads.

But yesterday I'd come home to find a Notice to Evict taped outside the front door. No amount of pretending was going to change that.

I'd dressed down on purpose. I'd hoped that the thin T-shirt and old shorts would help sell our need. So I sat there dressed in clothes that, after the appointment, felt so contaminated by the act I'd just committed I'd later toss them in the trash. I answered all the questions and, in between answering, sat mute, deferring to this stranger who would decide if we could eat this month or not. I put up with her quiet rudeness, her flipping on her little transistor radio.

She stopped the dial, momentarily, at a modern jazz station, and the ache of a tenor sax rolled across her desk. But, unsatisfied, she coaxed the dial a tiny bit more. A fifties, hipsterish voice filled our little corner of Human Welfare, coming across the airwaves in stark clarity. The man crooned, over and over, about his twitchy feeling, and she settled upon our file, satisfied.

And I filled out forms. I smiled at the kids and whispered to them that we'd be leaving in a few minutes. "Mommy is just about done," I assured them. I made them sit over in the play area with filthy plastic Fisher-Price toys they were too old for.

I pretended that they couldn't read, that they didn't know the meaning of the word—*Welfare*—stenciled on the door.

I crafted stupid prayers in my head, reciting them silently toward the social worker, hoping I could make her give us food stamps. But I knew, and I knew she knew, that she was one pen stroke away from marking our file REJECTED.

Bitch.

THE TILT-A-WHIRL SEATS WERE SO HOT THE METAL burned the backs of our legs. We couldn't bear to rest our hands on the scalding safety bar that kept us from hurtling out and flying across the hard, hot ground. New Orleans heat and humidity swallowed us whole. It was blazing, as if we had fallen into a pizza oven.

When the ride finally stopped, we sat for a moment, dizzy and drenched in sweat. Instead of being cooled by the wind that blew against us, we felt nauseated and hotter than ever. Our shirts stuck to our backs, and our hair was plastered in wet rivulets down our necks. We peeled the backs of our sweaty legs from the metal buckets as we climbed out. I saw a booth across a scrabbly dirt walkway and took a child's hand in each of mine.

"Can we have three cups of water, please?" I asked the plump girl inside the booth. A frosted-up machine whirled a red, icy mixture around and around inside its clear plastic box. We stood enraptured, studying every delicious, frozen molecule.

"No," the girl said. It was a school day, and I tried to figure how this sixteen-year-old with AC/DC airbrushed across her T-shirt had gotten out of school to work at an amusement park.

I didn't think I'd heard her right, so I asked again, "Three cups of water, please."

"We don't sell no water." The girl held a hose in her fist. She sprayed the concrete floor, rinsing away red, sticky sugar water. She watched her own work, her progress with pushing the red water pool out of her booth. The hose spat cold water in a hard line when she pressed her thick thumb over its end. "We got strawberry Frosties," she said and cocked her non-hose-working thumb back at the machine.

I eyed the glistening water spraying from the hose and glanced over at my son and daughter, who'd taken refuge in the shade. One Frostie was a buck and a half. I had one dollar left to my name. It was sweat-limp and folded inside my bra.

"We already bought Frosties at the other end of the park an hour ago," I lied. "We just need some water. Is there a fountain anywhere?" Wavy heat lines danced up off the tar walkway that lead visitors out of Funarama. It had to be a hundred degrees. The girl let the hose run over her flip-flops, over her toes, and looked up at me. "They all shut down. Just Royal Crown cola and Frosties. Extra ice costs extra."

The sound of the cold water flowing and splashing drove me mad. I calculated that either I had to find a way to get her to give me a Frostie for my wet dollar bill or we needed to head back to the Pinto and drive to someplace with water, which would take us at least thirty minutes. We were already dangerously heat-fatigued, dry-lipped, and parched. I looked at my kids and their beet-colored cheeks.

"Let me have that hose," I said and held my hand out.

She kept spraying at the floor. She moved the hose to the sticky strawberry Frostie cart. When she was done with that, she let the water pour over her feet again.

She wiggled her toes in delight.

"It's against the law to let people get sick in this heat and not have some water available somewhere," I told her. "This sugary crap will make us sick. It's too hot. We already bought those crappy drinks. Let me have that hose. We need water."

Flies dotted the booth's flimsy countertop. They lit in little black-dotted groups, then flew away. Then lit again. The kids, preoccupied with the giant Ferris wheel, tipped their heads back, hands shielding their eyes to watch the machine lift people into the sky. I was about to collect them, to rush back to the parking lot and open the Pinto's windows and let a swish of hot breeze circle around inside it before we climbed into its furnacelike interior and bolted. But I considered this for only a second because I'd just left the New Orleans Parish Human Welfare Office, where I'd had to tell a stranger who didn't give a damn and who had heard a hell of a lot worse that I wasn't making it, that I could no longer hold it together. I'd just left a woman's desk where I'd had to explain in excruciating detail that my husband, whom I'd loved, the only man I'd ever been with, had snuck out one night while we all slept and credit-carded his way across five states without ever looking back.

I'd had to explain to her that I didn't have a clue where he'd gone and that, no, I wasn't hiding him or preventing my children from seeing him.

He simply didn't want us anymore.

I'd had to see her blink back at me and make notes in her new "Beck" file that we were destitute, that we had no family we could turn to, that they had long ago gone their separate, often alcoholic, and sometimes suicidal ways. There was no one to help.

I'd had to wipe mean, hot tears from my face while checking to see that the kids weren't seeing their mother crying, and I had to keep answering questions: *Do you have anything of value you could sell? Any bank accounts? Any resources—or anyone—someone who might give you a loan or something? Is there a boyfriend who might help out? Is there any other adult living at your address?*

I'd had to force myself to keep from screaming, *No, you dumb fuck! If I had any of those options, don't you think I'd have already used them?*

I'd just had to push it all aside, and wipe snot from my running nose, and whisper hard so she could hear but my kids couldn't, whisper and insist, *Please* at her. *Please.*

I'd had to beg.

So instead of bolting, I lunged over the countertop to grab the fucking hose from this girl with all the water and all the power in her hand. Instinctively, she pressed her thumb to the hose and shot the hard stream straight at my face, a piercing, ice-cold, razor-sharp spray to my forehead, mean and freezing water bullets, like a water machine gun. The force made me fall backward.

I gasped, shocked. The girl pointed the hose to the floor and looked at me, eyes wide. I sensed my kids frozen near me, put both hands to my eyes and wiped water off my face, pushed back dripping hair from my forehead.

A laugh choked my chest. Then another. The girl put her thumb near the end of the hose and sprayed me again, less forcibly this time, and I stepped back and let the cold water hit me. My little boy grinned up at me, and I touched his face and laughed. He moved to stand in front of me and then turned in a circle until he was completely wet. Both kids opened their mouths, and the girl let the water glide up in an arc, and they drank hungrily. My daughter held up her pigtails and put her head in front of the spray and rubbed the water over her face.

The kids kept laughing in circles, letting the water pour over them. I laughed, too, allowing the tears to mix with the spray. Then it was all too much, and I openly cried, like I'd been slapped or something. I doubted we'd get the food stamps and felt the confusing and scary mixture of relief at being spared the indignity of using them and fear of not knowing how we were going to eat. I wondered if we'd have to move again to an even smaller, cheaper place, like we'd had to last year, and I wondered if, ultimately, I'd have to send the kids to the horrifying Lindenwood Public School No. 59, where twelve-year-olds shot up and a six-year-old had been stabbed and killed last year.

I turned to take the kids home. As we walked the midway, letting our shorts and tops and hair drip, I saw a heavy black woman walking toward us. She held a little girl's hand in one of her own. The little girl had a purple balloon tied to her wrist, and she bopped the balloon away from her with her hand. *BopBopBop.* The three of us approached them. We looked ridiculous, our clothes and hair drenched, but we didn't care. We were jolly in our cool relief.

My eyes met the woman's when we were nearly at the same spot, and we both slowed our stride. It was the Human Welfare office woman. She was not in the tight blue suit now but wore a sleeveless muumuu and open-toed sandals.

As we passed, her look shifted from recognition to something else. A knowing, an understanding crept across her eyes. She read me, read the scene she was watching; a very young woman with two little kids, all of us soaking wet, defeated. She read me, and then a little miracle. I read her. Her eyes were soft with empathy. She watched her little girl do another bop-bop with her balloon, then she looked at me, and her eyes skirted toward my kids. I knew then that we'd get the food stamps, that perhaps we wouldn't have to move after all, at least for a while, that we'd get to go to Schwegmann's and fill our cart.

For once, the Pinto was cool. The sun had shifted while we were in Funarama, and the car had been sitting in the shade. Someone had walked by and ripped the plastic tape off the broken window, and for a second I smiled at the vandal's disappointment when he discovered there was no radio to rip out. Air had had a chance to circulate through the missing window, and, as we climbed in, I felt the relief of my damp clothes against the heat. A second wave of relief rolled over me as the car started without its normal choke and stall.

The kids unrolled the remaining intact window and, as we pulled away from Funarama Fantasy Farm, I let my fear and shame shift off to the side. My daughter moved over to sit next to me, and, as I drove, we all absorbed how safe we felt. I knew we all felt it, the safety, the okay-for-now, because she put her small hand at the bottom of the steering wheel and pretended that she was steering, that together we could guide us home.

CHAPTER TWO

Waiting to Inhale

Fast-forward from that sweltering day at the Fantasy Farm and hold that fast-forward button down, zooming through years and years and then more years until you are smack in the middle of my tiny, basement apartment in the fall of 1994.

That fall launched a series of firsts. Though I was in my late thirties, it was the first time I had ever lived alone, the first time in my life I wasn't solely responsible for an entire group of people. I could come and go as I pleased.

I adore my children and they me. A child raising children creates a particularly adhesive familial glue, and I would happily cut off both arms for my kids, but I was also barely thirty-nine years old and *ready to rock 'n' roll.*

I was primed, honey, primed for hell and high water and illicit (or prescription, I didn't care) drugs, which I'd never had the opportunity to experiment with. I was primed for promiscuity and staying up late, for all those activities that I knew others my age had long ago partaken of and (mostly) abandoned but that were never, ever, not even for a month back in the seventies, a part of my existence.

For the first time in what seemed like a very long time, I didn't have to confine my friendships to my kids' friends' parents, adults usually fifteen to thirty years older than me. I could make friends with people who were younger or older or childless or scoundrels or any other damn irresponsible being with whom I wanted to keep company.

I could take a lover—a stupid one with cut biceps and a flagrant disdain for all children—if I wanted. I could walk around naked in my own house, and I could go out late at night or not come home at all. I could elect to not pay any of my bills on time and let them shut off all the utilities.

For the first time in my life, I wasn't one paycheck away from homelessness—but hell, they could evict me if they wanted, because there was only me to worry about.

I was just beginning the huge inhale of a long and very luxuriant deep breath.

Yippee! I was having a Big, Fat *Do Over* where I got to pick myself up, dust myself off with whatever cloying bath powder I chose, and start all over again.

I never did do any of that stuff, by the way. I paid my bills and didn't do anything that could have remotely got me arrested. Except for walking around naked and eating Corn Chex from the box while watching *Mork & Mindy* reruns, my life looked much as it always had.

But it *could* have been cool and James Bond–like. That's the important part. At any minute, I could have done any of the things I thought about.

I wasn't yet forty, damn it. There was a big, unmet life out there, and I was ready to jump in with both feet. I was ready to cultivate friends based on intellectual pursuits and fun and daring. I wanted to talk about good books rather than good grades. I wanted to eye a man's butt and comment on it to someone without feeling like Mommie Dearest gone porno. I wanted to jump on an airplane and land wherever the wind and jet engines propelled me.

But what I hadn't counted on, what I had not planned for or realized was this: I still had no one to play with. So I placed an ad for friends.

THE WEEK AFTER I PLACED MY AD WAS A DIN OF TELE-phone ringing and ringing and ringing. I put all the women who called through a spiel and seduced them into talking about themselves. *Where do you live?* I asked. *Why are you interested in a women's group?* (I was intent on weeding out those looking for group therapy. The very last thing I needed was some horror story in my living room.) Seven women seemed like possibilities, and they all committed to coming over on a Wednesday night for the first meeting. But an obsessive need for even numbers plagued me. I wanted that eighth member, so I continued to screen.

"I'm an artist," Denise said to me on the phone, a heavy Bronx bite in her words. She didn't introduce herself. She didn't say hello. She shot the facts at me as if she and I were already past all the small talk, like somehow we'd been planning on having that very conversation.

Sometimes—not often—when you meet someone, in that first hello, you are certain that everything thereafter will be altered. It's a dream of things to come that flashes somewhere in the back of the subconscious. So, while you open your mouth, expand your vocal cords, and try to begin, your soul smiles, already knowing the story to come.

I should have seen our future there in that moment.

"But my husband and I have a frame shop behind our house," she reported.

"Are you from here?" I asked, knowing full well she wasn't.

"Boulder's home," she said. "I've been here for twenty-five years. I'm forty-three."

"Where are you from? New York?"

"Weird you picked up on that," she said. "I've been gone from there for so long."

Like a couple of decades could dilute that accent.

THE START-UP NIGHT WAS AWKWARD. THE STRANGERS gathered in my home wore blank faces and looked about the room for something to happen. A tall, almost masculine woman arrived first. Then a red-haired, child-size, middle-aged woman knocked at the door. I had a hard time catching names as they all seemed to arrive at once.

"Hello, come on in," I said, and they did. Several others, including a very young one and a wild-looking woman with electric green pants. Different ages, different sizes. One took the rocking chair, others grabbed the couch. I carried one of my two kitchen chairs to the living room and handed the other to a woman with thick eyeglasses. The young one sat on a pillow on the floor.

All of them looked at me and offered variations of hesitant, timid smiles. In just minutes, it seemed, strangers were in my living room and I wondered what the hell I was doing.

I was nervous, aware that WOW was really nothing more than an awkward menagerie of strangers. But I was also unapologetically happy we'd bloomed into a group of real, live people. I wondered which one was Denise and how I was going to boot out the woman who'd arrived last, leisurely so. She reeked of entitlement.

We'll go around the circle, I thought, *and I'll ask some gentle, guiding questions. Where do you work? Do you have kids? A boyfriend?* Out of nervousness, I made a split-second decision to break the ice by opening up with myself. "I was out of the country for a few months and didn't have anywhere to land when I came back to the States," I said to the group. "So I stopped off in Indiana and stayed with a childhood friend for a while. I just got back to Boulder."

The one who'd arrived late eyeballed me, and I saw that she was itching to say something. But I continued, "Before that, I went to Russia for a few months. I've got two grown kids; they both live out of state."

"*You've* got two grown kids?" She finally found a way to interrupt. But I was used to the question. I'd been hearing it for years, so I gave everyone in the room the approximately eight seconds I knew they would need to calculate, to register my age against my children's, and to conclude that there was but a handful of years between us.

That's when it hit me. That voice.

It was Denise, and I looked at her more closely. She was pretty in the way that stubby Catholic girls with thin hair notice: long legs; a luxurious, curly mane; piercing brown eyes. She sat back in her chair, crossed her ankles, and squinted her eyes at me, her face a big question mark. "How *old* are you anyway?" she challenged.

I was irritated she'd interrupted me. I also wondered if she asked everyone their age inside ten seconds of meeting them. "I turned thirty-nine last month," I said.

"Well, how old are your kids?" Ms. Beyond Rude injected again.

I reaffirmed my initial conviction that I'd no intention of putting up with her beyond that night, despite our easy phone conversation. "They're twenty-one and nineteen," I said.

I looked straight at her to see if she was actually going to let me go on. "My Indiana friend and I were getting on each other's nerves. But it was time for me to leave anyway. I've been back in Boulder about a month."

I paused for a few seconds. Denise, too, was quiet, actually waiting for me to continue. Over time I learned that it was something she did for sport, asking people personal questions before they had a chance to warm up to her in any way. It was a diversion tactic, done with a hint of a smile, the tiniest upturn at the corner of her mouth, and within minutes of meeting anyone. I somehow knew that she did it to entertain herself, which I found entertaining.

But in those first few minutes of our initial meeting, long before everything that was about to unfold for us began, I looked at that New York–born artist sitting with perfectly suntanned legs almost into October, and I was wary, unsure that she was going to even allow me to tell my story.

Not that I knew exactly what my story was. I felt on the verge of something new, but I had no idea what shape it could take. Looking back at my old story, I felt like no one could ever understand my past, or care to, and I'd learned long ago that my circumstances made people tsk-tsk with pity, made them ignore me and my kids, made people leave. We were too close to rock bottom. But now I felt ready to launch something, though I didn't have a clue what. Kids and striving had taken everything I had for nearly two decades. I realized, as we began WOW, that I needed a new story. Looking around the room, I wondered if I was the only one.

I rushed to finish my intro. "For money, I freelance write and do research for lawyers representing women in a national class-action breast implant lawsuit."

It was a quirky mix of work, I knew. Over seventeen years, I'd moved from typist to paralegal, inadvertently securing a Ph.D. in How Lawyers Operate—New Orleans lawyers, a.k.a. third-generation blue bloods (or aspiring to be so), my specialty. No matter how big or small, a law office is a guaranteed paycheck. If you can type fast, they'll hire you, without even knowing your name (happened). If you can flirt, file, and fan a tail feather or two, bring along a brain and do research, maybe even prepare a deposition summary, they've got all the fifteen-dollar-an-hour days you can stomach.

"I do both part-time," I added. "Half the time I'm at the law office. The other half I write stories for the newspaper."

I was warming up to tell the group all about this more interesting side of my life when Denise, moved into the limelight again. "I have multiple sclerosis," she said. I didn't catch anyone else's reaction to this apropos-of-nothing interjection, because Denise waved all the horror away as summarily as she had brought it to our attention. "But it's the good kind, a very mild form. It's in remission."

I opened my mouth to respond, to say something, but I was forced to talk over the stomp!-stomp!-stomping of my insane landlady, whose living room sat directly above mine. Landlady Laura was middle-aged and anorexic, and told anyone who'd listen that she was an *artiste*. She came from Connecticut money, old dough that had bought her the building we both lived in. She'd been dating the same guy for fourteen years, and soon, she told me the day I moved in, he was going to marry her and get her pregnant. She also let me know that she could hear me and my new, personal-ad boyfriend fight— that's right, an *entire* life built of newspaper ads—that she heard every last detail through the furnace vents that led straight from my living room to hers. She made a point of marching around when she knew I was home. I liked to flush the toilet when I heard her shower running.

"Let's break for some tea," I said, though it was still early. I used Landlady Laura's obnoxious noisemaking above us as an excuse, but the truth was I needed to stop the action and look more closely at this woman who'd interrogated me, who'd ignored everyone else in the room, who'd announced she had a disease, and who looked like a movie star. Something was up with that chick, though I wasn't sure what.

"Okay," Denise said to me, chummy-like. "Tea sounds good."

Like we were the only people in the room.

DENISE AND I WALKED AHEAD OF THE GROUP FROM THE kitchen back into my living room, carefully balancing coffee mugs filled with Celestial Seasonings Red Zinger and honey.

"These are nice." Denise pointed to two oil paintings I'd paid a poor Azerbaijani artist five dollars for. They were treasures to me, and I knew, somehow, that Denise's compliment was not a shallow one, that this person didn't pay shallow compliments.

Before I could tell her anything about my paintings, one of the other women finally broke her silence. "Those boob-job women are stupid. They deserve whatever they get." I turned from the Russian paintings and looked past Denise's shoulder to the source of the statement.

"I'm Sharon," a woman said, reacting to my questioning look. She sported a wild mass of black, frizzy hair and outdated plastic eyeglasses.

"What are you talking about?" I asked, as we all returned to our seats. "I spend my afternoons assembling evidence for hundreds of women who have lupus or cancer because they got breast implants."

"They took that risk when they decided they had to have big tits," Sharon argued and then sniffed. "It's a stupid procedure. They should have known better. They deserve what's happening to them."

"They bought a *product*," I jabbed back. "If your mascara blinded you, you'd sue the shit out of Clinique. They trusted the FDA, just like you do."

The other women sat mute. You had to feel sorry for the tiny redhead sitting between me and Sharon, a miniature woman who tried to erase herself from the room, sinking back and into the furniture. She was perfect in a 1940s Nancy Davis (just before she met Ronald Reagan) sort of way: perfect hair, perfect outfit, curled up and back and against the couch like a little perfect kitten. Suddenly, she sat up and struggled to get a word in edgewise. "Uhhh . . . ," she said, hardly audible. "So, these women are really, really sick?"

I gave Picture Perfect a glance but didn't answer. I was furious at the ignorance of that butterball with a mouth, Sharon. She revealed later that night that she lived "up above the park," indicating the swankiest part of town, with a live-in boyfriend she paid a ten-thousand-dollar fee for from "an exclusive Beverly Hills matchmaking service." She and her thoroughbred padded around all day long in their twenty-two-room mansion, dealing with their investments. "My family's from old utility money." She snorted sideways at Denise, like that explained everything.

"Most of them will never see a dime from the lawsuit anyway," I said. "The deadline's passed to join the lawsuit. Most of the women are out of luck at this point."

Silence hung in the air for a few seconds. We were a pack of strangers with a whole host of hidden agendas and dysfunctions and brokenness, struggling to suspend our breathing against all the unused air in the room.

"We'll hold an art auction," Denise said casually. She even shrugged her shoulders a little. "We'll donate the proceeds to the Colorado women who didn't make that deadline, who didn't get into the lawsuit on time."

I'd felt a pull before, a deep resonance I didn't really get, but in that moment The Click happened. It was like a well-made buckle snapping together, a nice, solid sound. It felt comforting and smooth to the touch. We came together easily, like we were made to connect, two pieces designed to interlock, each built to accommodate the other.

I looked at Denise across the room, and she locked her eyes with mine. She looked into me, then through me, transmitting a signal that indicated I should have known that she was coming, that she would offer to do this. She silently sent a message that I should have expected this, should have expected her, that this was a blatantly obvious next chapter in both our lives.

For the first time that evening, I was at a loss for words. Eight heads all turned and looked at her expectantly.

"It's easy. The Art Walk is next month. I'll just put a few pieces out and auction them off."

Then, just as summarily as she'd dismissed her MS, Denise turned our attention away from the women suffering from breast implants. "What's your name?" she said to a woman across the room. *Okay, sister,* her eyes signaled to me,

37

let's get your goofy little group going, shall we? Let's have some fun with it.

And so we met the others with whom we would spend the next eighteen months of Wednesdays. Without saying anything aloud to each other, Denise and I took charge of the group together, leading them through introductions, secure in our alliance. Denise seemed to have satisfied her thirst for pointed questions on me and prodded and queried the others with more subtlety. I relaxed and actually smiled for the first time that evening.

"I'm Thomasina," a woman said in a whiskey-toned voice. She cast a glance about the room, projecting herself as a sad Ingrid Bergman, a Bergman in her *Europa* days—ash-blond, slender, with a beautifully boned face. "I'm a massage thera-pist, but my parents still help me."

Denise and I learned over time that Thomasina did give the occasional massage in her apartment, but we also discov-ered that her massages were as timid and ineffectual as her demeanor. Thomasina proved to be forever forlorn, rarely smil-ing, yet she wore her inner grief well, under a veneer of de-spondent loveliness.

"I need a massage," the frighteningly skinny woman next to Thomasina interrupted. I started to ask her name, but she beat me to it. "Malinda," she said, though offered up from her tiny bird's mouth, it sounded more like "malignant." We learned that she didn't have a job, a boyfriend, or a hobby.

When the Q & A revealed that she'd once dated an ex-boyfriend of mine, I grilled her on all the details. She never came back.

Denise queried Millicent, who, we found out, had just left her redneck husband of seventeen years back in rural Mississippi. "I've got six teenage sons," she said with a sliver of Southern twang to the room full of dropped jaws. "Four of 'em are from two sets of twins, and I'm finishing a Ph.D. in molecular biology."

Millicent lent a wonderful analytical mind to the group. But she looked like one more boy in her herd of boys, and as the months wore on, Denise and I speculated on how best to upgrade Millicent's looks. She was over six feet tall and leggy, and we were dying to get her out of those chinos and into a push-up bra, maybe even talk her into growing out that mannish haircut.

But as soon as we'd get going on a "Millicent rant," we'd instantly check ourselves. We admired Millicent's disregard for hair and clothes. She jockeyed all day long for respect and political gain in the male-dominated world of science. Then she came home to six boys by herself. She was brilliant in worlds we couldn't even begin to penetrate. *Who are we?* we'd say and shake our heads at our own foolishness. To our benefit, Millicent stayed throughout the life of WOW.

"I'm Harmony," a woman said in an accent that sounded suspiciously like Denise's. "I grew up on Long Island," she added. Harmony, formerly known as Gloria, slunk about my living room in kelly green satin pants and hot pink ballet slippers. She lasted but a few evenings.

Nancy Reagan's real name, it turned out, was Sandy.

We instantly, privately renamed her Size-Five Sandy. Sandy dyed her hair to a coppery red that glowed. She stuck it out those eighteen months, as did Ginger—the youngest member, in her twenties, a chain-smoking, hoochie-coochie-lookin' gal with a knockout figure and little common sense. She played caretaker to a voluminous family packed with alcoholics and early deaths.

Who knew what criteria those women met to end up there together? Were there unifying traits among them? Did each bring some element absent from my life that I hungrily fed on during the two hours we spent together each week?

Hell no. They were extras in our—mine and Denise's—script. We were Bette Davis and Anne Bancroft. The others were stands-ins from the Screen Actors Guild, mere background bodies.

Every Wednesday evening for a year and a half, Denise and I reigned as the understood bosses of the group—drawing out everyone else's stories, insecurities, dreams. We came to know who had money troubles, boyfriend troubles, kid troubles. They came to know ours. Little bits of ourselves dropped into the middle of a group over time created a natural intimacy. However, Denise and I fell to being a bit of a joint-hostess team. We tended, advised, shared, and supported. In doing so together, we created our own, private intimacy.

The women became our friends in a peripheral sort of way, and their lives became mirrors in which we viewed ourselves.

The thing is, you think that you've seen the worst of everything, that you've been to the mountain, walked through the fire. You think the hard part is over. And you think the peripheral people are just that—minor, unimportant, expendable—because the pal you're hanging out with will be there for decades. She'll be there forever.

But one day, the friend with whom you'd built a certain trust and confidence, the one who holds your heart in her hands, well, she's gone. The one to whom you've revealed yourself (the nastiest parts of yourself, the things you're most afraid of, the secrets that bring you shame) is no longer there.

And that's when you know: you haven't yet even *begun* to hurt.

A MONTH TO THE DAY AFTER THAT FIRST WOW MEETING, I watched Denise offer up a half dozen of her own works, even crafting an exquisite papier-mâché sculpture for her "little art auction," and miraculously raise—in one weekend—a stack of cash for the implant women. Despite my very vocal awe and excitement, Denise remained utterly indifferent to her swift and savvy fund-raising. She was calm, pure, detached somehow from the frenzy created by looking at her accomplishment in terms of the other women's pain.

"It's not like I gave them my *own* money," she said, dismissing my admiration. "Some doctor from Denver bought two pieces. The guy's loaded." Then she laughed. "He talked my ear off for over an hour. *That* part was painful."

CHAPTER THREE

Guttersnipes

I hadn't always been friendless. In fact, I grew up with loads of friends. But to understand mid-1960s, inner-city Catholic friends, you have to possess a fundamental appreciation of bingo and bill collectors.

In 1965, we navy-blue-skirt-wearing, Our Lady of Perpetual Sorrow grade school girls jockeyed each weekend to be chosen to waitress at Bingo. It was a tough gig. On Sunday nights, when most kids lay prone and freshly bathed on worn living room rugs, *The Wonderful World of Disney* flickering across their faces, we showed up at Perpetual Sorrow aching, hoping—often praying—for Father Francis Flaherty to pick us for the prized unpaid waitress positions.

We didn't give a damn about the lack of wage. It was the tips and the thievery we hungered after.

We'd show up every Sunday at 5:00 P.M. sharp, craving one of those shaved-beef sandwiches on a steamy hamburger bun, maybe a frosty bottle of Pepsi-Cola poured over chipped ice. We'd linger about the long, low cooler at the back of the

old-fashioned cafeteria kitchen, dressed in our school uniforms: wrinkled skirts and stale white blouses yanked from
dirty clothes hampers.

I needed to work Bingo every chance I could; my mother
depended on the money to feed me and my four siblings. But
some Sundays pressed harder than others, like when the
Beneficial Finance Man came.

Beneficial Man was tough, persistent, pervasive.

He'd telephone our house for weeks. I came to know his
voice immediately, even the breath he held before I whispered,
Hello? It made me jittery just to lift the receiver. Beneficial Man
came to hate me. He wanted an adult to pick up, but my mom
had long ago stopped answering the phone. So he grew himself a whole new level of determination, letting the phone ring
twenty-three times once. I counted. *Trillll! Trilll! Trillll! Trilll!
Trillll! Trilll! Trillll! Trilll! Trillll! Trilll! Trillll! Trilll! Trillll! Trilll!
Trillll! Trilll! Trillll! Trilll! Trillll! Trilll! Trillll! Trilll! Trillll!*

One Friday afternoon my three sisters and I sat parked in
front of *The Popeye and Merry Mary Show,* the late-day pab-
lum for Gary, Indiana, kids trying to come down from a
seven-hour school day. The woman with bad dentures and a
ragged up-do crooned to us: *Puff the Magic Dragon, lived by
the sea.* Even my mom watched, with our year-old, wall-eyed
baby brother on her lap. She watched because she loved hating Merry Mary. She loved to loathe Merry Mary's tinny little
nasal singing voice, loved to hate that, although Mary had a
television studio full of kids she sang to every afternoon before the Popeye cartoons began, she got to go home at 4:30,
got to hand off all those kids to someone else to feed.

BAM! BAM! BAM!

The fist slammed against the front door of our rented duplex, startling even the cockroaches. My heart slammed to my throat. I knew who it was. Our mom crushed her cigarette into the ashtray she'd been balancing on the couch arm. She grabbed the baby and swung him under her arm.

"Get into the basement," she hissed. "Move!"

We scurried down the steep basement steps, working to keep from falling facefirst into the damp blackness that we otherwise would never be caught dead going into. We were terrified of the basement.

We all turned and crouched beneath the damp staircase and, through a cracked window at ground level, watched as the trench coat paced our front porch. It was the Beneficial Man, and Dad owed him a lot of money. We held our breaths as he slammed his fat, thick palm against the door. The baby whimpered. *Sssssh!* Mom insisted into his ear.

"What's he—?" I started. She slapped her hand to my mouth, and I quieted, but not before I saw my best friend, eleven-year-old Eileen-Marie O'Shaunessy, walk up the steps behind him.

"They're not home," Eileen-Marie said to the man's back. He jumped out of his skin. "I know them," she added when he turned to face her. "They're gone."

He lifted his hand to hit the door again, and my mother and I strained to get a better view. We stopped breathing altogether, paralyzed in an agonized silence. The man hesitated, then snarled at the closed door, *Fucking guttersnipes.*

He pivoted roughly, nearly knocking Eileen-Marie down as he marched off the porch and away.

We all exhaled into the mold creeping along the basement wall.

EILEEN-MARIE O'SHAUNESSY HAD SEVENTEEN BROTHERS and sisters. Most all of them had wild mops of curly, burnt orange hair and freckles like endless rain spots on a sidewalk—so many freckles. They were the largest litter at Perpetual Sorrow.

Eileen-Marie and I arrived regularly for Bingo, early and eager. We bore our promptness like a virtue, certain that it increased our odds of being chosen. Though our uniforms were hand-me-downs, frayed and often stained and patched, we showed up ready, nonetheless. At eleven years old, we had few options.

Father Flaherty always arrived late. He was a nice, handsome man with a Bing Crosby comb-back and smiling blue eyes. He hummed to himself a lot, sometimes church standards like the *Salve Regina,* but more often the current Bing Crosby hits, "My Pet" and "It's the Natural Thing to Do."

"Hello, girls," he'd announce himself, and we'd stand up straight, maneuvering to make ourselves seen.

But he never selected the two waitresses he needed right off the bat. No, first he'd get us all to help him set up the cafeteria.

"Eileen-Marie O'Shaunessy," he'd boom. "Hand me that box of napkins," and Eileen-Marie would dutifully climb the stepladder to the shelf high up at the back of the cavernous storeroom that housed everything for Bingo refreshments, including the cooler. Father Flaherty watched her every move, scanning Eileen-Marie's muscular legs.

"Catherine—fill the cooler with soda pop," he'd instruct in his thunderous voice. I'd pick up the bottles from the wooden case, but I'd hold the back of my skirt tightly behind my thighs as I bent over, leaning deep into my pelvis, to line the bottles up in the cooler's cold, cavernous belly.

Then he'd send the other girls home. Eileen-Marie and I would try to relax. I'd work to think it a lucky night for us. Sometimes Father would pick Rose McGovern, with her jet-black hair and Elizabeth Taylor eyes. But often he chose Annie Walsh, who was well into puberty before any of the rest of us knew what a Kotex pad was.

"Maybe next week, girls," Father would say to the non-chosen. He'd move up behind me and place his hand on my buttock and pick up a Pepsi bottle and put it in the case. Then another bottle. And another. He'd help me with my assigned task, his large hard hand gripping me, holding my pubic bone fast against the cooler. Then he'd move back to the other side of the closet, to Eileen-Marie, and reach around her to help her load paper napkins into the metal dispensers, swiping the front of her chest in the process.

Eileen-Marie and I would work until midnight those Sundays, waiting on the fat Bingo ladies when they ordered hot dogs with pickle relish or coffee with four sugars or a shaved beef sandwich and a PayDay. We'd stagger home, drunk with fatigue, our hair and bodies soaked in the stench of wiener steam and cigarette smoke, our pockets weighted with nickels and dimes, half of which we'd helped ourselves to when the Bingo women weren't looking.

Father Francis Flaherty died a few years later, and all six hundred Perpetual Sorrow students were forced to attend his funeral, a High Mass where all us kids recited Latin, trapped in obligatory sadness.

"Such a saint," Monsignor Patrick McNulty wept from the pulpit, eulogizing the tall, egg-shaped man with a W. C. Fields nose, a man who'd led the Catholic Youth Organization for years. "Our lives will never be the same without him," the monsignor insisted. He pulled a tablecloth-size handkerchief from his robe and blew harshly, bellowing like an African elephant. I tried to look down, but my eyes flickered to Eileen-Marie's, and pained, convulsive laughter burst from our throats, like it had a life of its own. Our shoulders shook with giggles, hysteria trapped inside us like small caged animals. We tried to make our bodies squash the laughter and we choked and coughed, sending spit onto the kids' backs in the pew in front of us, but it only made it worse. So we weren't surprised when Sister Maria Divine yanked us out of Mass by our hair and condemned us to scrubbing every floor of the priests' rectory (plus their toilets) for a month. And we didn't care.

So there'd been friends. Once.

DENISE WAS ONE OF THE FOUNDERS OF WHAT SHE CALLED the Real Boulder. As a girl coming of age in the late 1960s and '70s, she fled her family's cramped, fourth-floor Bronx flat for a picturesque college hamlet set in the middle of the snowcapped Rockies.

In Boulder, Colorado, in 1970, students held passionate, give-peace-a-chance sit-ins and took their outrage at the United States government to the streets. Girls had sex with anyone they damn well wanted, any time they wanted, without a lick of guilt. The pill and marijuana and Janis Joplin were readily available and helped to unleash decades of pent-up desires, creating what Denise called "a perfect five-year period," a time when "true hippies" came to be.

"You missed it," she'd say to me pointedly, on more than one occasion. "There was this one window. It was bounded by Vietnam and Kent State. There was Robert Kennedy, who was very, very cute (she could not say "Robert Kennedy" without the "who was very, very cute" modifier), and Martin Luther King. There was Woodstock and there were head shops.

"I'm sorry," she'd add. "But you missed that window. You were born too late. Many call themselves hippies, but they're not unless they were born in 1950, give or take a year."

It was bullshit, but I believed her. I believed her because she was so bossy, so commanding, and so full of life. Plus, it felt good to be in the company of someone so ballsy.

Ho Chi Minh Trail, civil rights, and LSD were all abstract terms that my siblings and I had heard in the background as our dad lay sprawled on our threadbare couch glued to Walter Cronkite. Though Robert Kennedy's face was famil-iar to us, my three younger sisters and I were more con-cerned about shoplifting Twinkies and how raging drunk our dad got each night than about some far-off country with impossible-to-pronounce cities highlighted in red on the CBS world map.

I had a baby in 1973, before I learned such a thing as Planned Parenthood even existed. By the time I lost enough baby-carrying fat to slip into a pair of low-cut jeans, bell-bottoms were creeping out of style.

Those who were born in the 1950s formed revolutions led by Gloria Steinem and Abbie Hoffman. Those of us born too late had to figure out who the politically correct insurgents were and then hope to march on in their mutinous footsteps, as righteously as we could.

Denise firmly believed that her age-group was smarter and more historically important than mine; it was a point she lorded over me. I respected the fact that she used it selectively—albeit often—and well.

DENISE AND I COULD NOT POSSIBLY HAVE STRUCK UP A friendship any earlier than we did—say, in 1984 instead of 1994.

In 1984, Denise was still at the top of her game, an economic dynamo. She touched an idea and it exploded in money. Yet, as she'd later tell me, enjoying the tale, enjoying the telling of the tale, life wasn't all perfect for her in '84. She suffered a broken heart that year from a tall, blond, handsome man.

"I was devastated that whole year after he walked out on me," she said. "So I *ran* over to CU and signed up for graduate school.

"Then I went on the 'heartbreak diet' for two years," she added, dripping with tongue-in-cheek drama. "I was drop-dead gorgeous those two years—big boobs, no hips. I looked *incredible*." If we were in her kitchen during this particular telling, she'd dramatically hesitate, cast down her eyes, then raise them and point toward a cabinet where she'd taped a black-and-white snapshot of her 1980-something self: all teenage-bodied and doe-eyed with a big, sultry smile. "Then I started a business and made a boatload of money."

Her methods of making money were productive but not particularly interconnected. In today's bizspeak, Denise never felt a need to capture or dominate any particular business "space." Rather, as she once commented offhandedly, "I just look around. There're plenty of ideas. It's not that hard."

One day, barely out of her teens, Denise noted that no one in Boulder got *The New York Times,* so she called the *Times* that day and arranged to have it shipped out. She'd meet the airplane in the black of night and toss the papers into the back of an old station wagon she'd bought for change. She would deliver the papers all by herself until dawn, making a dollar profit per copy.

She did the same thing with the Boston, Washington, Los Angeles, and Chicago papers, plus *The Wall Street Journal,* cornering the market lickety-split, before anyone could catch on and copy her. She hired delivery people and socked away bags and bags of money while her waitressing peers flirted and cajoled customers in hopes they'd get more than a fifty-cent tip.

After the paper route, she had a barrette business. There was a time when every American woman under thirty owned one of Denise's barrettes—a strip of hand-tooled leather with a wooden dowel running through it to hold long, parted-in-the-middle hair in ponytails at the backs of their necks. Denise first made the barrettes at home and then sold them—all of them—on the street in two hours. Then she got someone else to sell them on the street. Then she sold them nationally from an ad in *The New Yorker*. Soon she had distributors and salespeople all over the country, display racks in department stores and head shops, and fifty worker bees back in Boulder furiously hammering out more barrettes. They flew off the shelves.

Everything she touched turned to gold.

Once, frustrated with my job and barely making ends meet, I tried to explain to her the notion that the rest of us don't automatically know how to get money, that we can't so easily see the ways to wooing wealth.

"You realize that you're lucky, that you've got a mind-blowing gift, don't you?" I told her, aggravated at her cavalier approach to cash. "I watch you wheel and deal, and to me, it's like you see a whole bunch of dough and you just reach into it, divert its direction toward you. Like you've got access to some special money switch."

She glanced up from matching frame borders against a really ugly painting. "That's some really touching shit," she said. "Are you through?" Then, without even a sneer or a snort, she went back to her work.

Denise saw a need for high-end, customized art frames in artsy Boulder. She saw true artists, trust-funders, a moneyed university, and middle-aged stockholders with big homes. She saw that all of them would happily pay for specialized frames that frequently surpassed the aesthetics of the art they encased.

I, on the other hand, had never possessed any such

overview of how the financial game worked, mostly because my goals were to keep us safe and warm and educated.

At age twenty-two, I decided never to have a car payment or the costly insurance that goes with it, in order to better afford a safer neighborhood to live in. Debt spelled trouble to me, and so I avoided it, unless I had a plan to pay it back. Student loans were secured only when absolutely necessary and never for my own college tuition, which was financed with Pell Grants and scholarships.

It made me giddy to dwell on Denise's ability to manipulate the money machine, to think of how, out of that talent, one more lucrative enterprise could grow—a mom-and-pop framing business. That she could create stunning art, and then sell it, that she could get people who liked their art framed to give her money for doing so, seemed like a secret recipe.

She didn't even know she was giving them to me, the secrets. But I lapped them up like a hungry puppy.

No, Denise wouldn't have had squat to do with me and my 1984 life of food stamps, fatherless kids, no education, and blue-collar boyfriends. I was so far removed from her 1984 world of rising-star Boulder babes, I would never have so much as registered on her radar.

It would take ten years, not to mention some unexpected, devastating circumstances, to align our stars. We collided more than met, and for four years hung on to each other for dear life, riding a violent, unrelenting vortex. And when the vortex finally, mercifully, released us, everything I ever thought I knew about controlling my life, about friendships, about hope—and about love—would be forever altered.

CHAPTER FOUR

Creamy & Delicious

Within days of meeting, we were going back and forth between each other's houses like we'd been doing it all our lives. Denise would stop to pick me up so we could run our errands together. I'd call her and, without introduction, speak dramatically into the phone. "Turn on Channel Seven now," I'd command. "Do you think I look like Bette Midler?"

"Yes," she'd reply, as if she'd been waiting for me to call. "Funny I didn't see that before." A second's hesitation, then she'd add, "Can you sing? We may be missing an opportunity." We'd watch the movie in silence, together, in our separate living rooms. "Tell me my lips aren't as gross as Barbara Hershey's," she'd insist.

"Never mind that," I'd answer. "Is Bette Midler pretty—or does she just look like Bette Midler?"

I'd always thought *Beaches* was sappy, all that "wind beneath my wings" stuff, but I couldn't stop watching it. There's Bette: chubby, hysterical, exuberant, so wanting.

There's Barbara: beautiful, stoic, successful. The comparison wasn't lost on me—on us.

Everything seemed so easy in those first heady months of our friendship. There was never any tentative getting-to-know-you with Denise. No delicate dance, no hesitation at calling and saying, *Drop what you're doing and come over. And stop at the five-dollar-a-plate Chinese place on your way.* It was all big, instantaneous, and action-filled from the beginning. It was "always-knowing" in the same way it is when you have a child, that once the child is born, it's impossible to recall ever not knowing that child.

One night I showed up unannounced—because it was an unspoken rule that I could—a warm, always-open invitation that satisfied fantasies I'd forever harbored about big, bosomy families who dropped in on each other without thinking about it. The idea of someone always glad to see me felt like warm, creamy butter.

"Does your husband want to join us?" I said with a nod toward the living room wall. I'd yet to meet Denise's husband. They had what I thought was a sophisticated living arrangement—sharing separate sides of a duplex. One marriage, two keys. It seemed mature to me, an unconventional way to acknowledge the need for intimacy and the desire for freedom. It seemed like Denise. Sometimes, however, it felt creepy, and I'd pause before I scooted up the steps and into her side of the duplex. Her husband's door, closed and impervious, gave me the jitters.

"Hmph." Denise reached down to tie her shoe. "Trust me. The last thing John wants to do is go to the movies with us."

I was curious about whether or not the absent hubby really existed (and what the hell did he look like, anyway?), because Denise was the only married woman in WOW. I had always believed that being married meant that you had it all wrapped up, that you didn't need friends, that you didn't get lonely. I wasn't naïve. I'd lived long enough to realize that many marriages were unhappy, maybe most were. But I remembered some of the comforts of being married, knowing who was waiting for me at the end of the day, who'd take me to the hospital if I had to go, and who, along with me, worried about the bills.

"Why'd you join our group?" I suddenly asked.

She kept fiddling with her shoes, taking time to arrange her clothing before she answered me. I wouldn't learn until later that MS would make her fingertips go numb and slow her down. I thought it was just a stalling tactic.

"Well," she said, "John doesn't do much with me." She gathered up her purse, reaching to shut off the television and lights. "Anyway, I was reading the paper one morning, saw your ad, and thought, Why not?"

I knew instinctively that this was only half an answer, and for a second, I considered pressing her. But I let the subject drop. Whatever the two of us had been seeking that Wednesday night, my sense was we'd struck some kind of bull's-eye.

Hell, though we kept the meetings up, we didn't need WOW. We had each other.

WE LAUNCHED OUR MOVIEGOING RITUAL ALMOST immediately—or, better put, I demanded right off the bat that she go with me at least once a week as part of my three-movies-a-week habit.

She wasn't the first I'd snared into my movie habit. I did the same thing with my kids. I remember insisting they watch *The African Queen* on television because I thought the writing and acting so important. And then waiting in line to see *Fiddler on the Roof* with free tickets I'd won. And then *E.T.* and *Ferris Bueller's Day Off*, the list goes on. Movies helped us have cheap fun. They helped us see other worlds.

Denise and I tried inviting Millicent from WOW, but she was too busy, and everyone else turned an initial invite down, content to see us at our Wednesday-evening gatherings.

So it was just we two, which felt perfect. We'd fill our pockets with miniature Reese's Peanut Butter Cups and M&M's, and tuck Diet Pepsis beneath our armpits so we'd have something to wash down all that candy with. We shared movie-theater-bought super buckets of buttered and salted popcorn because snuck-in microwaved popcorn just didn't cut it.

We liked the college lecture-room theater at the university's movie house, where each row of seats was several inches higher than the one before it. I loved those lecture halls. I fell in love with them when, in my twenties, I found myself miraculously taking one college course at a time, often on a Saturday morning, or one evening a week, but still. Those lecture halls full of thinking, full of invisible ideas, felt redemptive to me. They helped me balance, in my head, the demands of a life packed with work and responsibilities against the wants of a soul seeking betterment and hope.

One night, as we climbed the lecture hall stairs in the semidark, Denise grabbed my elbow to steady herself.

I'd been watching her for weeks. What I hadn't said to anyone that first night at WOW was that Eileen-Marie O'Shaunessy, my childhood friend with whom I'd briefly stayed in Indiana after my sojourn to Russia, also suffered from MS. Hers was pretty advanced, and I left because I couldn't bear to stay. I wanted to not feel the pull to take care of yet one more person. I wanted to be free.

I'm not proud of the sentiment. I justified my itch to leave by clinging to the knowledge that she had plenty of family, plenty of help. But I'd seen, firsthand, what MS could do to an otherwise absolutely healthy young woman.

So I'd been surreptitiously checking out Denise, scanning her body to see if she had the lurching gait I'd seen in my childhood friend, the chronic fatigue, the outright inability to get out of a chair. Though I'd noted Denise sometimes walked slower than I did, plenty of people walk slow, right?

When she grabbed my elbow, that was the first time I'd ever sensed that her MS was real, and I considered literally and figuratively letting go of her. But I didn't. Instead, I offered my full arm, made sure Denise had her balance, and kidded myself that, when it came to MS, there really was a good kind.

When Denise finally, mercifully, selected two seats, we fell into them. She turned her head side-to-side at the blank screen, testing the angle. "Mmmm . . . No."

"What?" I made like I didn't get that she wanted to switch seats and pulled a handful of M&M's from my pocket, popped open my drink, and turned completely around, opposite her, scanning the crowd and pretending not to notice her.

She heaved herself up and out of her seat. "We're moving."

I stood up and into the aisle and waited for her to get her bearings, to inch her way out of the row, maybe even to grab my elbow again. Then a lumbering teenage boy marched down the aisle, and his shoulder smacked my ear, leaving my head ringing. I held on to Denise for balance and followed her, slowly descending the theater's grade until we were directly beneath the screen.

"Too close," she said, and steered us both 180 degrees around. We re-climbed the steps until mid-theater and inched through a long row of empty seats all the way to the other side. She turned, checked the view.

"Nope," she said.

"Fuck this," I said. "Sit." I pushed her into a seat and smiled apologetically at the two women seated behind us. The women ignored us, and one of them kept chatting to the other about how hard it was to get her finger up and *far enough into* her dog's anal glands, thereby releasing a nasty, infectious pus.

Denise surrendered and popped her drink open with a loud *hisssss*.

"Hey, check that guy out," she said, loud enough for everyone around us to hear her. "His belly is big enough to sit on." She nodded her head toward a fat man across the aisle from us. I was mortified. Still, I stole a glance, just in time to see the man pour almost an entire box of Milk Duds into his mouth.

The trailers started. "Do you have those peanut butter cups?"

Her voice was big and invasive, like a church fart.

"Denise, shut up," I whispered.

"It's just the trailers," she said, pissy and even louder. She pouted and slumped into her seat. She was giving me the initiation into her emotional wall-building. She smashed her way through movie previews so she could resist the effect the movies themselves would ultimately have on her. She was trying to train herself not to feel, but I didn't realize that yet.

"Would you two *shut up*?" A woman leaned forward from the row behind us, her head between ours.

"Yeah, do you two *mind*?" her pal chimed in on the other side of my head, locking me tight in reprimand stereo.

Denise turned to face the women squarely. "Shut the fuck up yourself," she said. "You two haven't stopped yakking since we sat down—about *dogs*! Shit machines, that's what dogs are. Worthless shit machines."

"I'm leaving." I moved to stand up, but my head clobbered the outside woman, whose head, I'd forgotten, was still leaning in toward me.

The movie started, and all four of us, like prizefighters returned to our corners after the bell, leaned back into our seats, feigning a ridiculous reluctance at giving up our stances. I was glad for the out and sensed the others were, too.

I couldn't stand the movie. It was a long and self-conscious epic. But the thing had been hyped for months, and Denise couldn't get enough of it. Images flickered across our faces, spreading a moonlightlike glow over the theater audience. A soldier and his lover professed their ardent *amour* for each other over and over, but you knew they'd never get together because they were married to other people. I liked to look away from the screen and watch the sea of spellbound faces, eyes and brains and emotions mesmerized, held hostage, beneath celluloid and sound.

Denise continually reached into my coat pocket, grabbing handfuls of M&M's.

"I never eat these," she said in a loud whisper at my ear. "They're delicious." Later, when she reached in and found the pocket empty, I saw her face, glued tight to the movie, at the edge of her eye, a tear.

After the movie, when I took her home, she gestured for me to pull my car to the curb and park. "Come inside and meet my husband," she insisted. We sat for a moment in the front seat of my car and looked at her house, sitting above the street on a small knoll. The house was old and white and had two front doors and two front porches.

"You know that's John's side of the duplex, right?" she said and pointed up at one door.

I nodded yes. "It's a perfect arrangement," I said.

She stopped and looked at me. "I can always tell what kind of a person someone is by their reaction to the way we live."

"You know, Mary Wollstonecraft and her husband, William Godwin—their daughter, Mary Shelley, wrote *Frankenstein,* so you know they had sex—but they lived in separate houses, across the road from each other. It was such a relief to me to learn that," I said. "It's so perfect. It gives me hope. I fear that if I got married again I'd be freaked out that I'd suddenly be stuck in some little house with his poopy underpants and him coughing up loogies all the time."

I felt certain that in Denise and John I'd stumbled upon the one and only doable, perfectly arranged marriage on the planet.

WE WALKED A NARROW PATH BETWEEN BRICK HOUSES, and a light shone from a small building out back. She opened a screen door to a one-room studio, a converted one-car garage, and we stepped into a room crowded with T-squares and picture frames: a collage of colors in wood and metal and plastic. Large art pieces lay unframed upon a white padded table in the middle of the crowded room. A man stood at the table and steadily cut a long piece of glass.

"This is our frame shop," Denise said. "John, this is Cathie."

A Robert De Niro look-alike, John oozed pure charm. He was sturdily built: thick-shouldered, muscled arms. I figured that he was not quite five-ten.

His face was warm and sensitive. Behind his wire-rimmed glasses, I connected with intelligent brown eyes, and it was all framed in a shaggy head of salt-and-pepper curls. Denise had already let me know that her husband's father was Jewish, that he'd died when John was just a boy, and that his French, widowed mother had raised him and his two siblings as Catholics.

I concluded on my own—and later my conclusion proved to be pretty accurate—that he was the best of both of these worlds, combining practical, street-savvy insight with highly developed cerebral sensitivity and creativity.

He had easy, groovy Ray Charles beating from a radio at the back of the cramped studio. In one graceful movement, like an understated dance step, John turned away from us to lower the volume, then turned back to me and took my hand in both of his. "Hi," he said. He wore baggy shorts and a loose T-shirt. That he could use a haircut and a shave gave him a bedraggled, just-got-out-of-bed, sexy-man look.

"I told you about her," Denise told John. "She's the woman's group."

"We just saw this dopey movie that lasted three hours," I said to him.

"You went to the movies with *her*?" he said, pretending dismay, a wry smile.

"I was embarrassed beyond belief," I said. I could see he knew what I meant. "I nearly walked out. Inside of a minute she insulted a fat man and got us into a fight with two women."

"I quit going to movies with her years ago," John said. "I can't take it."

He glanced at Denise, then leaned into me conspiratorially. "You came along just in time." He grinned. "She's worked through everyone else—ain't nobody left but us chickens."

Denise laughed. She was the center of our attention. Her new friend got on with her husband, and she was happy. She jammed her hand into my pocket.

"You ate *all* of those M&M's?" she asked, in mock shock, but I didn't respond. I was distracted by the radio, by Ray Charles's lament for longed-for sweets and love meant for others. . . . *feedin' him ice cream and cake,* Charles crooned. *It shouldda been me with that real fine chick. You know, it shouldda been me eatin' ice cream . . . mmmhmm.*

John's comment—"nobody here but us chickens"—slipped by me slippery as the cool night air. He was giving me, at that moment, the state of the union address, the truth telling, the warning, the outright relief that I'd finally shown up—in a simple sentence. But I didn't hear it. I was caught up in the joke sharing, in our flirtation on Denise's behalf. As we commiserated about her loud, in-your-face personality—as we silently communicated to each other that she was, indeed, a complicated yet lovable pain in our respective asses—I missed what was plainly put in front of me. John was fairly shouting, "Look out!"

His sense of weariness glided right on by me. It was easy to ignore. There were, after all, just the three of us under the soft studio lights. There was our laughter and all the pretty frames and her handsome husband and the intoxication of a new friendship.

It was all I could do to drink all that in. It was all I wanted to do: soak it up, roll around in it. I just wanted to do what we were doing: laughing, grabbin' candy from each other, tapping our toes, just a little, to Ray Charles.

A chick walked out . . . She sure looked swell . . .

I gave her the eye . . . And started to carry on . . . When a Cadillac cruised up . . .

We were all still young enough, at our alleged primes, part of the big, fat, powerful baby-booming demographic—setting the proverbial world on fire, building stock portfolios and such.

Weren't we?

Mmm . . . hmmm, Ray Charles sang. *And "swish" she was gone . . .*

JACK LONDON WROTE A SHORT STORY ABOUT A FREEZING man who makes one last-ditch effort to build a fire to save his life. He struggles and struggles and finally gets a little flame going; then the flame grows and the man begins to warm. Suddenly a tree branch, high above him and laden with snow, lets go of its burden, dumping snow all over the fire, extinguishing the flames and his last chance to survive.

The story tells of how the tree feels the imperceptible disturbance of the fire building, the indistinguishable movement that jars the branches into letting go of months of snow accumulation, resulting in the loss of one last chance at warmth, resulting in the man's terrifying death from the cold.

The story haunts me—how an old tree kills that man, how his own tiny movements cost him his life.

Tiny movements.

The disintegration of a potent person, one brain cell at a time, is imperceptible.

There was no movie trailer giving us all a look-see of things to come. Had there been, I would likely have dropped her off after the show, said good night, and avoided her phone calls after that. No doubt I'd have dismantled WOW, chalked it up to making an awkward effort at manufacturing an instant community.

The little list in her step, her feather-light touch to my elbow to steady herself—like the tree branch barely altered, yet ultimately a death warrant—felt familiar, even inviting. Besides, falling apart is a comfort to those of us used to things routinely going south. A tottering woman, with an incurable disease, who insists she "has the good kind," is like a well-worn country-western song whistled softly in the dark: "Can't You Feel the Clusterfuck A-Comin', Hon?"

It's nearly imperceptible.

CHAPTER FIVE

I Dream of Jeannie

Just as I'd assembled a new life with friends acquired from the classifieds, I determined I was a restaurant critic long before I actually became one. I imagined myself an authority on what a decent cheesecake feels like, looks like, tastes like. I pictured myself a bread pudding expert, someone who not only would appreciate the raisins swimming in sugary goo but who could also discern a sultana from a sun-dried, a currant from a Corinthian. I would be smugly astute. I'd lick the rim of a freshly drawn stout, relishing the foam in anticipation of the ale's piquant charm. I'd be obsessive and skeptical, sometimes benevolent.

I'd be fickle but fair.

It had been eighteen years since my husband had left us and I had followed a friend to New Orleans. My young woman's whim resulted in me spending all of my twenties in New Orleans, a city that catapulted me far away from my midwestern culinary expectations (one roast + no salt + no pepper + unseasoned mashed potatoes = Gourmet Meal). In New

Orleans, each point of a four-point intersection offered up scores of unbelievable, mind-blowing menus, all of them vying to top the ones across the street: étouffée, shrimp as big as your fist, garlic swirling in golden butter, soft-shelled crab just minutes out of the Gulf—a gorging orgasm that made it impossible to select your favorite restaurant.

Hemingway wrote: "If you are lucky enough to have lived in Paris as a young man, then wherever you go for the rest of your life it stays with you, for Paris is a moveable feast."

Bite me, H.

If you are lucky enough to have lived in New Orleans as a young woman, you don't need Paris.

THINGS WERE OPENING UP, AND FOR THE FIRST TIME IN what felt like forever I was sensing a glimmer of possibility. Autumn's melancholy air cooled the Boulder flagstone sidewalks, lending a sweet longing to the late afternoon. Driving home with a fresh stash of Celestial Seasonings for that evening's WOW meeting, I saw it—a banner with "Boulder Bugle" scrawled across it. A new rag had, apparently, rented office space in an old building off Pearl Street in the center of town.

Holy hibiscus blend. I *had* read every single Wayne Dyer "you can do it" book I could get my hands on, but I never thought that shit actually *worked.*

I sensed a life-changing opportunity. Operating on gut rather than good sense, I parked the Plymouth and ran into a newsroom no bigger than a closet, schmoozed up the editor, and went home to write two mock reviews of restaurants that didn't actually exist. Then I took the last twenty-one dollars in my checking account and raced to Kinko's to create a full-page "Boulder Bugle Food Section" layout.

It was spectacular. It was colorful. It was smart. It made you want to *eat*.

I ran it back to the editor.

"We've got to do this," I insisted, and held the layout under his nose. I was tired of the old, of all-that-went-before. Could it actually come to pass that I might *never* have to type a legal brief again? Suddenly, everything I ever wanted, everything I ever imagined for a work life hung on this schlubby, bespectacled editor's whims.

I thought I heard him grunt.

"The *Camera's* old restaurant critic is dated and stodgy," I said, referring to his competitor. "He doesn't know a hush puppy from a hot tamale. See?" I pointed to the reviews and tried not to stare at his shiny head.

A second grunt.

"This will open wide all kinds of possibilities for advertising revenue," I added, instantly proud of my Denise-like thinking. I didn't mention all the possibilities it would open for me: eating and writing about food. The "in" I'd have with larger, national magazines as a Colorado restaurant critic would open doors to writing for those glamorous rags as well. Maybe, just *maybe,* I'd never again have to fetch one more cup of coffee for some boss-lawyer eyeing my breasts.

A tickle in my bones told me that I was behaving in a new, bold, and self-promoting fashion—grabbing an opportunity by the tail, brashly self-promoting—and that, somehow, rubbing up against Denise's business brain was breathing entrepreneurial life into mine.

And why not? I was sick of the dead-end toil. I vibrated with this new career—new life—possibility.

Suddenly, I couldn't breathe. *I had to have the gig. My entire work life, until that moment, hung on it.*

As I stood over the editor's desk, I flashed to the delicious anticipation of pulling Denise aside that evening at WOW with the news. *We're going to get fat for free! Start listing every Boulder restaurant you've ever wanted to try,* I would tell her. I knew that even her cynical, seen-it-all-before veneer would crack at this turn of events.

My eyes bore into his pink and balding scalp. I thought I might faint.

He looked up from his desk, put his pencil down, and unceremoniously nodded. "Okay."

NATURALLY, I PULLED DENISE FULL-FORCE INTO THIS new job. Naturally, we took ourselves oh so seriously from the start. I hid a tape recorder in my lap while Denise scratched illegible notes, her handwriting, her grip, weakening even then. *The wine's flat,* I whispered to the cassette tape whirring in my crotch as Denise hurriedly scribbled my insights onto the notepad hidden beneath her napkin. In the process she knocked a forty-two-dollar bottle of Australian chardonnay across the table.

About two dinners in, we got over ourselves and learned to ignore detail. Instead, we came to rely on our instincts and impressions, and we partied ourselves silly on newspaper-paid-for cabernet and calamari. It was all too perfect. I had a great, new friend, who was supportive and fun and wowed by this eating adventure. And because I'd had to wait until I was almost forty to land my dream job, I imagined—*hoped* was more like it—that my restaurant critic gig might spark just a wee bit of envy in other journalists. I knew I was being petty, but I didn't care. If those who had launched their careers at college age felt a little jealous, that was just the maraschino cherry on top.

Bliss.

Sometimes John came with us. He was the perfect dinner and review companion: not only did he know food (he had written a cookbook years ago) but he didn't drink much, so he could always recall specifics. Those evenings with John made Denise happy, as if he was going on a sort-of date with her. I understood her desire to have him with her, to laugh with her, to be adventurous and optimistic with her, but I squirmed at her obvious ache for him to join us, her raw want for his company. I didn't know if the cajoling, the flirting to get him to go out with us was a new dynamic between the two of them or if it had always been that way. Hell, I wasn't married. Maybe that was the way marriage works. But I came to realize that there was no one but John and me, that there was no close circle of friends, that her family didn't live close by, and that her framing customers were just customers, after all. So I went along and helped her in her efforts to exact her husband into our escapades.

Because that's what she wanted.

WE HIT A MOROCCAN PLACE MONTHS INTO OUR ALLEGED professional restauranting. Denise worked to stuff a poster-size, laminated menu into her purse in between the waiter's visits to our table, to help me recall entrée names for the column. I dragged along Judd, my current boyfriend, to make us an even-number double date. He was a whiner and a vegetarian, with a firm grip on a germ phobia, so sitting on the floor Moroccan-style made him extra nervous.

Someone blew a squawky wood flute in the corner of the place, and a chubby woman in an *I Dream of Jeannie* outfit wiggled out from behind a curtain, contorting and bending and sucking in her fleshy belly. She jiggled like mad and worked her way onto a shabby rug till she was in the center of the dining room. Falling into a back bend, she tried to make a penny flip over on her belly button. Suck *in*, push *out*, suck *in*. The penny didn't budge.

The flute played on, insistent and shrill. "Looks to me like she's dispelling afterbirth," I said loudly over the music.

A waiter pulled back strings of plastic beads in a doorway and delivered a large metal platter onto the table in front of us. In the middle sat a small and shiny whole chicken gleaming with fresh grease. Denise and I each snapped off a leg. Judd turned ashen.

"I'll give you a hundred dollars," I said to Denise between chews, "to get out there and belly-dance with her." The chicken was tender, oily, and delicious.

Denise laughed as John poured dishwater tea from an old metal pot into four small cups. A man came from behind the curtain in the corner, pelvic-thrusting his way to the center of the floor, and joined the belly dancer. He wore baggy, orange pants, and his skin and hair were as shiny as the chicken.

Denise chewed and studied the action.

"I'll give you *two hundred dollars* to go with her and dance," John said to me.

We laughed aloud, and Denise and I sank even deeper into the floor pillows, considering the cash possibilities. Denise leaned against the wall behind her.

"Too much trouble," we more or less said together.

I glanced at Judd. He was mesmerized by the belly dancer, though I guessed that he was grossed out by the restaurant and the slippery chicken. The funny thing was, Judd was actually a lot like that slick chicken: difficult to grab and even harder to hold on to. But he was the first guy I'd really dated as a woman without children living under my roof, and I was just learning childless dating. Judd could be very sweet to me. He'd stop and get flowers on his way to my house. He'd cut out an article he thought I'd be interested in. He wasn't without his niceness. But he found time to get together only once a week, and then he was hours late and wanted sex and little else.

Denise thought that he was cute, that I should be more stra-
tegic and try baiting him and sweet-talking him a little more.
But her endorsement felt false. It didn't feel like the savvy,
confident Denise. I wondered, if it had been fifteen years
earlier and she wasn't looking an illness straight in the eye,
would she think Judd so promising?

For the first time ever, I was groping my way into relationship health. I was just beginning to realign what I thought a
loving relationship might look like, should look like. I still
had no idea what it might feel like. But I knew Judd wasn't a
keeper. His last name was Wassermann, and I more or less
understood that I was a shiksa experience.

"These rugs are filthy," Judd said into my ear. He kept his
hands in his lap, touching nothing, including me, and nodded his head at the walls, where pseudo-imported rugs hung.
It was like a cave in there, I realized then, gloomy, maybe
moldy behind Denise's back where she was leaning, maybe
moldy beneath our butts, under the worn pillows we sat upon.

When we left, Denise grabbed a souvenir matchbook and
clung to John's arm, steadying herself, moving slowly at first,
a new habit, "warm-up walking."

Linking her arm securely through his, she basked in the
event of his being there. It was easy to see that she was forever
in love with him and why that was. He was masculine: muscled arms, broad back, strong legs. He could swing a hammer
and argue politics with equal ease.

Though he hated people and spent most waking and
sleeping hours on that self-built bunk bed of his, he was also
a perfect dancer and an exacting charmer.

"I remember going to this wedding," Denise once told me. "I had to drag him. It was the only time I can ever remember John wearing a tie—with jeans, though."

"He whirled every woman there around at least once," she said dreamily. "Women were coming up to him, cooing over him. They couldn't get enough. I'd never seen him dance until that wedding—and I haven't seen him dance since."

Outside the restaurant, she let go of John's arm and started jiggling, her hips awkward and slender. She was top-heavy, always had been, but that didn't stop her. I danced a little dance on the sidewalk next to her, and she flailed her arms, a full moon behind her breath-clouds in the frigid air.

We imitated the belly dancer mercilessly, pushing out our chicken-filled bellies, then bending way back like we were heading into back bends. Denise held the souvenir matchbook to my stomach and turned it over and over, and I obliged, pushing my gut out, pulling it back in.

We were hysterical, and so the men just waited at the curb. We didn't see anything. We were blind, staggering, holding each other up like trapeze artists, losing our balance and missing the wire and falling, nearly knocking each other down, clinging, gripping each other's arms.

"I'm cold," my date said, and we screamed with laughter, snake-, snake-, snake-dancing our way to the car.

WHAT JUDD DID NEXT WAS OPEN MY HEART WIDE TO John's former love for his wife, for what they'd once had. For a moment, just a second, really, they had their electric attraction to each other back. They had what they'd had in the eighties, when there was energy and spark, titillation and temptation. In that backseat, I saw a couple that once had a first kiss, a crazy-love make-out session, laughter, and longing for each other. I knew they'd once had all that and more because I saw it.

Judd left John with Denise and me still belly dancing on the curb and headed to the edge of the lot to collect his 1957 Chrysler New Yorker convertible. He was not a car guy in the average, car-mechanic sense of the word, but Judd possessed a brilliant engineer-wizard's mind, so he'd bought an old Chrysler years ago, when he was but a very young man with no money and no family in Colorado. Piece by piece, he'd restored the automobile, brought it fully to life, made it glimmer and purr. He'd coaxed and stroked and reengineered that magnificent car, making it glide on the road better than it had when it was new.

He almost never let it out of his garage. It'd taken him twenty years and countless bruised knuckles and cusswords and long, lonely hours with the hood propped wide open like a big animal's cavernous mouth to resurrect a car that rarely saw the light of day.

But that night, he showed it off to John and us appreciative girls, and he navigated the old-fashioned, oversize steering wheel, moving the car in a smooth float toward us like a monstrous pink boat, its convertible top folded completely back despite the chilly autumn air. Denise and I climbed into the backseat together, still snickering over the belly dancing, satiated with food and friendship. Then Judd steered the larger-than-life vehicle onto a busy street, and passersby honked and waved and called out to us like we were celebrities in the Macy's Parade. We adored the attention, and, for effect, Judd gunned the car a little. Even John couldn't help himself, and he turned toward the two of us and threw Denise a flirtatious wink. I don't know if the tears that sprang to my eyes were from the sharp wind cutting at our faces or from the knowing, the knowledge that Denise had everything she wanted, that she had—just for a moment—more than she could ever have hoped for.

From the back of the Chrysler, she laughed and waved to strangers like she'd just been crowned queen of the parade, wrapped tight in full-blown love and outrageous fun and in a body that, she forgot for the moment, didn't work. For those moments, she had the undivided attention and the unabashed admiration and the complete, unbridled adoration of her handsome, sexy, smarter-than-anyone husband.

CHAPTER SIX

Dead Women Talking

W hen not gorging on food, we gorged on gore. I couldn't get enough of serial killers because I was forever surprised I'd escaped them. Throughout the 1980s, I should have been, could have been nabbed, killed, maimed, and left to rot more times than I care to remember—if not by a serial killer then by some project crackhead, or any of the other beasts that lurked and lived at the edge of the Mississippi River.

Bridge phobia prohibited my driving over the New Orleans Industrial Canal Bridge, a monstrous, stadium-lit structure, a mile long and six lanes wide, built to support cars passing over the Mississippi River barge traffic. So at 3:00 A.M., done bartending, I'd drive under the bridge, all the way out from Canal Street, along the flat Almonaster Road—a ten-mile-long, forgotten strip of tar lined with abandoned welfare housing projects, broken windows hovering in the shadows like so many craggy, phantomlike faces. I'd race the Pinto at breakneck speed to get the frightening trip over with, sure that, among the junked-out car bodies, tires, and trash thrown about the deserted strip, the Pinto's 250,000+ mileage would finally give way. Racing, racing, shifting the car's gears like a pro, high-throttling it home in the predawn, certain one of the $13 retreads was about to blow.

Being so terrified of going over a bridge that you drive under it and through the scariest section of New Orleans—at the worst, the darkest part of night—makes you flirt with the fear, with the horror of those cars that never made it.

WE HARBORED OUR OWN REASONS FOR FEELING HAUNTED by violence. Many women do. They know the way that violence coats your soul like a rash does tender skin. They know that you don't shake violence, even the threat of it. It never leaves. It not only penetrates but moves in and resides permanently in your DNA, your voice, your demeanor, your dreams. It's like a film that can't be cleaned off with even the most abrasive cleanser, and so you're forced to allow it to adhere. You ever so slightly shift who you are to accommodate its menace. And you become obsessed.

Denise and I feverishly took up reading about murderers. It was our joint, tacit quest to figure out why atrocities happened. Reading about serial killers allowed us to visit our own pain, to look at it, at our collective unspoken outrage, from a safe distance. In this way, we could live with the injustice of it all just a tiny bit.

Ann Rule was our shared, decadently delightful obsession. An ex-cop turned true-crime writer, she pens tales of heinous murders, meticulously researching the myriad details surrounding the deaths of people who, as she'll tell you in her books, were just living their lives until somebody slashed their throats or burned them up in an arsonist's spree. She gathers the daily details of the husbands, the siblings, the children, the lifestyles, and wraps it all up in haunting stories about seemingly good citizens, got-it-together people who also happen to be killers: attorneys who plan their wives' deaths; cops who stop women for speeding, then stab them and bury them alongside deserted highways; creepy dads who set their daughters up to be hit men, then let the girls take the fall. You get the picture.

CNN news and my ignorance of Ted Bundy brought us both to Rule. Watching a report on the anniversary of Bundy's death, I asked Denise who he was.

"You never heard of Ted Bundy?" she responded in disbelief. "The college coed killer? They say he was so charming and handsome that during his trial women slipped him their phone number."

"That's insane," I said.

I checked out Ann Rule's *The Stranger Beside Me* at the library. On the back of the worn paperback was the story of Rule and Bundy's meeting, how the two of them worked in 1971 at a Seattle crisis clinic, where they shared the night shift answering a suicide hotline.

I curled up by myself on the couch and searched for clues to Bundy's devilish core in the black-and-white pictures that were glued to the center of the book's binding. I was particularly struck by the one of Mr. Handsome Murderer in his law school days, with thick, curly hair and a roguish grin as he leaned against a Volkswagen—the car he lured coeds into before he butchered them.

It was a quiet night. The landlady was out of town, so the house settled, still and solemn. I turned up the heat to take the edge off the chill that seeped into the corners of my basement apartment, then I turned out all the lights except the small reading lamp over the corner of the couch where I sat.

I studied the photos, titillated and horrified. The last was a full page, a striking picture of Bundy, dressed smartly in suit and tie, a regular guy next door who might offer to cut your grass or ask you to a movie. I thought of his parents, who watched this strong and thick-haired boy grow and who must have taken joy in their boy's documented academic prowess, who nurtured his maturation from gangly adolescent to robust, sculpted manhood.

When I lifted the book up close to study his face, the page loosened from the binding and slipped from my grip, falling away. A little start escaped my throat, and I snatched the page midair to stuff it back into the book's pages. Then I stopped short.

Bundy grinned straight up at me, and I held my breath, caught in his grimace. I remembered an Izaak Walton quote I'd written down and looked upon for faith and help as a young woman alone and overwhelmed: "If you can't be content for what you have received, be thankful for what you have escaped."

And I was. I felt overwhelming thanks for where I was, for my chilly apartment, for my children being alive and safe. I was struck by, and then consumed with, a wave of gratitude and awe at being free to breathe, to lock my door, to bathe in a warm bubble bath, and then to sleep soundly and safely.

SO THE TWO OF US PLUNGED HEADFIRST INTO AN ANN Rule immersion. We didn't just read her books, we waited like vultures for each new one, debated incessantly on which crimes Ann worked hardest to research and write. Denise said that Ann gave her women victims way too much credit in the smarts department, that she too generously described the victims as bright and got-it-all-together when she set up the story.

We analyzed her books back and forth, back and forth. Obsessively. *How do these guys walk around and slaughter and not get caught? Why are so many of them good-looking and smart?* These were the questions we tossed at each other. It was too juicy for us both. We were voyeurs, sneak-peeking into the lives of the victims, pretty women, we commented to each other, examining their photos in the books, women we pitied but also instinctively, self-protectively criticized for getting themselves into such awful hot water.

Our WOW friends laughed at our obsession. "Get real lives," Millicent said. "She's a cop who writes trash."

"Trash we devour," Denise quipped back.

But Ann wasn't trash. She was the victims' voice, and that made her *our* voice. Ann earned our mutual respect because we felt there existed an under-the-radar club of the defective and broken, and we were at the core of that club. We knew that really bad things happened every day to unsuspecting and innocent folk and that most of that badness never got talked about. We knew firsthand that people don't talk about—let alone deal straight out with—real bad shit. Gut-wrenching facts of pure, unbridled tragedy often paralyzed those of us who were just trying to keep the Subaru payments up. The facts might be horrific, but they were somebody else's horrors, and they were nightmares tightly bound and professionally packaged in a designer's elegant jacket.

All that containment was a comfort.

WHEN ANN RULE GAVE A BOULDER BOOKSTORE READING, we rushed to be the first in line. Though seeing Ann in person was Denise's idea—she called me twice at my office to confirm our plans—it turned out to be a hard night for her.

Finally ready, I headed out to pick her up. Her house was dark when I got there. I walked in and through her kitchen, flicking on lights as I went. Denise stood just inside her bedroom, off the kitchen, braiding a thick plait of hair. Though we were late, she moved slowly, steadily crisscrossing long chunks of coarse auburn hair. She eventually got it where she wanted it and secured the braid against the back of her head with a large, ornate barrette—a thing of beauty, a sculpture really, with copper and gold and silver woven through the design. She'd discovered it one afternoon at an art show and couldn't get away from it, going to other installations, admiring a painting and some photography, and then, without my knowing it, she had two of them—identical, one for each of us—wrapped in fine tissue paper; we were now middle-aged women with matching hair barrettes.

I could see that her hands were trembling. Recently, I'd seen several sure signs of the MS acting up. Each small symptom, every imbalance, seared my soul, took my breath away. Little fractures in my heart magnified when I'd witness the smallest struggle. But the honest truth, in that moment, is that I was annoyed. The signs threatened our chances of seeing and hearing and maybe even talking to the writer whose every story, every syllable we consumed with relish.

Not that either of us would have considered not going. Denise never made reference to her symptoms (which often didn't show), but then neither of us did. We pretended. We acted. We made grocery lists, did laundry, kept the car filled with gas. Neither of us knew at what point, how or when, denial became our modus operandi, but it was a strategy we'd each downloaded. We'd fine-tuned our ability to ignore the MS fallout to a sturdy yet delicate rhythm. If we didn't speak about the Illness with No Cure in our midst, then we were still simply two women enjoying ourselves as best we could. We didn't have to worry about numb fingers or blurred vision or vertigo. We were like anyone else.

Furthermore, my brain operated in a distinctly polar-opposite fashion. On the one hand, I noticed her hand tremors and her sweat-beaded brow and her subtle touch when she reached for a chair arm to steady herself. Who wouldn't? But I'd left my Gary, Indiana, pal not because of, but certainly in the thick of, her MS demise—disintegration exhibited with alternating bouts of rage and debilitating depression. And I'd just traded in a life of Goodwill furniture and chronic financial strife for one of independence and hope. My brain refused to merge these two worlds.

"Your hair looks good," I said, reaching for her wine goblets. I had to push aside three of the five blenders that stood at attention on her kitchen countertop. Denise created mush in the blenders, with newspaper and water and plaster of Paris, a gloppy mess that splattered everywhere. She dyed the paper pulp and ultimately molded it into fantastic, surreal sculptures, creations hard to envision while she was elbow-deep in the sludge.

I pulled two glasses from her cabinet and poured a little cheap Hungarian cabernet into each. I doubted the wine's quality, but Denise said that she'd read about it, that, even at the unspeakable price of five dollars a bottle, it was supposed to be "full of personality."

"I colored it last night," she said, barely managing to snap the hair clip closed, her hair was so thick, her fingertips so noticeably unsteady.

"You dye your hair?" I asked, dumbfounded. I had no idea. To me it was a believable, sturdy color. It matched her complexion and temperament perfectly. I felt duped and also hypocritical, because for years I'd also "helped" lift my tannish hair into varying shades of blond. "What's your natural color?"

She eyed me. "It's been snow white for fifteen years."

I stopped midpour. "It is *NOT. Snow* white?"

"It takes two boxes of stuff to cover it," she said proudly, turning back toward the mirror. "I thought I'd never get through it last night. I was so tired by the time I finished."

"How often do you do it?" I probed, still disbelieving. "I've never, ever seen one little hint of white roots showing. And I look at everyone's roots."

"At least every two weeks," she said. "*Of course* you never see my roots." She said this last line like I'd insulted her, then walked over to get her wine.

She lost her balance and knocked against the door frame between her kitchen and bedroom, but we both kept moving like it never happened. I fake-checked my purse for car keys so she wouldn't notice me noticing *her,* then turned away and busied myself by plugging up the wine bottle. She grabbed the door frame, took a few seconds to regain her balance, and downed the wine. She was right. It did have personality. A bitter, biting one.

I strained not to reach over and straighten the crooked barrette for her.

"Are you going to get her autograph?" I asked, trying to change the subject.

"Puh-lease," she replied with a glance, letting me know that autograph-seeking was pedestrian. "Hurry up," she ordered, then reached behind her kitchen door and casually pulled out a walking cane I'd never seen before. She gave me a nudge and shut her door behind us.

WE MADE OUR WAY TO THE FIRST ROW OF CHAIRS, RIPPED Reserved signs from two, and flopped down.

Our eyes were glued to the table just a few feet from our seats, where everything—bottled water, a microphone, and her newest book—was set up for our celebrity author. We vibrated with anticipation, elbowing each other with silent can-you-believe-we're-here! pokes. Charles Manson's presence couldn't have titillated us more.

Fans filled the bookstore. "Who *are* these people?" Denise asked. We were a little miffed by the large turnout. When Ann Rule, goddess of god-awful gore, finally walked in, her appearance threw us off. She looked like she had never spent a day in police academy training or the dark dungeons of the deadliest and most devious minds in the country. She was a gal you'd want for a neighbor—friendly faced, late fifties, tinted blond hair, and wearing the comfortable, blousy clothing that travels well and flatters middle age. "My next book is about a mother who sets her house on fire to kill her three children," she said, matter-of-factly. The entire room held its collective breath, all of us, riveted to her every syllable.

"She's an M.D.," Ann added. "She was seeking revenge on a husband who'd left her." Ann captivated her hushed audience, talking on about the way she researched, the criteria she required, the facts she needed like who was arrested for what and when, her strategies for making the story whole.

"The crime must already be resolved," she explained, "so I have to wait a long time to get the entire story for a book. It's a lot of talking—with victims' families, the FBI, lawyers.

"And yes," she went on. "When possible, I do visit the crime scene. And I always visit with the killers. It's important for me to hear their stories, to hear firsthand what happened. Often I visit them several times."

Denise and I grinned at each other.

WHEN ANN FINISHED TALKING, IT WAS HARD TO GET HER attention, to get her to stop autographing books, to just get close to her. But we ignored the line of autograph-seekers lining up in front of the table, and elbowed our way through the jutting arms clutching new-bought books. Denise, white-knuckled and leaning hard into her cane, worked her way around to the back of Ann's autograph table.

"Hey, take our picture!" I called to the first woman in line, thrusting a camera at her and ducking beneath the throngs to the author's side. Ann was sitting, so I had to squat next to her to get our heads at the same level.

"Wait! Wait till we're ready!" I called out to the photographer. Denise was having trouble squatting to get her head at the same level as ours. I looked over at them both, their eyes poised and smiling at our photographer, their grins waiting and expectant.

"Look here! Hey, you! Look!" Our photographer waved to get my attention. "Now—*smile!*"

I pulled my eyes from Ann and Denise, but I didn't want to. I wanted to keep looking at those faces: devilish smirks, shiny eyelashes, the overheated room leaving a moist blush on their cheeks. I turned away from them and found the camera's lens in the crowd, then smiled dead-on into it. The light exploded in my eyes, and I blinked several times, straining to see Denise, worried I'd lose her in the blinding flash. Now that we had the shot, the struggle Denise had been having all night rushed over me. *What if she has too much trouble getting back on her feet? What if her motor control really is failing?*

Then I thought, *Surely Ann will help us if I can't pull Denise up, if Denise can't right herself. She is only a person a little off balance, after all.*

I heard Denise laugh aloud, and I looked over at her, with her head thrown back and the wide swatch of snow-white hair at her neck. The glimpse of white hair softened some hard edge of my heart and made me beam at all our good fortune. I saw Ann reach out and catch Denise's barrette as it fell from her hair. In the next second, Ann held Denise's wrist and steadied her. Denise was tickled by the folly of us three, and then Ann, infected with Denise's giggle, began chuckling, and we all laughed together, united in our glee, in our communion, our understanding that nothing was as bad as it seemed, that it all could really have been a hell of a lot worse. One whole hell of a lot.

I MANAGED TO HOIST DENISE UP AND GET US SAFELY BACK to her living room: a room with fourteen-foot-high ceilings and walls covered with twenty years of her devotion to art collecting. On one wall hung Kandinsky-like paintings, oversize, surreal explosions built of electric colors. Watercolored cityscapes and one of Denise's own paper sculptures—a dozen rows of rolled and molded paper pipes with gold-leaf trim—covered one wall. Pastoral oil paintings and testaments to 1960s culture—an *Abbey Road* album framed and autographed, eyeglasses with pointy corners and metal frames, and a Lava lamp covered another. Tiny, recessed lights showcased one of John's works, a bicycle folded, bent, and crammed into a little cage and displayed upon a white pedestal. It was magnificent, mesmerizing. How'd he get that bicycle so *folded up*? It was hard to stop looking at it.

Since John's half of the duplex was a junky mishmash of old furniture and rusted file cabinets, he migrated some evenings to Denise's half to eat, to watch TV, to escape. "My sister once accused me of installing cable TV on my side of the duplex," Denise told me, "so that John would be lured over here." I couldn't tell if she meant to be sarcastic, honest, or both.

Sure enough, in our absence that night, John had wandered over to Denise's side and created a feast: roast beef in a reduced wine sauce with tender carrots and glazed onions. He presented his efforts, arranged on a beautiful white platter, and we oohed and aahed with surprise, grabbing plates and reopening the Hungarian swill we'd started before the Rule regalia.

"Well?" John asked and looked from my face to Denise's. "Was she scary?"

"Ann Rule is not scary, she's funny and nice—and she doesn't write fast enough. Her next book's not due out till next year," said Denise.

"We got a picture, look." I thrust our photograph in front of John's face.

"How'd you manage this?" he asked, smiling when he saw our three mugs grinning back from the Polaroid.

"Cathie pushed everyone out of the way and organized it," said Denise, sinking next to me on the couch. "I don't think Ann appreciated it."

"She didn't care," I said. "We're nothing. She's used to interviewing killers and rapists for hours. I don't know how she does it. How does she sleep nights? She said that she drives home alone in her car after interviewing a guy who gives her hours and hours of details about torture."

"Speaking of torture," Denise said to John, "we need a bigger television. Ann's new book is getting made into a movie; I want to actually be able to see it." Denise assumed a fake sadness and looked forlornly at her thirteen-inch set. "That thing's over ten years old." She nodded at the television and grinned at me. Something was up.

"Don't even think about it," John said. He knew well Denise's proclivity for being loose with a credit card, a holdover from her 1980s days of high rolling and moneymaking.

"Yeah," she called to him, "one of those high-tech ones, with lifelike resolution and a VCR built into it."

When I leaned toward the coffee table to fill my plate, Denise put her mouth to my ear. "Don't tell John, but I've already bought one. I'm going to tell him it was given to me. It'll fit great right there." She pointed to the one corner of the cramped room that actually had a few inches of furniture-free, non-art-displaying space.

"Sssh!" I whispered back. "Those things cost thousands, and John's going to blow a gasket when he finds out."

"Think of *aalllll* those movies we'll watch," she said loudly, a talk-whisper into my ear, not dropping her voice a bit.

"You two want some Ben & Jerry's?" John asked. He stood over us with a pint of soft ice cream in one hand and sipped from his wineglass with the other. We hadn't seen him walk back in from the kitchen.

Startled, Denise and I looked up at him and too loudly, guilt tingeing our voices, yelled *"Yes!"* together, our wide eyes fairly screaming our duplicity—and then we burst out laughing. John walked away, shaking his head.

CHAPTER SEVEN

BeCoz, Just BeCoz

Denise swore to John that the CU Athletic Department *gave* her the thirty-six-inch TV-VCR combo. "They were trading up," she said. But once she'd rolled it into her living room—jamming it between wandering Jews and philodendrons in desperate need of repotting—we all quickly came to love the television, sitting rapt as Orenthal James Simpson and his histrionic lawyer held court on MSNBC. Like those who come to the town square early for the public hanging, we watched hungrily and waited for the conviction we knew was imminent.

"He'll cook," Denise said. "His attorney's a clown."

"Too bad for him that DNA evidence exists," I said. "God, that's one smokin', sexy black man."

"Don't get attached," Denise deadpanned. "He's as good as dead."

When Saturdays rolled around and we couldn't watch the trial, watch news about the trial, or watch interviews of those who'd crossed paths with O.J., we slipped comfortably into the time-honored cavorting of garage-sale hunting. It was a ritual, and not just for us, but for what seemed like thousands of Boulder bargainers who woke up Saturday mornings and headed straight out their front doors to their cars. With one fist clamped tight around a grande low-fat latte and the other locked to the steering wheel, they'd cruise the pictorial, rolling Rocky Mountain foothill streets, one eye on the road and the other peeled to front yards.

Garage sales in Boulder, Colorado, are different from garage sales in, say, Des Moines, Iowa. In Des Moines or Amarillo or Kankakee, garage sales offer up loads of baby clothes, a pasta maker, and a dented bike or two. But in Boulder, a postcardlike village überpopulated by Silicon Valley defectors eager to blow their severance on the new crop of multimillion-dollar homes, garage sales took on an elevated, celebratory air. Middle-class bargain hunters reveled in the chance to sift through a stranger's oh-so-last-season, two-thousand-dollar ski outfits, their nerves tingling at the prospect of the score. Castaway custom-designed furniture and state-of-the-art biking and mountaineering equipment was standard stock at Boulder garage sales. Often the stuff had never been used.

That particular Colorado morning exploded with springtime showing off in Hollywood Technicolor: aqua blue sky and brilliant red mountains jutted shockingly upward. It was a backdrop so stunning, it had the backlit quality of an Imax movie screen. You wanted to reach out and touch it.

We'd been driving for barely ten minutes when Denise pointed toward a luxurious, solar-panel-roofed home rising straight up from a mountainside. The mansion was set against the exquisite Chautauqua Park, with its artists' colony of cozy cabins that once played host to Allen Ginsberg and Jack Kerouac. A tiny sign half an acre down from the house announced the inevitable: ESTATE SALE.

Denise threw open the car door before I could kill the engine. She was as eager to haggle, to snag the rich people's throwaways, to get as much as she could for nothing as everyone else. This was an Olympic sport for Denise. She wasn't cheap, nor did she necessarily need or even want the stuff she brought back. She was just so skilled at getting people to *give* her their goods that she couldn't resist the challenge. At one point I wrote a full-page newspaper story on her devotion to Boulder garage sales.

Denise loved the story. The picture on the front page of the Lifestyle section flattered her and listed all the booty she'd snagged for free. "$300 designer handbag, cost to super bargain hunter Denise Katz—$0" read the caption underneath her smug and smiling face. She'd talked someone into giving it to her (then she promptly threw it in a closet and never used it).

I laughed at her after the story ran. She'd bragged in the interview about secret Boulder neighborhoods full of excellent garage sale stuff, crowing she'd later regret, as her big mouth ensured the secret was out.

That morning was no different from any other Saturday morning as I followed breathlessly after her. The sunny day tricked everyone into forgetting that summer was still a few months off. Denise wore dark green khaki shorts that showed off her shapely, tanned-looking legs, limbs that appeared youthful, athletic, without defect.

The lawn she scaled was massive, a professionally land-scaped masterpiece that, until a few years prior, had been little more than a rocky hillside covered in scrub weed and thistle. That day, an expanse of weekly-fertilizer-fed sod spread across the incline like an eerie green blanket. Slender aspen starter trees formed little groves on each side of the man-made creek that ran through the front lawn. A redwood bridge spanned the little creek, and I couldn't help thinking that East Boulder Landscapes certainly hadn't had dozens of roaming bargain hunters in mind when they designed the rickety little bridge or the Disneyland oasis.

I parked the car and ran-skipped after Denise to see what'd caught her eye. When I tapped her on the back to let her know I was there, she spun around. "Check these out!" she exclaimed in a hushed voice. She leaned over a bunch of boxes containing glass and dust. "These chandeliers would cost a thousand dollars in an antiques shop," she whispered.

She turned to a woman with a blond globe of hair and a diamond ring too big for her bony finger, who fake-smiled at us. "What are you asking for these?" Denise said nonchalantly, turning away from the boxes as if she'd lost interest.

"Aaah," said the blond globe. "These are some of my family's heirlooms. They came from our Atlanta home," which came out *Ahtlaantah huume*. The woman was no dope, but neither was Denise, who had already turned her attention to some Pier 1–looking crap: three margarita glasses and a matching pitcher.

"Mistah Wellington would just *die* if he saw me getting rid of them." The woman leaned into Denise, trying to snag her into husbands-are-sooo-troublesome commiserating.

Denise had already moved on to a set of snowshoes, one of which she picked up and turned over and over, scrutinizing its tightly woven threads. "These don't have a price," she said. She had never snowshoed in her life.

"Those light fixtures don't work in Colorado," Denise said to me, plenty loud enough for Mrs. Wellington to hear. "We have different electrical codes here."

"Well," Blondie started. "Would you like to make an offer? They're both almost seventy-five years old."

"And heavy as hell," Denise said. "And probably need special wiring."

"I feel certain an antiques dealer would—" Blondie tried.

Denise butted in. "Maybe in the South. Colorado's too modern." Denise knew even less of the South than she did of snowshoes. Even though her heart and home had been in Boulder for twenty-five years, she harbored an almost familial pride in being a native New Yorker. Given the opportunity, she'd intentionally mix up Louisiana and Indiana in reference to any geography west of Wall Street, entertaining herself with her New Yorker's dig at the irrelevancy of anything beyond the Island.

Yellow Hair gave her a look that said: *It's sad that Coloradans with their Buffalo Bill tastes can't begin to appreciate beautiful Southern antiques.*

"Oh," Denise said, and she glanced down into the boxes again. "Those little glass icicle things will be impossible to replace, so even if you *could* find a way to hang these mon-sters, they won't look right, they'll be missing pieces." She said this toward me, though I had not contributed a syllable to the conversation. "Maybe fifty bucks." She shrugged like she was finished and bored.

Globe Lady put her well-manicured and diamond-studded hand to her throat.

"But I don't know," Denise said, again, at me. "I hate to take junk home that I'll just throw in the garage." Like she had a garage. "But throw in those glasses and that heavy pitcher, and ..." She turned toward Mrs. Wellington and hesitated like she might change her mind. "And, okay, it's a deal." Denise whipped out a fifty-dollar bill and put it under Globe Lady's nose. The next thing I knew, Denise was handing me a box loaded with tinkly-sounding glass. She grabbed the pitcher and glasses, carefully placing them in the other chandelier-laden box, and together we hiked the long slope down toward the car.

We were gone before Wellington's wife could understand what had happened to her *Ahtlaantah* antiques.

YEARS LATER, THOSE CHANDELIERS WILL TRAVEL THROUGH two turn-of-the-century Colorado homes I end up living in. They'll be dismantled, packed up, and replaced with crummy Home Depot fixtures as I leave one house and move to an-other.

Also years later, the chandeliers safely installed in one of those houses, I'm running errands on an off Saturday afternoon. With time on my hands and a notion stirring from some subliminal recess, I pull my car to a curb in the South Broadway Antique Row section of Denver. A shop sign has caught my eye: ANTIQUE LIGHTING.

Right inside the door—purposely hung at the front of the shop to lure in passersby with their magnificent, intricate design—are duplicates of the very chandeliers that hang in my house, one in the dining room, the other in an oversize foyer. Their price tags: $1,500 and $2,000 apiece.

Each chandelier is nearly three feet wide, and every spring I dismantle the hundreds of crystal droplets, dip them in ammonia, and wipe them down, cussing all the while at how tedious and time-consuming and positively mind-numbing this rite-of-springtime cleaning is.

Then I'll wait until the late-morning sun beams in from the south-facing windows. I'll watch the larger one that hangs in the dining room as a stream of sun catches one of the fixtures, at the tips of those hundreds of crystals, tossing brilliant prisms of purple and gold and red and ice-white light across the room. I'll sip excellent coffee, no grande or latte anything, more like what they percolate in Des Moines, with texture and heavy, fresh cream, and I'll think of those sturdy, athletic legs. And I'll remember.

MIDMORNING WE PULLED INTO A SINCLAIR STATION, AND while the gas pumped into the tank, I looked around at the waiting area. It was sparsely furnished: an ancient, humming cooler crammed between a torn vinyl kitchen chair and a counter holding a manual cash register. I pulled open the cooler door to find two bottles of dust-draped Orange Crush, which I hated. "I'm going to that 7-Eleven across the street to get something to drink," I said to Denise, who sat in the passenger seat circling garage sale ads as fast as her marker allowed.

When I returned, I stopped short. A 1965 Mustang, lemon sherbet on the outside, supple and silky black bucket seats inside, was parked at the side of the station. Next to the Mustang sat a 1958 candy-apple-red Corvette. It was a convertible, and the top was down; the whole thing glimmered like a ruby in the sunlight. I pressed my face to the Mustang's window and saw a shiny gearshift, a dashboard that glowed, it was so pristine.

"There's only forty-seven thousand miles on that."

I stepped back, and a silver-haired man with luminescent blue eyes smiled at me.

"The odometer's turned over," I said to him. "That's more like one forty-seven, probably two hundred forty-seven thousand miles."

"No," he said, still grinning. "This car's been garaged for fifteen years. That's forty-seven thousand miles—total."

Denise poked her head between us. Beaming, she took a swig of Orange Crush.

"Both of these cars are his," she said, nodding her head toward the smiling man. An olive green mechanic's shirt strained against Blue Eyes's belly. MERLE was stitched across the shirt's pocket, and Denise's look told me that she and Merle were great buds—that my crossing the street for a few minutes had left me decidedly out of their very exclusive loop.

I couldn't help but gawk at the cars, wanting to eat them both, they were so smooth and liquid-looking, washed and polished clean as two freshly bathed babies.

"I call this one Tweety Bird. Just bought her," Merle said, gesturing toward the Mustang. "She sat for fifteen years in one of my customers' garages. It was her husband's, and he's been dead that long." Merle was pleased to tell me this, a half smile on his face. "Let me show you two what I just bought," he added, knowing a captive audience when he saw one. He popped the hood, and we had no choice but to admire the car's shiny innards.

"How long have you had this station?" Denise asked.

"Going on twenty-two years," he answered from under the hood.

A dachshund shuffled out of the station's waiting area and stopped at our feet.

"That's Coz," said Merle. "Short for Cosmo."

Denise stooped down and petted Coz as if she doted on dogs every chance she got.

"*Ooh, Cozzy,*" she crooned, swiping that little wiener-dog head. "Your daddy promised me a ride in his Corvette." She looked at me out of the corner of her eye. "We're going to the mountains tomorrow—want to go, little doggie?" she baby-talked at Coz, picking him up and planting a loud *smack*-kiss on his tiny, hairy ear.

I gave her a look to remind her of the dogs-are-shit-machines movie fight. She ignored me and cradled the dog in her arms.

"Are these cars for sale?" I asked for the sport of it, to be nice.

Merle laughed. "Nope."

"I'll bet that Corvette's fast," Denise said, popping Coz another kiss on his little head.

I looked at her and her blatant flirtation, her faked-out swooning over that dog.

"So," I said, "if someone walked in and offered you thirty thousand dollars for that Mustang, you'd say no?" Like I had thirty thousand dollars. It was easy for me to joke with that mechanic, that old-car aficionado. He embodied many of the men in my extended family. He was friendly, capable of talking easily with others, loaded with secrets he held close. He was likable, and I could hear—in the little clip in his voice, in the way he wrapped his mouth around his vowels, soft and malleable—that he was from the Midwest.

Unfettered by any heavy man-woman political dynamic, we teased each other almost like we were related, and it was easy to see that the ease between the two of us pleased Denise.

"You offering thirty k?" Merle said jokingly.

"Well, we can't buy, but we can ride," Denise said. "Cozzy's saying he wants a ride." She put the dog's mouth to her ear like Cozzy was whispering his want-a-ride request. My look told her that, if she didn't stop, I'd projectile-puke on her and the dog.

Merle called to another mechanic back in the shop that he'd be out for a while, and then we were all in the Mustang. Denise had wanted the Corvette, but we couldn't all three fit. The sun blasted a steady stream of warmth through the windshield, making everything glitter: the metal-filled dashboard, the sleek bucket seats, Coz's red coat—and Denise's eyes, which caught mine in the right side-view mirror just as Merle shifted Tweety Bird's engine smoothly, expertly into high gear.

It was just like Denise. She saw something she wanted, and then *click-click-click,* her brain took over and came up with a plan to get it.

Merle drove a little too fast that morning, and it was thrilling. I shut my eyes against the wind as we blew down the street, rushing against the air and picking up speed. I knew their affair had begun and settled in, ready to give in to the car's magic, to shake off all our cares of the moment.

But I couldn't.

CHAPTER EIGHT

Urethra's Got Two

"I've booked us at CUNT," I said. Chez Universelle Natural-Beauty Training, where we got facials, pedicures, and manicures—a half day's primping—for just twelve dollars. CUNT was our made-up beauty school name (and acronym) for a franchise of alleged fancy schools we thought suspect in their academic quality.

The twelve-dollar bargain was supposed to be a onetime-only offer, but we got around all that by changing our names each time we went.

We hated that the Chez Universelle students paid loads of "tuition" money and that, once trained, they went on to work in the Chez Universelle shops all over town—hoity-toity salons tucked into exclusive neighborhoods like Cherry Creek, where the John Elways and Coors brewing founders lived and spent. *Real* salon clientele (versus we beauty school guinea pigs) got charged $250 for a haircut, largely because you got a *team* at the real salon. Two people, often a gay guy with clips and combs hanging off his shirt paired up with a

Broncos-cheerleader-looking dame, stood solicitously by, hemming and hawing over exactly What It Was *Your* Hair Needed.

We just got to the CUNT alumni before they hit Cherry Creek.

I drilled Denise on the way downtown.

"You're Deb," I told her. "Got it? My name's Aretha."

She gave me a little snort.

"Listen! I reserved you under Deb. Deb, Deb, Deb." She acted like she wasn't listening. "*Think:* Debbie Reynolds, Debbie Does Dallas."

Our grooming scam played out perfectly for us both because it was inherently what we knew how to do best. Denise scored deals all day long, and she prided herself on her ability to figure out what people really, really wanted or what they needed (or what they thought they needed). She'd then step in and offer them whatever it was they couldn't live without.

And we both knew about needing a pick-me-up and getting it for nothing.

But that's not the whole story. The whole story is that we laughed at what we devised for entertainment. We made fun of ourselves for crafting crap to do. We created diversions that had us racing toward the next adventure with blinders. We knew that, whatever it was we were headed toward, it promised even more twists, turns, and total surprises than anything we might have planned. We weren't stupid. We knew there was a price to pay for giving young, apprenticing beauty professionals access to our bodies. But what the hell? Our bodies had seen a lot and would continue to see a lot. Abdicating them for twelve dollars and a couple of hours

to girls and boys and their scissors and chemicals felt luscious.

Because we had such a damn good time doing it.

That day I splurged, adding a three-dollar styling to my
tab so that a girl could dry-cut my hair. She grabbed a clump
in her fist, held it out, and chopped. Her face registered confu-
sion as my hair fell to the floor. Either that or she was stoned.
I couldn't tell.

"Let's go over here and wash the rest," she said.

I looked up her nineteen-year-old nostrils and watched
five silver rings wiggle along her nose as she sudsed my head.
The cold bowl felt good on my neck, and I relaxed against the
porcelain, reveling in the fact that I was playing hooky from
a temporary editorial job I was sick to death of. It was a weird
trade-magazine editing gig, with a staff built of fundamental-
ist Christian family members, mostly men from Oklahoma.
I wondered if anyone would notice I was gone.

When the nineteen-year-old led me back to the cutting
chair, I stopped and watched a young black woman dig the
grout from Denise's big toenail. I thought there were long green
worms or something on the pedicurist's hands, but when I
looked again, I saw that she sported six-inch fingernails that
curled in dramatic neon swirls over the ends of her brown
fingertips. She was holding Denise's foot on her knee with her
knuckles.

"I do nails, nothin' but nails," she said when she saw me
stop to watch. She picked something from a corner of Denise's
toe and wiped it on a towel. I saw Denise's balance waver. She
grabbed the edge of her seat with both hands.

"Ooooh-WEE," said the pedicurist, "I couldn't wear this color in a million years. Honey? This color'd look like *nothin'* on me." Denise showed me the Rose Mauve Blush she'd chosen from a bin of nail polishes.

"So when are you getting married?" Denise asked the nail girl.

"Oh, I don't know. He's still married, so we got to take care of a few things." She studied Denise's toes, then took the towel and swiped between each one.

"Four stepchildren. Do you know how much work that is?" Denise asked.

"You got kids?" the nail girl asked back, not looking up from her work.

"No, but *Urethra* here's got two," Denise said. I threw her a look.

The girl either didn't hear or didn't care about the Urethra moniker. "My momma, she raised eleven of us," she said, lifting Denise's foot toward the light. Denise grabbed the chair arms to keep from falling. "I suppose I can do four. These feet need a good soakin', girl. Your heels got them big ol' pads on them. They lookin' like you got big ol' biscuits on the back o' yo' feet. You ever use a razor on these heels?"

MY HAIR WAS BOY-SHORT, AND I WAS FREAKED. I KEPT running my hand over my scalp, feeling for the missing weight. I asked Denise for the fifth time, "Does this look good?" She glanced at me, and I saw the itch to smile at the corner of her mouth. I thought she was going to make a crack about Millicent's mannish hair, her nearly shaved head and mine, which would have sent me over some edge.

I snapped the rearview mirror askew and pointed it toward me, examining my head over and over in the reflection. Like a movie on a continuous loop, I saw the repeated image of shocks of my hair falling to the floor; the surprise hit me anew when I looked back into the mirror and saw yellow spikes jutting like sunflower petals from my head.

Yes, it was just hair, but something about the bizarre MTV-inspired spikes made me a little nuts. So without so much as a second's thought, I drove past our exit and steered us north toward the edge of Boulder County, to Longmont.

Longmont was a town that, in a few years, would host a country club for the nouveau riche and an exclusive golf course to match. But that day it was still a hamlet, still all-American and rednecky, just a few miles up the road from Boulder and populated with but a few thousand people, with real estate still priced for regular folk.

I didn't tell Denise we were heading out to house-hunt, partly because I didn't know. I'd made no plan. I hadn't gone over my scheme to buy a house with anyone—not with a real estate agent, not even with Denise. And I didn't say anything as I barreled down the highway past our regular exit. I didn't have to, because we often detoured from whatever plan we'd made, and this was one time I wanted to be in control. Besides, she was enamored with her Rose Mauve Blush toenails, wiggling them admiringly, so she didn't even notice that I'd bypassed our regular route.

I don't know. Maybe it was the hair. Maybe I felt vulnerable and exposed. Or maybe I felt the conflict of promise and fear. Whatever it was, I knew I needed action. I needed to make a move.

But first, I needed a plan.

I HAD BEEN THE FIRST PERSON EVER IN MY FAMILY TO own a house. It was years ago, before my so-called husband snuck away in the dead of night and I learned that he'd not made payments for months and the house was in foreclosure. For my entire life, I'd watched from afar as relatives and friends' parents managed to move their families out and up and into clapboard and tract houses. Those houses had built-in barbecue pits that people partied around summer after summer. They had yards that, groomed over time, became showpieces. Our parents, conversely, got us kicked out of over a dozen rentals in as many years for not paying the rent, for setting the kitchen on fire, for screaming and fighting so long and loud we'd be evicted.

I'd managed to get my name on a mortgage with a husband who had access to a VA loan. We were twenty and twenty-one years old, respectively, when we bought it, and we were already living lives meant for forty-year-olds, complete with full-time jobs and two kids and a drawer full of bills we hadn't a clue how we would ever be able to pay.

Then one night he pulled a suitcase full of clothes from the dark of our bedroom closet sometime after 1:00 A.M., slinking off into the night, pretty much never to be seen or heard from again. What struck me about that night, the thing that will never leave me, is that I'd spent the entire day washing and drying and folding and ironing all the laundry: four people's underwear and socks and shirts and linens and towels and even tennis shoes. It was a job that, by the time I slipped the last little sock into my baby son's dresser drawer, had consumed a good thirteen hours. Chevy Chase was announcing on NBC. "Live from New York!" Chase yelled. "It's *Saturdaay NIGHT!*"

With his suitcase full of fresh-smelling, beautifully folded clothes, he booked into the black night (all that starch and bleach and All-Purpose Cheer lost and gone), and overnight I was forced to sell the one place, the address I often gazed upon when I retrieved our mail, that I'd figured would be my kids' address well into their teens. Imagine. The same address for years. I had to sell it swiftly to an investor who'd left a flyer rubber-banded to the front porch doorknob, just to keep me and the babies from being thrown, literally, onto the streets.

Denise had her own house-owning meshugaas. Her mother-in-law, Edith, was very French and very vocal about her ownership of the duplex Denise and John shared. "I've told Edith, several times over, that she should deed this house to John," Denise told me. "She acts like she can't understand English, like she can't hear me when I say that. She starts talking about the news or something. Someone'll have to pry that damn deed from her dead little French fingers before she'll ever let go of this place.

"Your man, your guy, whomever that may end up being," she advised me, "will provide you *your* house. You don't have to worry about it."

I found that thinking archaic, sexist, and fundamentally not true. And I couldn't believe that this hellion, this business pioneer believed what she said. But I didn't say that to her. I kept silent because I somehow absorbed the unspoken fact that, years ago, when she struck her marital deal, Denise still had it in her to be able to buy all of Momma's houses and then some. It was fine, back in the eighties, to marry knowing she could earn plenty of dough and let's live in momma's duplex. At that time, moving into the mother-in-law's compound was just a convenient, momentary setup.

That the deal had turned into a trap was something Denise would never admit out loud.

But I wasn't waiting for anyone ever again to share a mortgage. Denise's lack of real estate ownership, the crystal-clear fact that the roof over her head, which she then needed more than ever before, which she had painted and decorated and gardened into loveliness, ultimately belonged to someone else, not even a bank but a mother-in-law who resented her—it all made me rabid to buy my own place.

And then there was Size-Five Sandy. She'd lived in her rental house for years. She'd spent a lot of money fixing it up, and there was a naïveté, a trust she had in her landlady that sent chills up my spine. "Oh, my landlady looooves me," she said, more than once, at WOW. "She wants me to retire in her house and it's so gorgeous and I've planted all that purple columbine in the back."

The idea of relying on a landlord's benevolence for shelter when I'm elderly, when I might need a roof over my head the most, felt to me akin to accidentally coming out of anesthesia in the midst of surgery: it's scary, dangerous, and being in that state could cause even worse damage than whatever ailment you're in the middle of fixing.

At almost forty, I was terrified about morphing into a version of Size-Five Sandy. Ten years from now, would I be throwing a thousand dollars a month of perfectly good mortgage money at a landlady who knew a good tenant when she saw one, soon to be followed by the event of turning sixty-five years old and owning not a lick of equity?

So, with no down payment in hand, and only marginal employment in work that was, for the most part, loathsome, I made the decision to buy a house.

LONGMONT IN THE 1990S WAS A HODGEPODGE OF NE-glected blue-collar neighborhoods, where engine shops operated from illegally zoned repair garages attached to low-rent apartments that hid illegal, mostly Hispanic, immigrants. The whites lived in dated subdivisions erected on cow pastures. Their cheaply built tract boxes were peeling faded blue, mauve, and beige paint. The whole scene was worlds away, yet just minutes from, the heart of Boulder's multimillion-dollar Victorian gingerbread houses. Those showcase homes, trimmed in fancy latticework and hip color schemes of Yankee blue and eggshell, during the 1980s had been just old houses real estate agents couldn't give away.

Thomasina, the beautiful, ballerina-like member of WOW, lived in Longmont. I knew because I'd gone to her condo for my one Thomasina massage. I'd never bothered to make the ten-minute drive from Boulder before that, but it stayed with me that there was a place to live outside of Boulder, yet close.

The drive took us past farms and pastures that were being swiftly consumed by developers. Pastoral foothill valleys were getting bought up and then regurgitated as cookie-cutter "golf course communities." The area was turning into a rolling morass of aluminum-sided houses that were overpriced, boxy, and about as interesting as pureed peas.

I drove to the center of town, past the gun shops that lined Main Street, the diners and the old Dickens B&B and ended up on a side street where turn-of-the-century houses sat close together. They were quaint old homes that the Silicon Valley moneyed, those who'd moved east from the California coast, had yet to sniff out.

I mindlessly cruised the street, turned a corner, and put on the brakes. A FOR SALE sign sparkled from a front yard and I stopped in front of it. The house looked to be a hundred years old. It was white, it was stucco, and it glowed like a back-lit orchid against the late-afternoon sun. I whipped the Pontiac to the curb, and we marched up steps to a porch that ran across the front of the house. Before we could knock, a dark man with a winning grin, a smile at once shy and glorious, threw the door open wide.

"I am José." He swept his arm into the house, almost bowing his introduction. "I have worked on this house for seven years with my own hands," he said, with a Mexican accent and carefully chosen English. "I created the woodwork myself."

He held out his arm as a welcome to come in farther, and we did. A grandfather clock in the foyer chimed deep in its belly. We gazed about, drinking in the house. Warm mahogany, rubbed to a glow, gleamed from antiques carefully selected and placed. A Queen Anne table under the window held a brilliant bouquet of tulips. A settee nestled against a wall was covered in a supple, caramel-colored brocade. An oak bar ran the length of the dining room and sparkled with crystal glasses. It was inset with a full and heavy-looking, six-foot-long mirror.

"This place is like a museum," Denise said, almost in a whisper. Then she got her voice back. "Where'd you get all this stuff?" She was matter-of-fact, almost coarse, and I breathed deeply, fearful she was going piss him off. But he was tickled by her.

"I go to auctions," he said, chuckling. "But wait. You must see this." He ushered her to the back of the house. I followed them to a large solarium—the walls, the ceiling, everything was made of glass. Denise and I gasped together as we stepped into a living Land of Oz, where brilliant red azaleas and exotic black-purple iris bloomed. A six-foot-tall tree sprayed dozens of cherry-blossomed limbs in a twelve-foot-wide arch, sweeping the floor like a glorious pink wedding gown.

Denise and José were a unit then, their heads bent together to admire full-flowering, purple clematis spreading wild about a trellis. "Someone was throwing these glass panels away," he explained. "I took the pieces and made a room, a year-round garden. But then my wife decided we needed a bigger house."

He had Denise where he wanted her, and it was a thing of beauty, their communion. Somehow, without ever having met her, he had gripped her at her weak point, her heart. She nurtured little opium plants in a tiny corner of her backyard, where she thought no one saw them, and cultivated un-heard-of colored tulips, ordering the bulbs from catalogs that charged obscene prices for their hard-to-get varieties. She had houseplants twenty years in the growing. I struggled to keep a houseplant for longer than twenty days.

No corner of the room was left unnurtured, uninspired. Tiny flowers we didn't know the names of ran round our feet and along a flagstone walkway built into the floor, which continued out the back French doors and onto a patio. A half hour later we were again on the front porch, thanking José, who took my hand and gently kissed the backs of my fingers.

I knew he was just trying to unload his house on me, and when he shut the door, I saw that a grimy machine shop operated out of a garage across the street and that there was a turkey-processing plant just two blocks down, which I was sure sent putrefying scents that way when the wind was just right. Train tracks ran two hundred feet behind the house, too, but none of that mattered, because I was in love with every last splinter of the place.

I began scheming about how I'd make the mortgage, vowing to get ten roommates if I had to. I'd sleep in the basement, curl up next to the washer and dryer if necessary, rent out the whole second floor, including the makeshift bathroom built beneath the staircase (a room I was certain was not up to code). But the house would be mine.

The comic Chris Rock does a stand-up bit where he talks about the gated community, the multimillion-dollar mansion he lives in. He says that no matter the money he's made, he's always got a "mental bag" packed and ready by the front door. He's certain someone's about to tell him to get the hell out.

Me, too. The important thing about figuring out how to get José's house was that no one could ever make me leave again. If I painstakingly planted flowers and then perfectly painted the front porch and then got a dreamy hot tub installed in the back, I wouldn't wake up one morning to find an eviction notice on the front door, or the hot tub boarded up because it was never really mine to begin with.

I could finally tell the landlords of the world to go to hell. Because that house would belong entirely and only to me. And I'd die a slow and agonizing death before I'd ever let anyone so much as act like they were going to take it away.

"IF YOU SLEEP WITH HIM, HE'LL COME KEEP THAT INDOOR garden up for you," Denise said. We were decompressing, driving the town's main drag and going nowhere but a little crazy, because of the way I wanted that house.

"It's you he couldn't take his eyes off of," I said.

"I was just workin' him for you," she said. "You're the one he kissed good-bye." She glanced over at me. She knew I was obsessed. "He'd probably even come cut the grass and keep that climbing clitoris trimmed for you. Fuck him on a regular basis and you've got yourself an on-call repairman."

"I want that house, Denise." It was pretty much all I could say. I wasn't in the mood to banter bad-girl sex talk. "And that's climbing clematis." I gave her a look.

"Then you'd better put an offer on the place. Or just blow him this afternoon. In which case, you'll have the keys in your hand by suppertime."

THE HAIR AMPUTATION—LET'S FACE IT, A BUZZ CUT WITH full-on bald patches—had me racing up Denise's steps and into her house, where I flopped down and sat Indian-style and riveted to the six-foot-tall, unframed mirror propped against her dining room wall. I couldn't get away from it. I thought, *I've got that phantom-limb thing that amputees get after they lose an arm or a leg,* and so I turned my head from side to side, side to side, looking, looking, then looking ... *again.*

Denise strode into her living room confidently, with grace, one foot in front of the other. She wore sandals, though it wasn't yet June, and her toes glimmered, all pinkish and clean, against the early-evening springtime light that followed her. Her heels were as soft and tender as a puppy's belly. Her left leg wasn't dragging that day, so each stride she took looked solid and earnest.

"Why do you do that?" I looked at her feet, watched her walk toward me.

"What?" She reached the dining room and leaned against the mirror, facing away from me and looking back out the still open front door, toward the Rocky Mountain foothills—a blue-purple backdrop. I saw her pretending she wasn't trying to catch her breath. "Do what?" she said again.

"Paint your toenails." I looked at her feet, then unfolded

116

my legs in front of me, checked my own toes: plain, white, chubby, and utilitarian.

She shrugged her shoulders. "It's my indulgence. It makes me feel good. Besides"—she glanced out the front door, made sure John wasn't walking in, then lowered her voice—"I've got a date."

I didn't think I'd heard her right. A date? Like, with an accountant or something? Then it hit me like a huge barn door slammed in my face. *Oh my God. With Merle the car guy.*

I blinked twice at her and tried to absorb what she was telling me. That after fourteen years of marriage she was officially stepping out.

Alarm rang through me. Denise wasn't the type to cheat. She came from loving parents, a solid family, and Jewish tradition that showed the world there was joy and untold promise in marriages of forty and fifty and even sixty or more years. Denise might have been part of the True Hippie brigade, she might have smoked a joint or two in 1970, she might even have marched against the Vietnam War, but beneath all that revolution and revolt was a woman of unmitigated loyalty, a woman of her word.

I was frightened. Something was terribly wrong.

"You're going to get caught," I told her. I crawled on my knees to her wine rack and grabbed a bottle of Bulgarian cabernet.

"No I won't." She collapsed on her couch and began opening the mail that was spread all over the coffee table, and then her front door opened and John was there. I squatted over the wine bottle, anchoring it with my feet; the corkscrew was lodged sideways.

"You won't *what*?" said John, grabbing the bottle from my grip and effortlessly popping the cork.

I let him open the wine and watched my eyes tear up in the mirror. I pulled the first glass from his hand and drank a long, large drink, emptying half the glass.

"What's the matter?" Denise stopped behind me and looked down to where I sat cross-legged, staring at myself.

It was all too much.

The irretrievable hair. Denise's impending infidelity. The fact that my children had never lived one night in a house their mother owned, I so wanted to make up for lost time. I wept openly, then bawled in big, ugly gulps, the snot flowing freely, and I didn't care.

I pined so much to be like a regular family, to have continuity, to experience family traditions, even if I had to invent them. What I'd never told anyone, not even Denise, was that I felt the dull ache, a black hole that had opened up a long time ago because I and my siblings had never gathered as a family since each of us left home. Not once.

There was never a place to go home to, no parents wishing we'd visit. Our parents had moved us almost every year for seventeen years, then split up when we were teenagers, going their separate, miserable, transitory ways. There were never any Christmases, never any homecomings, never so much as an invitation.

The realization that I'd not been able to provide this cohesiveness, this comfort and security for my own children—it crushed me. My insides shattered into a million pieces.

"My kids are never going to live close by," I sobbed at Denise. "When Heather came back for the summer last year, she had to sleep on the living room floor because I don't even have a spare room.

"You don't know what it feels like," I said and then noisily blew my nose. She stood stock-still and listened, and something about her paying solid attention, something about it being the first time I'd ever said aloud what I was telling her, opened wide a gulf in me. "Once they graduate," I wept, "they'll never move back here. They're gone forever." I dropped my head into my hands, beyond defeated, utterly beaten. "Because I can't even buy a goddamn house like everyone else." I blew hard into the Kleenex, then pressed my fists to my eyes and gulped for air.

Sure, they were away at college for the moment, but if I had a house, maybe they'd move home after graduation and anchor in Colorado. Maybe we'd all end up living near each other, and everyone and their spouses and my future grandkids would be close because we'd finally have a homestead, a place to gather.

But maybe it was too late.

John walked in with a platter of cheese, poured himself some of the Bulgarian cabernet, and bit into a piece of Gouda. He looked at me, ignored my crying, then turned to Denise. "You won't *what*?" he asked once again, this time directly at her.

Shit. We'd completely forgotten we'd been talking of her affair.

CHAPTER NINE

Happy Birthday,
Mr. President

I abandoned altogether my past of temp and part-time jobs, then dramatically batted my eyelashes at Mr. Oklahoma of the trade publishing company I was temping at and took a full-time gig. It was my first ever, if you didn't count secretarial work, which I didn't, because even when I "accepted a position" (which always sounded pornographic to me), I'd already calculated exactly how long I'd have to keep the job to reach whatever money goal was at hand: treatment for a child's toothache, a car without rust holes in the floorboard, rent and deposit money.

No, this was a real job that was supposed to be full-time, 8:00 to 5:00, came with an office and, most important, a regular paycheck. It was a eureka moment. Finally someone was paying me to spend my working days writing and editing.

However, I'd also spent those years imagining a newsroom with smart, quirky characters like Mary and Ted and Lou Grant. In my interview for the executive editorship, I was told writing and editing experience were necessary, and I did meet a crackerjack colleague or two. But it took about two days to figure out that, if you were related to the owner of the company and you were a construction worker, a never-employed, very overweight woman, and/or a recovering alcoholic, you had perfectly good qualifications for being hired as a staff writer, even given full editorship of a magazine.

That all worked perfectly for my lack of a robust writing résumé. Though I had the restaurant critic's job and a degree in journalism, I was trying to change careers from law office hack to professional writer and editor.

BowlingBiz magazine proved to be the career-switching ticket; it was a publication completely devoted to bowling: people who sold bowling paraphernalia; folks who owned, ran, and worked in bowling ball manufacturing plants; and people who owned little mom-and-pop bowling alleys in places like Burnt Corn, Alabama, and Buttzville, New Jersey.

Furthermore, a family-run trade pub that encouraged the hiring of all unemployed and largely unqualified family members made my slide over to a writing career even smoother. Granted, it wasn't *The New York Times,* but, given the relatively low credentialed standards of the little publishing dynasty, my years of typing and editing legal briefs suddenly, miraculously came in handy.

This grown-up, full-time job had to not just transition my career but qualify me for a mortgage for a house I couldn't afford, which was how I wound up cowering and cajoling, practically on my middle-aged knees blowing Jack—the boss, the publisher of my magazine—who was right, white, and twenty-five years old. A *Star Wars* poster covered one full wall of Jack's cube, exactly like the movie-themed sheets my son used to have. Above Jack's desk hung a big wooden crucifix, complete with Jesus and blood and his crown of thorns. The sign on the other cubicle wall read: Winning isn't everything, it's the only thing—VINCE LOMBARDI.

"Would you mind if I crafted a letter for my mortgage company from you?" I said to him tentatively without knocking. It was hard to knock on cubes. "And got you to sign it?" I leaned, but not too hard, against the open spot in his cubicle in an attempt at nonchalance. "I need to tell them that I've got a good future here. I'm trying to qualify." He and his wife and his (three already!) kids had just bought a house, so I posited mutual house-buying angst into my voice.

His phone rang, and when he turned to answer it, I heard mine ring from the other side of our shared wall, so I raced around and caught it.

"I think you should marry Merle," Denise said before I could say hello. It was the middle of the workday. Lately, she'd been taking lots of breaks from the framing shop, calling me any time she wanted.

"I can't talk now," I said low. I could hear Jack still on his phone.

"Merle talks about you. He'd buy that house for you, you know."

"You're the one sleeping with him—remember?" I pulled my skirt up to my waist, took a shaky step onto my swivelly office chair, and clung to the cube wall with both hands, straining to pinch the phone between my shoulder and ear as I reached to see Jack. I couldn't hear him talking anymore.

"I can't even begin to think of him that way," I said in a forced hush. "He's a car guy. He's got a huge belly. He looks like every male I've ever been related to."

Jack swung around the corner and into my cube, and I leapt from the chair. As the platform sole of my shoe caught the chair arm, my nose slammed into all-terrain carpet that worked like sandpaper against my right temple. My skirt knotted into a ball at my waist, and my ass lay in full view for my boss. I couldn't remember if I was wearing nice or ratty underpants. I managed to get upright, then snatched up the phone. I gave Jack the just-one-sec-and-I'm-off sign, smoothed my skirt down, and wondered if there was blood on my rug-burned nose. I smiled hard at Jack and made like I was on the phone with the most exclusive interview *BowlingBiz* magazine could've ever hoped for.

"Sure, we'd love to write a profile 'bout y'all," I said loudly into the phone at Denise, in the hope of throwing Jack off. My ten-year New Orleans stint allowed me to lapse easily enough into a dialect handy when chattin' up a born-and-bred Alabamian. "I didn't realize y'all had those commemorative bowling shirts and matching balls all these years. Send me a picture. Better yet—let's get together at the trade show next month." I smiled into the phone and glanced up at Jack.

"You're stupid," Denise said, ignoring my Southern-drawled, bowling blabbing. "He'd be a really good husband for you. He's got that gas station. I love being with him, but it's you he wants. Trust me. What time are you leaving there, anyway? I need to do a Big Store run."

"O-key-DOKEY," I said with a loud laugh, wearing my we're-doin'-some-business-now! face. I needed Jack's letter. The mortgage company wouldn't even consider my application without a written guarantee that my salary would increase soon, that I was not going to quit, that the office that churned out monthly pamphlets of schlock loved every syllable I wrote. "That'll be great. It's a date. You're buying!" I practically screamed into the phone, so loaded with bowling enthusiasm I might take up the sport myself. I hung up with an emphatic clang and looked to be sure that Jack had caught it all, that he saw my *proactive* way with interviewees who might transform into paying advertisers, that he got how devoted to bowling and bowling devotees I was.

But Jack was long gone.

DENISE PULLED AN OVERSIZE SHOPPING CART FROM A long chain of carts, and so did I. Shoulder to shoulder we headed into the massive, fluorescent-lighted Big Store, a triple-football-field warehouse that made you pay an annual fee just to shop there. I thought the fee was weird and never would have bothered, but Denise loved the place and insisted I go, signing me up as an employee of her framing business so I got in for free.

I followed behind her and her big cart like a child in an amusement park, pointing out ketchup in jars as big as doghouses and six months' worth of toilet paper packaged and stacked on pallets to the warehouse's ceiling.

"I know what I want for my birthday," she said as she studied two-hundred-foot-long garden hoses, coiled high as big green snakes. "I want to go out to dinner."

"We do that all the time." I couldn't take my eyes off fifty-pound boxes of Miracle-Gro, red roses big as watermelons splashed across the fronts.

"No, I don't mean you and me doing a restaurant review," she said, "though you'd better never even *think* of doing that without me. I want you and me and Merle and John to go to Le Central, that new French restaurant. You know, like two regular couples, going out," she said, stroking a flat of twenty-four football-size muffins, mixed assortment.

"You want us to double date?" It took two hands for me to lift the three-foot-long foam package of skinless chicken breasts. "That's sort of stupid. Why do you want them at the same table?" Chicken blood oozed from the package and dripped on my sandaled feet. I heaved the poultry out of the cart and chucked it back into its cooler. "What if John figures it out?"

"It's my birthday present to myself," Denise said and threw a tub of guacamole into her cart.

"It'll take you till Christmas to eat all of that guacamole," I told her.

"Actually, I lied," said Denise. "It's not really a double date. You won't have a date." She grinned when she said this and marched—there wasn't anything wrong with her gait that day—two aisles over. She came back with a box of Le Claire feminine douche big enough to service any brothel for a year and a seven-pack of black lace teeny-bikini underwear.

"They're both my dates," she said, beaming at me. "Remember?"

I SWEATED AND STRUGGLED TO GET THE FORTY-POUND container of laundry detergent through the front door, the wire grip slicing my palm. The phone was ringing when I popped the door open, and the corner of the plastic tub caught my big toe squarely as I raced to answer it, but the machine caught the call. I fell onto the couch, used the tub as a footstool, and leaned back to listen to the message.

Miss Beck, this is American Mortgage. You're aware that you've got an outstanding unpaid utility bill on your credit report. We also note that you've cosigned on a car loan, which potentially lowers your credit score, a man's voice announced into the machine. *Call me as soon as possible.*

I shifted my feet on the laundry detergent footstool and absorbed the lay o' the land, the house-buying scheme and all of its ridiculousness: that I didn't have a down payment; that I likely didn't make enough money to qualify for a mortgage that could secure even a closet in a bad neighborhood; that there was no one in the world who might even consider cosigning on a loan for me; and that the one thing I was counting on, *at least* a good credit rating, had—in one, disinterested telephone message—become laughable.

My entire body felt made of lead as I sat listening to my credit rating demise—something that had never been more important in my life than it was right that second, when I wanted, *needed,* to buy a house, to have at least a little control of the roof over my head.

The machine hiccupped, stopped, and the recording repeated: *please hang up and try again.*

I let my head fall against the back of the couch and tried not to cry. Eyes still closed, I reached over the end table and slammed the machine twice with my fist. The cassette popped out like a Jack-in-the-box.

PERHAPS I WOULDN'T BE ABLE TO HANDLE THE PAYMENTS on a house with a 100 percent mortgage. Maybe I'd get seriously sick and end up in a Section 8 apartment or a halfway house or a hospice and the whole house-owning thing would go to hell anyway. It could happen that Denise and I, while bright women, might end up indigent and homeless, broken women who, for a variety of reasons, couldn't and wouldn't ever own their own houses, like my entire family—collecting eviction notices like empty pop bottles.

But just once, I felt like my life depended on, was screaming for, one chance to own a bloody home of my own. I imagined holding it, wrapping my arms around it like a lost lover, a missing child. I knew that if I could ever, just for a split second, get my hands on it, I'd never lose it, never let it go.

Without the credit rating, I understood that my one shot was gone, and I realized how outrageously I'd been behaving. To think that taking a stupid job I hated might give me a chance at undoing generations of homelessness, might get me—and thereby my kids—that one chance was ridiculous beyond measure. I now understood that.

Off-the-charts ludicrous.

WE WERE SILLY, DRESSING FOR DENISE'S BIRTHDAY DINner like schoolgirls heading to a low-rent prom. Crammed into her tiny bedroom, I sang, "Happy birthday, Mr. Prezzi-dennt," campy, sashaying here and there in my underwear. It was late August, hot and moist outside, a damp veneer everywhere. That night was her second to last birthday, but neither of us knew that then.

She acted aggravated when I was in her way but laughed, too. "Can I wear these?" Hundreds of earrings hung from a wooden holder. They were works of abstract art: triangles and circles and dangly squares in every color, some three inches long.

I wiped off two red bulbs on silver chains, then stepped into a red sleeveless and backless dress. I was ambivalent about this escapade, but there was an infectious gaiety in our getups, a daring in the plan that was fun. I knew that night that it was her show, that she craved raw fun.

There was also something more important, something left unsaid; I knew it, Denise knew it. It was an evening built to celebrate her womanliness, and that required men, men who knew her well.

MS, like many a chronic illness, can erase sexuality, douse the fire. It's a loss that has nothing to do with sexual performance. It's much more. It's a universe that's been misaligned. The loss is about the dimming fire within, the departure of youthfulness and vigor. These are things felt, tectonic-plate movement, unwelcomed and alarming, from somewhere dark and constantly shifting.

"When are we leaving? I'm starving," John yelled from the frame shop's doorway and through the open bedroom window.

I pulled back the curtain. "We're just trying to look beautiful for you, *monsieur*," I singsonged and sent him kissy-kisses with red-painted lips. He was camped deep in curmudgeon mode but let go a half smile nevertheless as he struggled to edge an oversize frame job through the shop's door. He stopped to look up.

"Jesus Christ," he said, squinting. "You look like a Toulouse-Lautrec whore." He, on the other hand, wore his uniform: shorts and a T-shirt that happened to have a long, white glue smear across the front.

Yet John managed to turn on his half-French charm at the dinner table. He was meeting car guy Merle for the first time, and you could tell he was impressed. He laid the car talk on thick, even adopting a car-guy vernacular. "How long you been racing?" he said.

"Let's get calamari," Denise said, looking with lover's eyes across the tablecloth to Merle. But Merle didn't notice; he kept up his end of the car talk, giving John one of his race car stories. Merle had left the gas station early to get a shower in. He wore a fresh work shirt and pants, and smelled of Lifebuoy and motor oil.

"Let's get this Chilean cab," I said. It was eighty-five dollars a bottle. I felt like I was on holiday—at a restaurant with no review due, a side job I wasn't letting go of. I didn't know who was paying, but I decided that we were splurging.

"Sweet forty-six and never been kissed," I sang. "Happy birthday." We all clinked wineglasses except Merle, who held up his highball glass full of whiskey.

"I didn't know calamari was French food," I said and slipped squid past my lips. "Have you ever seen Denise in a dress?" I wanted them to quit the car talk. "Doesn't she look stunning?"

"Hmmph," John grunted and eyed her wraparound dress. "She looks like a dyke wrapped in toilet paper."

At first I thought it a mean remark, but then I realized that it was meant to be a quip, stand-up-comic style, and something about him, about him that evening, caught my attention. I was taken by the low-grade sorrow I felt for John, for his rickety life with a questionable future. I was sad for the deception I was a part of, for his wife stepping out, and for her longing for him to still love her as he had in the beginning, for the confidence in them both at the start of their marriage.

Without letting the others know—I laughed at their banter, I poured everyone more wine—I secretly studied John, who that night appeared a nice, handsome man, a guy who was delightful company, a wonderful addition to our little foursome. It was easy to forget that he was failing his wife.

That she felt it necessary to cajole him, most times, into joining us for a restaurant review, for an evening on her side of the duplex, made me see the chinks in their marriage armor.

That their intimacy was failing, perhaps was over, was apparent in her uncharacteristic launch of an affair with a man she'd never have looked at twice back in the days she was MS-free.

She felt adrift, unmoored. She'd thought she would never know that brand of uncertainty.

Of that, I was certain.

It was almost possible to forget that Denise was cheating, that, though she'd never been unfaithful in her marriage until then, she was, nevertheless, sneaking over to Merle's house, sidling up to him in his Corvette after an afternoon's road trip, after their adventures. I could almost forget that she rushed into his apartment, then into his arms, then into his bed.

I feared her getting caught, worried that her vitriolic way wouldn't let her continue to contain her secret. I feared for her because she'd announced her deception at WOW the previous week—a move I never saw coming.

WHEN OUR WOMEN ON THE WAY MEMBERS SHOWED UP ON Wednesday evening, I demanded that every one of them walk outside to admire the gargantuan sunflower blooms.

The sunflowers grew from seeds that were odd and walnut-looking to begin with, contraband I had snuck back into the States from a dacha outside Chernobyl. They were huge seeds; one nearly covered my palm. *They will grow, they will grow,* my Russian gardening friend, Natya, had promised, stuffing a small bag of them into my backpack as I hopped onto the Aeroflot plane and headed home.

In semi-arid Colorado, with fancy fertilizer and even fancier dirt, they grew to be twelve feet tall by midsummer, their magnificent heads already heavy with seeded weight, car-tire-size blooms atop tree-trunk-like stems, luring birds all day long. The newspaper wanted to photograph the flowers, feature them on the front page—the True Russian Mammoth Sunflowers—blossoms over two feet wide.

We all stood in the pressing summer evening heat with our hands on hips, our faces to the sky. Birds flew high above our heads, annoyed that we were there, preventing them from feasting. When I felt satisfied that everyone had oohed and aahed enough, we headed inside and collapsed into our ring of seats, leaving the front door and a side window open, hoping for a breeze, pouring ourselves big glasses of ice water and iced tea in the meantime. We sat in our circle fanning ourselves and pinning sweaty hair up off our necks.

The heat was oppressive, even in the relatively cooler-than-outside basement apartment. We all had wet cloths laid across our necks and chests. The women took turns going to the kitchen and rewetting their cloths, and I kept turning my one, lone oscillating floor fan to get a wider breeze going.

"What's new?" I asked the group. I was wilted from the heat, wilted from living in that apartment.

"I have something I'm upset about," Denise said. I had no idea what she was talking about, so I paid attention.

"I'm having an affair," Denise said.

"You are?" Millicent asked.

"Yup," Denise answered, matter-of-factly. "And I don't feel guilty about it. John won't have sex," she added.

"He won't? Or he can't?" gorgeous Thomasina asked. She swung out her long, shapely legs, then recrossed them, the effect beautifully distracting.

"Oh, he *can*," Denise answered. "But he won't. I've usually been the one to initiate. But now, he's just stopped. He just doesn't want to do it anymore."

"So I don't see a problem," said the ever-pragmatic scientist Millicent. "Sounds like mission accomplished."

"I don't know," Denise said. "I don't know. I just felt like mentioning it."

An awkwardness spread about the room. Nature hates a vacuum and so do I, so I moved to fill it by changing the subject back to the flowers. Besides hating vacuums, I hated understanding that, unless she were very ill, unless she felt a doom, an end, something terribly, terribly wrong, Denise would never have cheated on her husband in a million years. I hated that this knowing kept hitting me like the thundercloud we all desperately wished would appear outside. I wanted to race away from the thought.

"The newspaper wants to do a story on those flowers," I told the group, nodding toward my grove out front. "They're sending a photographer in the morning."

"I won't have photographers parading around on my lawn!" came the screech from Lunatic Laura, outside my screen door. I didn't know how long she'd been standing there. I saw her cover her eyes and squint through the screen, and I could tell she couldn't see into the room, but that didn't stop her. "I just came to tell you to water the yard. My *fiancé*"—she had the annoying habit of using the word *fiancé* with emphasis, like a flavoring—"my *fiancé* and I are going back east," she said. "So be sure to gather up my mail. There's a substitute delivering it, and I don't trust him." She pressed her face closer to the screen, peering harder to see us. "Make sure you collect it."

The WOW women stopped talking and gaped at the source. Laura's voice was penetrating—aimed rather than delivered.

"It's *one* photographer, *one* guy," I told her. "He'll take two, three snaps tops."

"I *am* an artiste," she said back at me through the screen. "I teach. I won't be made a spectacle."

When our meeting ended, I walked with the women outside, and we all drank in the sweet, dark summer air. The full moon cast a silver glow against the mountains and our faces. Everything was dramatic and soft all at the same time.

At the end of the yard, we stopped short. There we looked, seven heads turned in unison. Sunflower stumps stuck up from the ground, barely visible in the moonlight. Each flower had been slashed at the base as if with a sharp ax. They were gone. A few dark seeds remained, scattered on the walkway, and I looked up to see birds soaring about in empty space. They dipped down and up and then down again, looking to snatch seeds from the orchard of blooms that was gone, that simply no longer existed.

"That bulimic bitch," Denise growled.

"YOU DO LOOK VERY NICE," MERLE SAID TO DENISE ACROSS the dinner table, but there was no sizzle in his voice, no delight at his lover's beauty, at her glow, at the secret he shared with her. His compliment sounded false, like he was being solicitous with an elderly aunt, and at that moment I realized their affair was already ticking to a close. It had been just a few months since it began, but Merle had no plan to keep it going, and I wondered how the end would look.

When the check came, John was slow to find his wallet. Merle gripped a roll of cash big as his fist. He peeled away a fan of bills, dropped them on the table. As an afterthought, he added another to the pile.

"This one's on me," he said and leaned sideways to shove the wad back into his pocket. I saw black grease beneath his fingernails.

Denise smiled at Merle's generosity and looked pretty doing it, wrapped in a leopard-print dress that wound around and ended in a sarong-like knot at her hip. I'd never seen her wear anything but Levi's, except once when we went to second Seder at Bonai Shalom. She had turned very Jewish on me that spring night, donning a dated skirt and frumpy sweater for the holy day while chastising me for my snug skirt and tailored jacket. "There's a rabbi at Seder, you know," she'd said, walking out the door. Eyeing my butt, she'd felt compelled to add: "Isn't that skirt a little tight?"

Denise smiled at everyone. She was a priestess that night, her lover-and-husband-filled birthday all about her, her hair at the late-night wild stage, barely tamed by an orchid pinned above her ear. She'd orchestrated a birthday party for herself full of love and longing and lusty food and liquor—and she'd gotten it. I knew she was wearing a pair of those lacy Big

Store bikini panties, the black ones, made for a Saturday night, a Saturday night full of men and what men think of.

She was showing me the Way. I learned that evening that putting on blinders, focusing on fun, and crafting memories is salvation. That we can transform how we feel merely by transforming our circumstances, even if just for an hour or two.

That evening, her face glowed in the varied hues of a woman's moist skin in candlelight. When dinner was over, she was the first to get up and leave, tossing her hair behind her shoulder and leading us across the restaurant's dining room: all movement, grace, high heels, and strut.

CHAPTER TEN

Got Bail?

We didn't set out to steal John's money. Until the house-buying business, we hadn't given his checking account a thought. Then one day I noticed that Denise was poring over her mail with even more relish than usual. She had this relationship with her mailman—he was her neighbor as well as her mail carrier—and the two of them had just wrapped up one of their frequent animated yak fests about schlepping mail, delivering mail, sending bad mail back. All of their mail fervor signaled to me that Denise was about to take a break from framing. So she sat in front of her huge rectangular coffee table with that day's mail spread about in front of her, like a fortune-teller rolling up her sleeves.

"The bank told me I have to have three thousand dollars sitting in my checking account when they process my mortgage application," I said to no one but the window. My self-pity was dug deep as ticks on a hound dog. "They said I have to have a down payment sitting there, that I can't borrow it."

Across the street, little yellow-haired boys raced around a Catholic school yard, white shirts hanging outside navy blue pants, piling on top of each other, shrieking. "It's a kind of house-buying trick," I said to her. I felt pissy toward her and the world. "Must be nice," I said, "to have a husband—or a husband's mother—*give* you a house." I let that statement sit for a second or two. If I were her, I'd have reached over that big coffee table and smacked me. I didn't dare look away from the school yard. I didn't have the guts. I let out a long, breathy sigh and then picked at my fingernails. "I have to *look* like I have a down payment just sitting there waiting, or they won't give me a mortgage."

"Are you sure that's all they're going to want?" She leaned over and lifted her purse from its end-of-couch hiding place (like a burglar won't search there?), then rummaged around in it. She pulled a deck of credit cards, held fast in a thick rubber band, from the depths of the bag.

"No," I said. "I'm sure they're going to want other costs covered; they said something about me having to pay an appraiser. But for now they're telling me that at least three thousand dollars needs to be there or they're going to throw my mortgage app in the trash.

"Oh, and I've got an old utility bill I didn't pay, so my credit rating's shit. Kaput," I told her. "And I guess you're not supposed to cosign for a kid's car loan either. It lowers your credit score."

Christ, I hated this. All of it. Mostly, I hated that my past was still my present.

Denise snapped the rubber band from the deck and spread plastic pieces like tarot cards across the table. "This one has my taxes on it. So it's about five thousand dollars down," she said thoughtfully, tapping her finger on one of the Visa cards. "We'd better not use that."

"You put your taxes on a credit card, Miss Econ-o-*mist*?" I was being pissy, all right, but I looked with curiosity at the table and the cards, then added, "You're paying nineteen percent interest on money you owe the government? You know what that's costing you?"

She ignored me. "This one has a two-thousand-dollar credit limit. We could get a cash advance. That could be part of the down payment."

A bell shrilled in the school yard, and the kids stopped dead in their tracks, like someone had flipped their Off switches. I watched them fall into a line of sorts at the school's back door. They were barely able to contain themselves, slapping each other and laughing. On top of everything else, I suddenly, massively missed my kids.

Denise ripped an envelope open and fanned the papers out on the table. She studied its contents.

"John's got three thousand dollars in this account." She held up one paper in front of me: WESTERN SAVINGS & LOAN. Then she smiled. "Guess who's got his bankbook."

She wrote the check quickly, like she did it every day. "Pay to the order of Catherine Beck: Two Thousand, Nine Hundred, and Ninety-five Dollars." When she got to the signature line, she moved the pen to the margin of a newspaper on the coffee table and practiced:

After a couple of scribbles, she signed his name—hesitant at first, then with a flourish, the pen gripped tight by her fingertips.

The children were gone, the school yard full of laughing echoes. The foothills rose like cathedrals behind the school, shaded in blacks and reds, shadows sliding down their slopes, framed by the late-afternoon sun.

"Let's get out of here," Denise said. She held the freshly forged check to the light and examined it closely. Her eyes took longer and longer those days to focus. Often, she threw the newspaper or magazine she was reading down in disgust. Now, however, she acted satisfied and thrust the check toward me. "You'd better get this into your account this afternoon."

"This is going to look suspicious," I told her.

"He'll never even know his statement came to me," she said with a dismissive wave of her hand.

"No," I said. "Not that John will find out. The mortgage company says they checked my account balance and there wasn't enough money in there. All of a sudden I've got three thousand dollars in it? They'll know something's up. They told me I couldn't borrow the down payment."

Denise looked straight at me, studied me. Her scrutiny made me squirm. "Do you *not* get that this is how things are done?" she said. "How do you think those idiots bought all those ugly houses they're ruining the foothills with?" She looked at me with true incredulity, like I was a child she must both admonish and counsel. "Their families give them money. That's how. Oh, and forget that dumb utility bill and that you cosigned on a loan. Pay the stupid bill off. They haven't reported anything. They called you first."

Ten thousand pounds of concrete lifted from my chest, my back, my shoulders. I didn't know that I'd been carrying it, that it was so heavy I'd been unable to breathe, and I choked in my chest with gratitude. I couldn't swallow. I couldn't catch my breath. I was so taken—so taken by the first pure and selfless gesture to change my life I'd ever known—that my relief was physical. I was at once light-headed and lighthearted, and it was too much to take in. That someone had taken on my problems, solved them with a deck of credit cards and an innate understanding of what needed to be done—that someone could take all this on for another human being and make all the years of hurt and heartache and hopelessness vanish— was a gift so large, it was almost too much to bear.

I wasn't worried about our using John's money. I knew that, between the two of us, it'd be back before he knew it was gone. In that moment, I trusted Denise in a way I'd never trusted anyone in my entire life. *Ever.*

For the very first time, I knew and experienced and absorbed pure unselfishness, the raw movement of one human tending the needs of another.

It was love, at its pinnacle.

I was tempted to conclude that she felt perfectly calm paying nearly 19 percent interest on taxes she owed the government, though it went against every economic tenet, every molecule in her DNA, because she could see the future—and all that interest and those taxes were *its* problem. It was easy for me to believe that she thought it right to give another the opportunity to hold title to the roof over her head—and felt at peace putting her financial self at risk to do it—because money, at the core of this penny-watching princess's core, had become negligible.

But had I drawn these conclusions, I would have been wrong. She granted me the ticket to my needed mortgage because she damn well felt like it.

IT WAS ONE OF OUR MOST MEMORABLE AFTERNOONS. Denise ripped John's bank statement into shreds and stuffed the ball of ripped paper into her purse to be tossed far away from the house later in the day. Then we raced to my bank to deposit the money. It was secretive, illegal, a frenzy of fun. We moved quickly, like bandits. I endorsed John's check, put it in the deposit envelope, and we watched it drop, irretrievable, into the slot that sent it, ultimately and not a little mysteriously, into the account that had on it this name: Catherine Beck. The weight of our actions tempered our mood momentarily. *What will happen if we're caught?* And then, *How soon can I pay the money back?* But we recovered quickly when

Denise said, "Let's pick up a large order of those sickeningly sweet BBQ ribs to go and take a drive."

I steered the car north of town, resisting the temptation to head straight toward what I then knew would be the first home I'd own since being of legal age. We ate and rode along the two-lane road, greasy sauce on our chins, on our shirts, beneath our fingernails. I drove with no hands on the wheel, my right knee steering easily, while holding and gnawing at a long, meaty rib I gripped at both ends. It was a trick I liked to show off.

Denise used to grab the wheel when I'd do this, nervous and chastising. "You're going to do that once too often," she'd say, and I'd tell her, "Get your hands off the wheel. You're gonna make us crash."

But she had come to ignore my no-hand driving—had even come to expect it—and so, relaxed and smiling, she scooped potato salad from a carton and offered me a big spoonful. I kept driving with my knee and leaned across the seat and took a bite.

She unrolled her window, and I did the same. There was nothing but farms and mountains and a rose-colored horizon around us. The wind whipped my hair straight up; hers blew out the window in a whoosh, like a thick brown blanket.

"So how many stars are you giving this rib joint?" she yelled over the wind.

"Hey," I shouted back, "I'll put John's money back as soon as I sign the house papers, okay?" She acted like she didn't hear me. "Put your seat belt on," I yelled.

She licked her fingers and tossed a bone into the bag, calling, "You want some baked beans?" just as the wind snapped a paper napkin from her hands and out the window, where I watched it in the rearview mirror, fluttering in the underwind for an instant like a strange white bird.

I slammed the gas pedal to the floor, and the acceleration threw us back against the seat; then Denise leaned her whole body out her window and screamed into the wind, *"WHOOOP! WHOOOP! WHOOOP!"* a wild-animal sound, and I grabbed the waistband of her Levi's as the car raced forward, and I knew I couldn't hold her, I knew I couldn't save her if she fell.

Yet inwardly I glowed, like a tiny lit church candle. It was pure and delicious. It was happiness. For the first time, for as far back I could remember, I felt that maybe, just possibly, life could be very, very good.

CHAPTER ELEVEN

Plastic Babies

"I love how smooth this is," Denise said. She had her face barely an inch from the bathroom mirror. It was a beautifully lighted bathroom mirror, in which I looked very good, no matter the time of day or night—and she would've looked beautiful in it, too, but she was screwing her mouth into a tight lip clench. She ran a finger over her upper lip and shifted her mouth from side to side.

"What did it look like before?" I watched her watch herself in the mirror. "I didn't even know you had anything done."

"I had tiny creases that looked like I smoked before Elliott Goldman got to me," she said. "Just enough lines to make me nuts." She turned her head to one side, scrunched her mouth into a pout, turned her head to the other side, pouted again. "It's a mitzvah, what Elliott did for me. Now it's smooth, smooth, smooth."

"HERE'S MY IDEA." SHE FLOPPED BACK ON THE COUCH, propped her head in her hand. She was glued to *Seinfeld*, but there was a commercial on; otherwise she wouldn't have talked to me.

"You should write a newspaper article about laser skin re-surfacing," she said. "You know, where they take a laser beam and erase your wrinkles? Elliott is wonderful. He's young, Jew-ish—*married,* but adorable nevertheless." *Seinfeld* was back on, so I watched the screen with her. Elaine was ranting at Jerry. I didn't catch the plot but noted that Elaine looked really good, even as she was screaming. A pop culture fetish of mine: I al-ways thought it amazing how movie stars look good even at their worst. I loved that. Sometimes I forgot the story or ig-nored the dialogue when an actress looked damn good, espe-cially when she was crying or screaming or dying. Fascinating.

Denise turned back to me from the television. "You write a letter to Elliott, that's *Doctah* Elliott Goldman," she said. "Tell him you'll write a big newspaper story about his state-of-the-art laser machine. He's trying to drum up business. That's how I got him. I went to one of his introduction semi-nars and he agreed to do this for two hundred dollars." She tapped her finger against her wrinkle-free upper lip, then pushed her face under the lamplight and made kiss lips so I could see how good she looked.

"So what?" I said. "A story about your plastic surgeon. Big fucking deal." The idea made me stew about the freelance writing I'd sold to local newspapers in the past: hundreds of hours researching, conducting interviews. Throwing in fea-ture story photo shoots I charged nothing extra for, I figured I scored about fourteen cents an hour all told. "Do you know how much work that is?"

"Shush." She flapped her hand at me. She was riveted, watching Elaine try to unload a weekend boyfriend. Elaine grabbed a suitcase and stuffed everything within arm's reach into it. The boyfriend lollygagged in bed. Elaine was hysterical, screaming about him missing his flight, flipped out because her alarm didn't go off, sure he'll miss his flight and she'll be stuck with him for another twenty-four hours. The scene made me think of an old boyfriend who once surprised me with a four-day visit that felt like four months.

Denise couldn't get enough. Her head thrown back, she laughed large, rocking laughs. She forgot I was even there.

"No, *no*," she said, sitting up straight and hitting the Mute button on the remote. I watched the soundless screen as a smiling woman rode a bike; then she stopped to kiss a man also riding a bike. 1-800-UHERPES flashed across the bottom of the screen. I thought about how the commercial's writers had managed to link VD with bicycling. Then I thought of how those hard bicycle seats must irritate genital herpes sores. Didn't the focus group at the ad agency consider that?

"*You* write the story in exchange for a *free* full-face laser skin resurfacing." She turned and looked hard at me so I would *finally get it.* She waited a second, then said in slow, baby-talk syllables: "Tell—him—you'll—do—a—big—sto—ry—on—his—tech—nique, a story about his place, you'll do photographs of him. In exchange for that kind of publicity, you'll be his guinea pig."

The *Seinfeld* friends were together, sipping coffee at their favorite diner, and Denise couldn't get the sound back up. I yanked the remote from her hand and pressed the Volume button, and already I knew that I was going to do it, that it was a slick, Denise-inspired plan that'd give me a new, slick face to go with my new life—an all-around new lease on life. It'd be fun! I knew I'd make the pitch to Doctah Goldman with some of the newspaper's letterhead I wasn't supposed to have.

I laughed along with my friend as a disheveled Elaine rushed out in her nightgown to drive her schlubby ex-boyfriend to the airport, to finally, finally be rid of him. She looked beautiful doing it.

A collision of thoughts hit me at once. After two years of her shoving Jerry Seinfeld and Julia Louis-Dreyfus and Jason Alexander down my throat, how could I not watch when Denise glued herself to the show daily? I was now tuned in to, hooked on, relating to, and had otherwise become just one more viewer lining the already monstrously lined pockets of Jerry Seinfeld.

I realized, then, that Elliott Goldman would go for Denise's free plastic surgery ploy.

I realized that I was learning to think strategically, tactically, as Denise did naturally.

And I realized that, for all that, I was not one bit sad.

IT WAS HALLOWEEN AND 5:00 P.M. THAT'S ABOUT ALL I knew because something dreamy was dripping into the needle taped to my hand. I was extremely happy about everything: I knew, for example, that I'd normally *never* even *consider* letting the newspaper's adorable, twenty-three-year-old photographer put his camera lens in my face like he was doing. If I was on top of things, I knew I'd never let Elliott see my greasy hair pulled straight back with a worn old headband like it was then. Elliott had popped metal contact lenses onto my eyeballs, and I was entirely cool with those eyeball covers, knowing Elliott would never make me go blind with an inadvertent slip of the laser beam.

I wrote my Pulitzer Prize winner's acceptance speech in my anesthetized head as Denise sat next to me, holding a humming tape recorder.

"Breathe, Cathie, *breathe*," Elliott crooned. Denise was right. Elliott was tender and nubile as a schoolboy, sensitive as dappled sunlight, and I was in love with him.

I proudly took the deep breaths Elliott told me to, drawing exaggerated drags into my lungs just to please him. Denise giggled next to my head. I heard the recorder's hum.

"So what's that feel like now?" she said to me. "He's finished your eyes."

"Ah cahn feel iss ahlready smoother," I lied. I was just a little bothered that my mouth and brain were misaligned and then decided someone was holding a hot hair dryer to my forehead.

"Aah tried . . . tell you . . . anessteeza duzn't work on meh. . . ." Little, hot toothpick pricks ran along my brow; then there was a warm drag along my cheek. "Hot," I managed.

I remembered I was working. "Put dah recahdah near my mouth." Ian, the child-photographer, click-click-clicked his camera.

Denise laughed. "The recorder's right here. He's running the laser over your chin now. Just talk gently; the recorder's here."

"Dah-neeeeze." I wanted to tell her something important, but it just went away. Heat burned the hell out of my earlobe, and I remembered that Elliott had promised he'd erase a weird wrinkle that'd appeared there in recent years.

"Da-neeeeze," I began again. "You aah sooo buteeful to me, can't . . . see?" I sort of sang, or thought I was singing.

"Whah iff you . . . fuch-up, Elliott?" I said. He ignored me, which irritated me a little, and I wondered if I really wanted him to leave his wife after all. He told Rebecca, his nurse, something I couldn't understand, something far away on the planet they were all on.

"Aah could sue you, Elle . . . ott, know daht? . . . We won't woowee 'bout daht now, will we?" I thought he could see my brain smiling so he'd know I was joking. I'd never sue someone I loved as much as I did him.

"Deep breaths, Cathie." There was an edge in his voice, and I wanted the sweet, solicitous Elliott to come back. I gave him the big inhale and exhale he wanted, thinking how proud he'd be of me. I knew I was his best patient ever.

"Stop talking," he ordered. "I'm going around your lips."

Denise laughed, the recorder whirred, the camera lens clicked.

I heard Denise's stuffy nose, the phlegm in her chest. She had a cold coming on. *Let me see,* I mused. Suddenly, the "local" anesthesia wasn't so fun. An alternative to "general," which puts you all the way asleep, the "local" floated my concerns in and out. Angst drifted into my brain. MS is *not* viral, right? *Is MS . . . immunological?* And the MS and her cold and Denise's immune system mixed up together in my head and I mildly worried that her cold might be a warning that something worse was coming on.

But then I thought about how Elliott would take care of us both if something went wrong, that together Denise and I could surely move into his house, and then the three of us could all take care of each other.

I felt warmth near my mouth and knew he'd just erased a wrinkle there that I'd told him not to miss. "Okay, Cathie." Elliott was so far away, I wondered if he knew he was supposed to be erasing my face.

"You did good, Cathie, sit up," said Rebecca. I felt the needle tip slide out from the back of my hand, and the reclined table I'd been leaning back on sat me upright in one smooth, mechanical move.

"I know a song about this," I said. I noted that my brain and mouth were beginning to realign.

"It's okay to sit up now," said Rebecca. I decided she was the best nurse ever. "But don't get off the table; you might feel a little nausea."

"It's a song just for you, Elliott," I said. "It's about plastic surgeons. I used to sing it when I was ten years old. Want me to sing it for you?"

My mouth'd never felt so closed shut, but I was determined to sing.

Early one day in the month of May,
I went down to the beach,

I started.

There were cuties and beauties in little bathing suities
and all of them within my reach.

Elliott handed me a mirror, and I was aghast: I saw a monster's blown-up face, swollen and drum-like taut. It looked like a horrid solar blast had exploded in that person's face, and I felt sorry for her. It was pretty much killing me to stretch my mouth skin around the words, but I was full of my own singing voice and wanted to make sure everyone knew how good a singer I was.

Now a 38-24-36 miss just happened to be walkin'
my way.
I said, "Please don't think me nervy but you look so
very curvy,
Tell me how you got that way."

The chorus appeared upon my brain like Teletype:

She said, "It's plastic!
Oh yes, it's plastic!
It's as pretty as can be,
but you know that it ain't me because—"

Elliott laughed. He'd stepped back from my operating chair and held his mask with one hand, bent over at the waist, and held his stomach with the other. I didn't know if he was laughing with me or at me but decided it didn't matter. I couldn't sing loud enough, remembering words that'd been thirty years gone. It was a little miracle, I thought, remembering that song, the one my sister and I used to sing, standing on the front porch banister and wiggling our prepubescent butts. It was like I'd been saving it up for that moment.

Denise smashed a fat wad of Kleenex to her mouth and laughed and coughed, heading to the bathroom so she could make it through the ride home—it was a dicey maneuver those days, getting her from one place to the next, hoping her bladder and bowels could hold out. Elliott and Rebecca made me stand up, which I didn't appreciate as I really liked the reclined table chair, plus I could sing better lying back. I couldn't see a thing through swollen-shut eyelids.

In the backseat of Ian's car, heading home, I knew it was late, after dark, but didn't really give a damn. The way I figured it, I'd soon have a great, young face, Elliott would get lots of that Boulder money fueled into his practice after my story was published, and Denise had had a good time, seeing me make a fool of myself.

Then I was sitting on my own living room couch, and Denise sat next to me with her hand on my knee. The plan was that she'd spend the night and be my nurse, which was something I really wanted to see.

"How do I look?" I said and tried to smile, tried to look pretty. I touched the top of my head and felt the slick of my short, Vaseline-coated hair. Elliott had globbed the stuff all over my face post-laser. I thought that I probably looked like my father, who combed Vaseline through his hair every day of his life.

"You're going to look incredible. This is exciting," Denise said. I could tell that she meant it, that she was incredulous at what my face was going to look like, that we'd pulled something off, that wiping away years of wrinkles was a damn good thing.

WHEN THE DOORBELL RANG, I LEANED MY HOT AND greasy head against the back of the couch and let her answer.

"Trick or treat!" Through the slits between my eyelids I saw a little boy in a T-shirt and the bottom half of a skeleton costume step into the living room. An even smaller little girl with a plastic witch hat pointing sideways off her head stepped in behind him.

Half Skeleton got a load of me on the couch and stepped back, horror-struck, against the witch. When the witch regained her balance, she turned to bolt.

"Wait, wait." Denise chuckled and delivered the kids a menacing grin. Denise, who'd never cared about Halloween, who, she freely admitted, had played the crazy old woman of her neighborhood on Halloween nights past—shutting off her lights, going to a movie to avoid trick-or-treaters, passing out loose change to kids when she'd forgotten the date and therefore forgotten to get candy—Denise clamped Little Witch's chubby arm in her fingers and reached for a bowl of miniature 3 Musketeers at the same time.

"Here you go," she said and held the bowl under their chins. "Take all you want." All that candy just for the taking—but they didn't even see it.

Vaseline dripped in stringy globs from my chin, landing in grease plops on my chest. My face was so hot I couldn't stand it. "Wheh's daht pain stuff Ell-ee-oht gahv you fo meh?" I said, which was torturous because my mouth was swollen shut and hotter than hell. Little Witch used her full little body power to yank her arm from Denise's grasp, slamming Little Skeleton back against the door in the process. Together they fled, leaving Denise offering the bowl of candy to nothing but thin air.

"Trick or fuckin treat yourself," I said, which came out "Trrr rr fnnn trr yrsssf."

THE POWER DENISE HAD OVER ME—THE POWERHOUSE SHE was at that time—could have stopped runaway trains, made rivers run backward. She was freewheelin' and fun-lovin' and piss-on-everybody gutsy, and that was just what I needed. Others might have felt overwhelmed and intimidated by Denise. Not me. I needed a partner in crime, a brilliant partner, who used the F-word without apology, who was smarter than I, who knew worlds unknown to me.

Denise felt like a trip to a foreign country to me, an exotic journey that I'd waited a lifetime for. And she felt like coming home.

She was an equal who could and did challenge me, dare me, up my ante. She was a voice of reason and confidence, someone who'd steered me through negotiating an editor's salary higher than I'd ever considered or knew I might get—because she insisted I demand it.

Holy shit, we were girls and we were *winning*. We were reveling in a perfect fusion of life circumstances: we were neither very young nor very old, but at powerful prime ages.

This was magic. It was but a moment, but it was also monstrously, gloriously real. The world, for the very first time, *was* my oyster, despite all the certainty with which I was emphatically told, at age seventeen and pregnant, that my life was over, that I was a goner, that I was not worth the paper my welfare checks would be printed on.

MY SENIOR YEAR OF HIGH SCHOOL, I SAT BAREFOOT ON the floor—white, fluffy-blond-haired—and as comfortable as any eight-and-a-half-months-pregnant, about-to-graduate high schooler could be. Like a sort of baby-shower mood music, my dad's RCA console TV with the broken horizontal droned from the next room. The United States continued to pull out of Vietnam, a weary-sounding newsman lamented, and gas had topped forty cents a gallon. Abortion, a new constitutional right, he added, continued to draw controversy.

I lit my third Marlboro 100 of the hour and looked down at my rock-hard belly and my new outfit. To get ready for the shower, I'd slapped my mom's plate-size powder puff down my chest, so Prince Matchabelli's Stradivari rose like a cloud around me. I'd smacked the dusting powder mitt between my legs for good measure.

My younger sister had sewn a stretchy, pregnant panel into the front of my pants the night before. I wore a matching blue top. The ensemble, a spongy, bell-shaped number, slid easily over my bell-shaped, five-foot-one, 160-pound frame. The Preference by L'Oreal champagne blond hair color (because I was worth it) gave my thin, waist-length hair temporary volume.

I was quite the package.

The house we'd rented had plenty of rooms, but we didn't have the furniture to fill it, so the baby shower room—what would have been any other family's living room—had oversize hippie pillows thrown about the floor and no curtains.

So there I was, sitting in that rented house on that highway, waiting for a party that was for someone else, a strange party for a person not even there. Our party was three: me, my sister, and Merrybelle, a girl in our new school. There were no parents. I don't know where my mom was; my dad was rarely home. Merrybelle was way sexy, with a flat stomach I envied. She pulled a joint from her cleavage and lit it.

The front door opened, and we all looked up. I expected to see Merrybelle's boyfriend, but instead my dad's long and lean frame fell through the doorway; then he paused against the door.

I sat up, frozen, and watched him.

"Who parked . . . in my *spaccce*?" His words slurred together, but my sister and I understood. We didn't answer. We waited to hear what might come next, which would tell us a lot.

"I toll *youuu . . . ,*" he started, but then he tried to stand up straight and collect himself, and the rest of the sentence was lost.

"Mr. Beck!" Merrybelle flicked the joint's ash into an ashtray tucked behind her pillow, then hid the joint among the cigarette butts. She popped up, and I was amazed at her agility. I recalled how light a body was with an empty front.

My father looked toward us, rheumy-eyed and unfocused, and then he spotted Merrybelle coming toward him. This was the first we'd seen of him in three weeks. He sold plastic signs from the trunk of his Chrysler to mom-and-pop businesses hidden along country roads and in small towns. Mostly he sold the signs to bars: VIV & SKIP'S LAST CHANCE INN, THE WHISTLE STOP.

We were always a little surprised when he returned. Sometimes we were hopeful. We hoped that he'd sold some signs and that maybe the sales had put him in a buoyant mood. Mostly, we hoped he had some cash.

Merrybelle propped her shoulder under my dad's armpit and grabbed his back. He stood six feet three, was thin, and had Elvis Presley hair. She struggled to hold him up.

"You're just in time for the party," she said up to his face while steering him toward the living room. "It's a baby shower," she added. I prayed that he was so wasted, so hammered, he wouldn't understand her, that he didn't catch that the party was to celebrate me having a baby. He'd quit talking to me months ago.

"You're . . . ," he started, and he searched for more words, his eyes closed as Merrybelle brought him into the room. "...*va va...voom*," he finished. Spittle popped from his bottom lip to Merrybelle's cheek, and she swiped it away with the arm not holding him up.

"Sit here, Mr. Beck." Merrybelle steered him toward her pillow. I grabbed the ashtray hiding the joint and pushed it behind my pillow.

"You'll sit on my lap?" My dad opened his eyes a little, grinned at Merrybelle and her chest.

She let go of his back, and he lurched forward, found the pillow, and fell into it. His awkward, long legs buckled and one bent, leaving the other splayed out in front of him.

"We're going to play games," Merrybelle said to his drooping head.

"You wanna make a baby?" My dad chuckled toward Merrybelle and kissed the air, then leaned his head back and shut his eyes, like he needed a break from every last thing on earth.

"Want some chips?" My sister's look, the desperate one, full of alarm flickering about her eyes like little firecrackers going off, helped me make my decision to try to get my bulbous stomach and all the rest—the swollen legs, the throbbing back—up and off the pillow. My stomach had grown unforgiving. I'd come to hate the up and down of life. Once you're down, with an extra forty pounds on your front, it takes considerable prethinking to get up again. I'd made the decision to get me and my load upright and on my puffy feet.

My sister worked to give Dad something, anything, that was good, that might be the magic thing he wanted. Keep him pacified until he passed out.

"Hand me . . . ," Dad said. One eye flicked open. He lifted a long finger and pointed it toward a corner of the room. I thought for a second that he'd seen the joint.

Merrybelle followed his pointing finger and picked up his guitar, an old guitar that had stood in some corner of every house we'd ever lived in as far back as I could remember. She handed it toward him while keeping her distance. She'd figured out not to step closer.

"I'm gonna sing you a song, Martha," Dad said, eyes still closed.

Nobody corrected him. No one bothered to even whisper, *Her name is Merrybelle.* We all sat stone still, like we were paralyzed. My sister and I were used to waiting like that, wondering what would happen next. We knew it could be anything.

But I could tell that Merrybelle wasn't used to that kind of waiting, the kind with no definition and an unsure purpose. It was like time stopped and we all just hung there, waiting for *Roe v. Wade* to take effect. Or waiting for our lives to begin, waiting for childhood to finally be done, waiting to be adults. Maybe waiting to be free. I saw Merrybelle put her hand to her mouth and giggle a little. It never dawned on me to laugh. Never.

Merrybelle stood holding my dad's guitar out to him like a decoy, so he wouldn't lunge at her. My dad didn't move at first. Then he slowly unbent his leg and stretched it out in front of him so his legs spread in a V.

"Want to join our party?" Merrybelle asked him tentatively, naïvely.

My father sat upright, adjusted himself to lean back against a bare wall. The thing was, my dad liked parties. He had an artist's sensibility, favoring beautifully designed Chryslers over perfunctory Fords. He'd fixed up the least used room in that eleven-room house, his office, which he was never in. It was lovely, deep amber-painted walls and abstract-print curtains. An odd room, lending stark contrast to the other sparse, mostly empty rooms.

"Party?" he said to Merrybelle. Then he turned to me. His eyes shut, and he worked to reopen them. "Hmph," he grunted, opened his eyes, and found focus on Merrybelle. "She doesn't deserve any party. Look at her." He tried to chuckle, tried to be the funny man, the clever one for Merrybelle. "She already had her party, see? She's like the niggers on welfare." He nodded toward my stomach and passed completely out.

Grabbing the wall for balance, I slowly stood up, shook a leg that'd fallen asleep, and snapped the newly made pants' pregnant panel against my round, concrete-like belly to give me some air. White powder poofed off the waistband, and Stradivari dust flew from my crotch like an inner-thigh-manufactured cloud.

I waddled toward the TV room, awkward and overheated, brushing off the clumps of thigh-sweat powder from inside my legs. On my way past the TV, that blaring thing no one was watching, the black horizontal line rolling, rolling, rolling, I popped the console's Off button with the bottom of my heel so forcefully, I smashed the knob, and it fell to the floor in pieces.

Then, a month later, my wrists and ankles were leather-strapped to a delivery table after nearly sixty hours of labor. Then there was a baby.

That afternoon, alone in a recovery room, foggy-headed, I peeked under a sheet and stared at my belly, a belly that had been so tight and frightening and swollen. Deep purple gashes zigzagged down the side of my stomach. It remained puffed up, the skin jiggly and loose.

I reached down and touched it with my index finger, like it was someone else's stomach, cringing at its tenderness. It hurt to touch it, yet I did again. I wanted to soothe it; I wanted to tell the skin that it was over, that it could go back to just being my stomach again. I wanted to tell the belly to calm down, and ask it why it was still so swollen, so much bigger than it was before a baby lived in there.

Instead, I dropped the sheet quickly, and as I did so, an involuntary gush of something warm and wet and thick moved from inside me. Immediately, I was lying in a pool of it. It seeped beneath my butt, and the volume forced it up my back, where it oozed, then turned chilling and cold.

I knew with all my heart, with profound certainty, then. My dad was right.

TWENTY-PLUS YEARS LATER, IT WAS HIGH SAILING, HIGH tide, and Denise and I were riding atop the biggest wave. I got a glimpse of how life could look because she took me there, because there was not one thing she was afraid of, and because she saw in me—without hesitation, without flinching—a winner. That's it.

Denise knew I was *not* the circumstances I'd been dealt. She knew me, and she championed me. She celebrated where I'd come from and that I was still there—and bigger and better and brighter than ever. No human being had ever seen, let alone celebrated, that part of me until that moment, Vaseline-dripping face and all.

CHAPTER TWELVE

Everything's Free in America

The thing that was so hard about our Jamaica-Cuba sojourn was absolutely everything. Our regular, workaday lives had us starting the trip already tired, and not one thing was convenient—not getting there, not getting food, not getting rest. Denise and I started fighting the second we stepped onto warm sand and quit fighting at the end only because we'd pretty much stopped speaking to each other.

But that's getting ahead of the story.

"WE'RE GOING TO JAMAICA," DENISE ANNOUNCED, STANDing inside the frame shop.

"And when might that be?" I asked. It was 3:27 P.M., and I was getting to where I skipped out on the magazine editing gig earlier and earlier each week. Passing through the house and heading back to the shop, I'd thought to yank a bottle of four-dollar Ecuadoran cab from the rack. I poured us each a full glass, tossed off my shoes, flicked the radio on, and let Nat King Cole leach into every last one of my *BowlingBiz*-frazzled nerves.

"When do you want to go?" she said. "I made a deal with a woman who owns a resort there. We can go whenever we want."

"What sort of deal?" I asked, taking a couple of pretty good sips.

Nat's "Unforgettable" was doin' me right, laying out my psyche very nicely, but I couldn't quite believe we were heading to Jamaica for free.

"I'm doing framing for her," Denise said. "It's for real. When should we go?"

"Next month," I said, letting the details of the bargain slide. "My face will be completely healed, January's colder than you know what, and we'll be sick of the snow, even more than we are right now. Plus, that'll give us plenty of time to brag about Jamaica to everyone."

"Merle says it's over," she said, laying a piece of purple mat next to a painting. She studied the color without looking up.

"What's over?" It took me a sec to get what she was telling me. "You and Merle?"

"He says that once he met John at my birthday dinner, he hasn't felt right about seeing me." She laid wood and copper frame samples against the painting. "He thinks John's a great guy."

"But that was months ago," I said. "It took him long enough to figure that out."

"Not really," Denise said, aligning the frame against the canvas. "He's been avoiding me lately. I've called him three times and he hasn't called back. That was two weeks ago."

"Yikes," I said. "So we made a tactical error." Though the affair was her crazy notion, I somehow felt we were in it together. I tried to see her face, see how she was taking it. "Having them both at dinner, I mean."

She threw the mat and frame samples on the table and collapsed onto a stool.

"I'm going to *make* him keep seeing me," she said. "He doesn't get it about John, that John's lazy, that he won't touch me anymore, that John wants nothing to do with me or my MS."

I turned the radio up to better hear Nat croon *inCRED-i-ble*.

What I said was "So let's go lie on a beach."

What I was thought was *Nat-man, you don't know for shit.*

OUR FIRST EVENING IN JAMAICA WAS MAGIC. WARM, damp breezes swept our cheekbones as we stepped from the plane and walked—I walked, Denise hobbled, her MS made worse in the heavy heat—into a third-world airplane terminal. An anxious man asked us, "Ah you Deeneeze?" and we said yes.

After a two-hour drive up one curvy road and down another, we finally arrived in the slate black of past midnight and predawn. We could tell, as we swept low-lying palm trees out of our way, that we were maneuvering through a kind of hut commune, sitting back several yards from the beach. We made sure the Caribbean—a thing we heard but could not see—was indeed there and flopped into an octagon-shaped hut hosting two twin beds pushed together and made up with sandy, mismatched sheets.

Midmorning, I stepped outside and viewed our straw house and the blinding, aqua blue water. Midwesterners were everywhere, their doughy legs and arms packed into crisp Gap Bermudas and shirts. They were paying $2,500 a week apiece to stay in their mini straw cabins, and you could tell they were feeling pretty exotic, sleeping under those straw roofs and having blue-black people cook their fish at night. I felt separate from the tourist crowd, mainly because we weren't paying a penny to be there.

The bar hut part of the commune was thirty feet from the hypnotic ocean beachfront. First, I had myself a piña colada made with what the chubby, flip-flop-wearing owner, Fred, told me was Jamaican rum that is "excellent, unlike anything in the States." He was right. Then I had one of those Jamaican beers, and capped it off with a second, seductive piña colada. I fell back into a hammock chained to a palm tree and shooed away a pack of children peddling beat-up bananas. Mmmmm. Jamaica *mahn*.

We took our supper that evening at yet another hut, where the same Jamaicans who'd mopped our rooms at midday were pushing plates of food out of what looked to me like a Burger King drive-through window.

That's where our trouble started. I ordered a glass of wine and watched Denise eyeball my glass, then cross her arms as she leaned over the table. Lowering her voice and not entirely meeting my gaze, she said, "Maybe you shouldn't drink any more."

Not drink any more?

This was my first one of the evening. This was thousands of miles from any responsibility I had ever had, currently had, or ever would have. I'd never been in such a vacation frame of mind in my life. This was Rastafarian, chronic-dope-smoking-to-the-max land. This was Jamaica *mahn,* for cris-sakes.

Okay, if there was a drinker between the two of us, I was it. Though lately, I'd been able to bring Denise up to snuff a little. She could, for example, pretty much share a bottle of wine with me. And when we bought any chocolate-flavored frozen drink mixer at the liquor store and whirled it up in the blender with ice and cheap rum, she could, on a good night, down three pretty-good-size goblets full.

But it was still my old neighborhood, not hers, that had hosted Our Lady of Perpetual Sorrow, the Dew-Drop, the 10-Pin Inn, and McShane's, all within walking distance of each other. It was my dad who lived at any and all of them, depending upon which night of the week it was, and it was my mom who sat in the living room lusting after Dean Martin on our old black-and-white TV, waiting for my dad to come home.

Once, he didn't. At least not for several weeks, so she quit her chair and took, instead, to lying flat-out on the couch. There she'd be when she sent all five of us to bed at night, and there she'd be still when we got up and got ourselves dressed for school the next morning: prone, chain-smoking those long Kool menthol 100s and staring hard at the ceiling. When we'd call "bye" and head out the door, we knew she heard us because she'd lift her smoke and suck in a hard drag.

Denise, on the other hand, grew up squeezed into a fourth-floor walk-up in the Bronx. It was a bland brick building with tiny windows, where she and her two sisters fed daily from the freezer of her aunt the confectioner. "Auntie brought home everything she didn't sell that day," Denise once told me. "Sometimes it was too much to fit into hers or my mother's freezer. So we'd just sit down and eat whatever— cakes, cookies—all those sweets in one sitting."

I asked Denise once if anyone drank alcohol in her family. "Sure," she said. "Mother never let a Seder pass without a new gallon of Manischewitz."

DENISE AND I WENT THERE ONCE, TO THAT BRONX APART- ment building. A shop on the ground floor sold egg creams, and she had to have one. It was a long subway ride from Manhattan, then the train, then walking down people-packed iron stairs to the street. Denise looked so at home heading down those dirty steel steps to the street, to her old neighborhood, that my psyche pitched back to a time in the late 1950s or early 1960s, creating its own little picture: I suddenly saw a young, limber girl skipping down those steps from the train and into the throngs of Hispanic and black and white faces heading in and out of shops with names like Rasofsky and Cohen painted on the doors.

The egg cream shop was covered in mirrors to make the space appear larger than it was, mirrors that also forced you to confront an unnerving, infinite number of reflections of yourself.

The second our creams were set in front of us, Denise moved from our booth to the one across the aisle, where four elderly women sat in their fur hats and cloaks. She scooted herself into their booth, and I watched an immediate and seamless conversation ignite—five women talking, laughing, slapping the table like they'd been waiting for her to arrive.

"Denise, aren't you going to introduce me?" I called, and though Denise glanced at me over her shoulder, I was soon ignored.

Thirty minutes later, she called me over. I couldn't finish the egg cream, the thought of a raw egg in a glass, whether there actually was one or not, bothered me, so I was glad to leave it.

"Cathie, this is Dorothy," Denise said. "She lives below the apartment where I grew up." Dorothy weighed ninety pounds, including her red, heavily rouged cheeks. She gave me the once-over from shocking blue eyes framed in a fascinating face of wrinkles layered upon wrinkles. "We're going to walk her home. These women have their own charity club. Elsie and Frieda here knew my mother years ago."

We'd come home to Denise's launchpad, to her beginnings. We'd arrived in a place that was so intimate, so automatic, so natural for her, she seemed to float in and about it, moving back forty years.

She needed to be there, I knew, as I watched those women with their comfortable bank accounts and uncomfortable joints bragging about their long-dead husbands, their charities, their kids who were now stockbrokers and lawyers and world travelers. I watched her listen to the women speak of their grown children who, like Denise, had left years ago for places far more glamorous than a borough that used to be a cow pasture.

She needed to be there, to hear of her father, who died of a heart attack while at the racetrack when she was a teenager. She needed to hear how funny and optimistic her mother always was, no matter what. She needed to drink in the memories—hers and theirs—as sharp and vivid as if mere days instead of decades had passed, recollections retained by those women, whose memory banks preserved Denise as a scholar, a thespian, a beacon of promise to her parents and to the entire generation squeezed into that booth.

She might have crafted a sharp and unwavering persona of blasé independence back in Boulder, but there in the center of the Bronx, Denise tapped into her core, one full of history and heart and vulnerability.

"Oy, your legs were so long," Elsie said. She was a regal woman, tall, with a ballerina's neck and a perfectly coiffed bun at the back of her head. She placed her long and wrinkled hand over Denise's. "We used to wonder if you'd ever stop growing."

"Do you remember that day you went missing? You went all the way to the boardwalk by yourself!" said Frieda, who looked exactly like Golda Meir. Frieda sat next to Denise and leaned her stocky, fox-fur-wrapped (little fox heads with popped-out eyeballs) body against Denise to make the point. "Your mother was a wreck. She was heading off to call the police when you came walking up eating peanuts. I remember seeing you from a block away, just strolling like you were on holiday. I watched you closely because I didn't know if your mother was going to kill you or kiss you."

Dorothy announced that she had things to do, had to get home, so Denise and I headed outside to help her navigate the icy sidewalk. I hoped that Dot—Denise and Dot were tight by then—and her walker didn't end up in a pile on the concrete.

"Dot just had her ninety-first birthday," Denise told me.

"You look wonderful," I said. "Amazing."

"Oh," Dot said, "I never leave without putting on my face." Dot worked the walker forward a few inches, hesitated, moved it inches forward again. I wondered how far we'd take her, thinking it'd be dark before we got there.

"But it's getting harder to see," Dot went on. "So I'm never sure if I've got my face on straight." In the fading, wintry Bronx sunlight, I examined Dot's smudged, ruby lips and drawn-on eyebrows.

I stopped short. I was seeing a vision of myself, I realized.

I'd get to grow thick in the middle and hang out all day eating whatever I liked and enjoying my daughter's tenuous patience in driving me to the grocery, though it would likely be the swanky Whole Foods, not Sal & Skip's Value Village. I'd likely get to watch my kids marry and make me grandchildren. I still had the chance to go to Africa and to fall in love and to hike the entire Natchez Trail. I would get to become Dot, to grow old and have a history to talk about.

Not everyone in our threesome would.

Watching Denise watching Dot, seeing Denise hanging on her words, and laughing at Dot's thrill at our company, made me lose focus. I could no longer catch their conversation, I couldn't even be polite and nod and agree at appropriate moments. Denise and Dot were leaving there soon—or at least it'd likely be sooner than I—perhaps even at times close together.

They were on their own voyage, and I wasn't invited and no one else was either, just those two, whose respective pasts had been built and were then wrapping up. Their lives had peaked—Denise's prematurely, Dot's naturally, yet seemingly in a sort of tandem—leaving haunting echoes even as we stood on the Bronx sidewalk. I wanted them both to stick around, I wanted my grandmother to stick around. I felt a mighty urge to reach past Dot and grab Denise's arm and insist that she not join Dot's departure, that she break herself away from Dot's chatter. I wanted to race back to the train.

Then Dot touched my cheek, her fingertips as soft and dry as feathers. "Her mother adores this one," Dot said with a nod toward Denise, and Denise's pleasure was palpable; she gripped Dot's walker bars, ostensibly to steady the device so Dot wouldn't fall, but it looked more like a grip meant to steady herself. Then Dot said, "You don't think I look a day over sixty?" She plastered a wide grin across her face, poking fun at herself, full of charm and joie de vivre.

"You look incredible," I told her. "We should look so good at your age."

"Why don't you have a husband?" Dot demanded of me. I looked at Denise, registering that she and Dot had had much to talk about, including my singleness, across that egg cream aisle. "I had my Lenny for forty-four years," Dot added, and she pushed the walker forward another six inches, then said, "I like to go out, but it can be hard to find good men my age."

Dot stopped dead in the walker's tracks and looked at us both. "You two know any good men over eighty?"

I NEVER MET DENISE'S MOTHER OR HER SIBLINGS OR HER one, lone niece or her brother-in-law, who loaned us his terrific, unused Manhattan apartment for that trip. I knew that Denise loved her mother and sent her money every month, even as she struggled to make ends meet herself.

I knew that Denise's mother had cherished her as a little girl in those claustrophobic Bronx neighborhoods, that she was there as Denise got forever hooked on sweets thanks to her aunt's bakery, and I knew she was there when, at age eighteen, Denise had to flee that walk-up for the mountains of Colorado. I knew that her mother's mere existence, the fact that she lived in that senior citizens' apartment in Florida, was often what kept Denise going.

"I couldn't quit," Denise once said. "I had to try to deal with this, though when I was first diagnosed, I immediately thought about just killing myself. Just getting some Valium.

"But I couldn't," she said. "It would kill my mother. I didn't do it because of her."

Aaaah. So she *did* have the will once to face a chronic, debilitating illness straight in the eye. She *could* look down the gun barrel at a life violently altered, an existence that had been alarmingly and statistically abbreviated with one doc's viewing of an MRI.

She didn't throw up her arms at the diagnosis. And once she had made the decision to fight the good fight she didn't quit when the symptoms increased, not just in duration but in variety. If for no other reason than for the grief her family would face if she didn't.

That take-it-in-the-chin resolve came at the starting point, however, when the news was new. The continuing moments of unfolding, of coping, of having to suck up years of irregular symptoms had been unraveling long before the Caribbean and Flip-Flop Fred and the jungle. The juju of time was unrolling in front of her, like a crazy welcome mat, shepherding her toward a questionable future.

"WHAT IN THE HELL ARE YOU TALKING ABOUT, *NOT DRINK any more*?" I snapped. I took a good, long pull on that glass of Jamaican chardonnay. The ocean was backdropped by a purple-blue sunset, waves constantly, languidly, slap-slap-slapping against silver sand. I looked at Denise; she had her head down, studying the hairs on her arms.

"Well," she started, "I just think it would be a good idea if you didn't have another drink." I realized then that she hadn't enjoyed a cocktail the entire day, except for the complimentary mango-flavored Kool-Aid thing handed out to tourists in the afternoon. Her abstinence ran counter to our normal party-time tempo.

"This is a vacation," I insisted. "What are you talking about?" I emptied my glass and stomped back up the spindly stairs to our room, leaving the half-raw fish on the plate. *How dare someone count my drinks when I'm on vacation!* I was good and hot. And then a new thought hit me: Maybe this mouthy bitch was staging an intervention—an intervention in *Jamaica,* that was true—but an intervention nevertheless.

It was a touchy subject. I'd micromanaged my alcoholic intake my entire life. I counted my drinks. When I was in my twenties, an evening out with two cocktails would propel me to the therapist's couch to analyze if I was denying a drinking problem. My kids used to make fun of me when I'd keep an untouched six-pack in the refrigerator for months to see if.

I didn't. I always forgot about it.

A counselor had once burst out laughing when I told her I'd had three margaritas over the course of a four-day weekend and did she think I should join AA? "Stop it," she'd ordered. "You've got crap to deal with like everyone else. Alcohol isn't part of it. I'd know it and you'd know it by now."

I was relieved to hear her professional assessment, and more or less relaxed and forgot the worry. But every once in a while, out of the blue, the notion that she might have been a drunk herself, in denial and enabling me, crossed my mind.

Denise took a long time to return from dinner (she admitted later she'd ordered and finished both desserts), dragging that foot of hers. I could hear her thump-rest-wait, thump-rest-wait gait outside our door, and I knew she was clinging to that thin bamboo railing with both hands, like it was a life preserver. Finally, she opened the door and shuffled in, nearly missing the bed as she collapsed, with a loud groan, onto the sheets. Her wild hair spread like a huge, dark halo around her head.

After a few minutes she said, "Look, Harriet and I made this frame trade."

I was in the bathroom.

She called out, "That fat guy's her husband, Fred. He's not up to speed."

I still wasn't getting it.

"*What* are you talking about?" I called back.

"I have to figure out how I'm going to pay for this," she answered.

I looked around the corner and saw she was lying flat, her eyes shut. She opened them and gazed at the straw ceiling. Her face was a scary, throbbing red. It had taken everything out of her, climbing those stairs.

"Wait," I said, pulling the underpants' elastic away from my thigh and swiping the sand off my butt. "*How you're going to pay for this?* You did framing for Harriet and this is the 'everything-included' payback."

I checked my naked butt in the room's weird, wavy mirror. I didn't see any sand, but there was a grainy feeling there anyway. I swiped, swiped, swiped, trying to brush off invisible sand.

"Harriet and I talked about a certain number of posters I'd frame for her." Denise opened her eyes and looked at me. "This is the husband. He thought it should be more work and that we should pay for our drinks and food as we go. I don't know what he'll charge us for this room."

Instantly I swapped relief that I wasn't caught in the midst of a Denise-led intervention for incredulity. "You don't have this all set up? You're telling me that, at any moment, we could either be kicked out of this sand trap or ordered to fork over twenty-five hundred dollars *each*?"

I was pretty much screaming then.

"Why don't I just pay my bar tab at the end of the week! I'll be damned if I'm going to walk on pins and needles 'cause this guy thinks I owe him money!

"You've been framing like a madwoman for nearly a year for this trip," I screeched. "Food for a week in this mosquito mess will cost us a thousand dollars each. This isn't a vacation, it's a trap!" I stomped out the door and down the steps, then marched to the beach, which was arresting in its beauty. Warm, moist air swirled above and along the shore, soft water rolled in, licking my toes and dissolving at my feet. A silver moon, like a shimmering dime, hung waiting over the ocean.

Squatters, held prisoner by a big-bellied Boulderite in dime-store flip-flops, I mused. We didn't have five grand. We didn't have one grand.

All I wanted was a nightcap. The bar hut, when I finally walked back, was sealed up tight as a drum, locked with more locks than I'd ever seen in one place. I counted eight before I walked away into the coconut-scented night air.

CHAPTER THIRTEEN

Do You Like Piña Coladas?

The Flip-Flop Fred incident liberated us somehow, gave us both an oh-what-the-hell feeling, and so we rented a motorized scooter and headed down the road to a travel agency. We'd been thinking of landing somewhere other than Jamaica anyway and had spent time back in Colorado, shoulder to shoulder, poring over maps and travel books. One afternoon, before we left the States, we'd looked hard at a map of the Caribbean and seen that Jamaica was within spitting distance of Cuba.

Keep Jamaica, we said to each other at the piña colada bar, full of righteous indignation. We were heading to Cuba. So what if it was illegal for Americans to enter Cuba? That only made us dig in our pretty, Jamaica-tanned heels.

Before leaving Boulder, we'd learned of Celia and her Havana apartment for rent through one of Denise's clients. An exchange of e-mails had ensued, and finally we'd arranged an international telephone call to Celia. Denise's client worked as our interpreter over the two-thousand-mile phone line, struggling to interpret Cuban Spanish with her native East L.A. Spanish. ("They keep dropping syllables!" she complained.) On little more than a grand leap of faith, we'd arranged on the phone to connect, to somehow find each other in the Havana airport, if, while in Jamaica, Denise and I decided to hop on over to Cuba.

Mr. Flip-Flop helped us elect to hop.

DENISE MANAGED TO GET HERSELF STRADDLED OVER THE back of our scooter, but it was everything I could do to get us that mile down the road in one piece. I had to drive on the wrong side of the road and hold steady Denise's 175 wobbly pounds. Cars passed us, impatient and honking, as we crept along at a shaky ten miles an hour. When a driver cut too close in front of us, we nearly wiped out.

"Fuck you!" Denise screamed at the driver, and I accidentally pressed the gas button instead of the brake. I'd barely gotten us eased back into our lane when a truck passed our shoulders in a loud *swooosh!*

"Denise, shut up!" I yelled. As I steered us down that tarmac, I felt Denise and I were beginning a soundless, ethereal power shift, much like a middle-aged woman and her mother who undergo that moment when the aging mother becomes the child, and the child the mother.

The Jamaican "travel agency" turned out to be a dark-skinned woman behind a folding table on a screened porch with a telephone and a 1983 IBM computer. She sat in the center of the mostly empty room and wielded a large, filthy flyswatter, smashing big horseflies flat as we walked in. The room smelled like coconuts, despite the dead flies speckled about the floor.

She spoke chunky-sounding Spanish and fifteen words of English, so the three of us spent the next forty-five minutes getting her to understand that we wanted to fly from Montego Bay, Jamaica, to Havana, Cuba—a tiny, ocean-covered, ninety-mile stretch that we had to show her on our map. We also had to explain that, no matter what she thought, we weren't rich Americans.

"Aaah, Montego Bay á Havana, Cuba?" the agent asked, eyeing my American Express card.

Her avocado-colored Princess phone cradled against her ear, she spoke to someone in Havana. She jabbered for another ten minutes, and Denise and I couldn't decipher so much as a word, even though Denise had spent the entire month before leaving the States proclaiming, "Oh, I took Spanish in high school. I sure was great at it—we'll have absolutely no problem." The words we *did* understand were *"no, no, no!"* and *"americano."*

Finally, our agent secured us tickets that had us leaving for Cuba the next morning. We were stuck with the scooter for the entire day, so we headed back to the rental shack to get a map. Why not spend the day exploring the island? Nagine, our scooter-renting guy, was still there. Shiny black and twenty-something, he was ripe and dark, a pair of cut-off shorts the only thing between him and the heat.

"My friend, he is tour guide," said Nagine when he saw us looking at maps. He pulled another Rastafarian-looking native from a chair and presented him to us. "Ramón, he will show you the *real* Jamaica."

We were weary of Bermuda-wearing Minnesotans at our hut commune and eager to see the real thing, so as Ramón eased his scooter out onto the road, we climbed back on ours and followed him. He kept glancing over his shoulder at us and was repeatedly forced to slow down and wait. We could tell he was impatient with our unsteady putt-putt-putting along—and then he had us on open roads of brilliant sunshine lined by blue-green vegetation so lush you wanted to lie down in it. I more or less got the hang of the scooter, and Denise sat bone still and hung on.

After an hour, Ramón turned his scooter to the side of the road, and the three of us sat beneath a rotting wood canopy, drinking up the shade and the water.

"I show you the largest waterfalls in the world," said Ramón. "It is not far."

And we were back on the road again, the vegetation getting thicker, the mountains appearing closer, like huge green anthills. Another hour of riding left my arms aching, so I sped up a little and signaled to Ramón that I needed to stop.

He smiled back at me and called out, "Close, very close."

"I hope you know the way back!" Denise yelled into my ear just as Ramón turned down a dirt road. Overrun with weeds and canopied with palm trees and bushes, a prehistoric-looking, wild-ass jungle of thigh-thick vines wove in and around it all. I struggled to keep up and to keep us balanced. After fifteen more minutes of riding, I decided I was stopping no matter what, but before I could pull over, a man stepped out from the bushes and Ramón shut off his scooter.

"This is Jaime," Ramón told us when we peeled ourselves off the sticky seats. I grabbed our water bottle and guzzled. Denise couldn't stand up; she collapsed to the ground in a heavy sweat, her face so scarlet it scared me. When I offered her the water bottle, she shook her head no, lay back on the ground, and shut her eyes.

"Jaime, he'll take you on a good walk through the village *mahn*," Ramón said.

"Where is this waterfall?" I said. "And how far away is this village?" The humidity was palpable, wet and thick as the inside of someone's mouth. The sun seared everything in a striking white heat. We had two swallows of water left.

"Oh, close," Ramón said.

Denise managed to heave her body up onto a fence post. She followed Ramón and Jaime slowly, putting one foot forward and more or less dragging the other. I brought up the rear as we headed along a mud-baked path. Though the shade was soothing, it was scarce, the unrelenting, heavy heat, crushing. Twenty minutes into the slow stroll, Denise collapsed in a heap.

"I can't make it," she said, breathless, and I knew she was right.

"Jaime, where is the big waterfall?" I asked. My T-shirt was sweat-soaked, and I had no clue where we were or what roads had gotten us there.

"Oh, it is not far," Ramón answered for him, not even turning to me to answer.

"Ramón," I said in a commanding voice that finally made him stop. "You have to walk down, get your scooter, ride it up here, and ride Denise back down. She's sick, and she can't walk."

"Oh, *noooo,*" said Ramón. "Bike cannot be on this ground." He stomped a clump of weeds to show me how nonnavigable the trail was.

"Then you'll have to carry her down," I said, and all three of us looked at Denise, her hat askew, her breathing labored, her body flat-out on the ground.

"I will see," Ramón relented, and he and Jaime turned to walk back down the path.

For the next half hour Denise and I lay in the shade. I watched her for signs of recovery, but she didn't move. Then we heard the shrill buzz of a scooter's engine.

"You ride Denise down," I said to our guides, wondering if she could sit upright. "I'll walk and meet you at the start of the road."

Denise heaved herself on behind Ramón, and he lurched his scooter forward, nearly losing her off the back. When he got it that slow and steady was the only way to make progress, they were gone through the thickets.

As I began following them, swatting away flies as big as my thumb, it came to me that we were killing ourselves trying to prove to no one in particular that we were just vacationers. On the surface, we were like a maddening drumbeat, persistent in our effort to be two relatively young women on a Caribbean lark. Beneath our vacation façade, Denise was nearly comatose from dehydration and a tropical-heat-induced, MS-fueled exhaustion. The fact that we were in a jungle with no allies or resources or language capabilities washed over me.

I wondered if I should try to find a hospital. Alone and despite the heat, I trembled, frightened for us both. Stronger than my fear, however, was my guilt. I felt responsible for wanting this vacation, for feeling like I'd carelessly encouraged her to take the trip. I should have been the wiser one— less needy, less wanting a huge adventure to make up for everything I felt I'd ever been denied.

I'd pulled Denise into an escapade we had no business being in. If she were well, clear-thinking, and strong, she never would have allowed those two hooligans to drag us into a jungle in the middle of nowhere. She wasn't well, but I was, and when she'd said that afternoon way back, "We're going to Jamaica," I should have found excuses to at least put off the trip, to wiggle out of it, to make sure she stayed close to home.

But I didn't, because, as much as I craved adventure, I knew that she craved it, too.

Denise was born fearless.

She knew she'd better live large *then and there,* and that's what she was doing. With equal fervor, I sought out the daring, if not the outright dangerous. We were like two parallel-track, runaway trains. The more I thought about it, the less clear it all seemed. I no longer knew who was in charge, who was responsible.

I knew that she could collapse, perhaps irretrievably, in that jungle. And I knew I needed to take charge and figure it all out. I needed to make sure no one got hurt—or died—in the process, and I needed to do it immediately. I didn't know what the hell I was going to do.

Would John have to fly to Jamaica and get us?

WHEN I CAUGHT UP WITH THEM AT THE START OF THE road, Denise and Ramón and Jaime were all in a circle. Ramón and Jaime were intense, talking at the same time, like they were trying to convince Denise of something. When I walked up, they stopped talking.

"Is there anywhere to get some water?" I said, and Jaime opened a cooler that he had not revealed until that moment.

"These are five dollars," he said to me, smiling and pointing to hot Pepsis at the bottom of the cooler.

"We must get our payment," Ramón said, with a steady eye straight at mine. "My friend Jaime here is the best guide on the island."

"Payment?" I asked, eyeing the hot soft drinks and resolving to die before I'd touch them.

"She agreed to pay us one hundred dollars each for this trip," he said with a sneer and cocked a thumb toward Denise.

Her face displayed bewilderment and utter exhaustion in equal proportions. "I thought it was a hundred dollars for the both of us," she said in a low voice.

"Ramón, draw me a map for getting back to the hotel," I said.

"Ah, mahn, we must have payment," Ramón said. The two men looked at each other, then at me. They were steady, rooted to the ground, their muscular arms crossed firmly against their chests.

"Denise and I are going to talk," I said and pulled her away.

"How much money do you have on you?" I demanded in a whisper. I was shaking, but I didn't know if it was from fury or fear.

"About sixty dollars," she told me. She didn't look good. Her pupils were dilated, one eye slightly askew. It was a symptom I'd only recently learned of, one that showed up when MS was aggravated. It was an indicator of overload, hard to notice, which made it all the scarier.

I looked at her face, beaded in sweat against the outrageous heat, the sun cooking both of us, charring our skin to an angry red sheen. My dry throat swallowed roughly, and in an instant, I could not speak. I scanned her face, her misery, and inside, I railed against getting jammed up in that jungle.

I looked her in the eye, put my hand on her shoulder, and swallowed. Then I found my voice. "I've got about fifty dollars. I'm going to offer them fifty dollars and tell them we'll pay the balance back at the hotel—but don't you give them a dime. I'm going to report their asses."

"To whom," Denise said with a look. "Tarzan?"

Her ability to joke at all costs flooded me with relief, pouring relaxation down my spine.

We turned back to the men. Jaime smiled and pointed at the Pepsis. "We've only got fifty dollars between the two of us," I said. "But a deal is a deal. I didn't know Denise had arranged everything with you. We'll have to give you the balance when we get to the hotel. How do we get back?"

Ramón took the money. He didn't look happy. Reluctantly, he sketched a route in the dirt. I wondered whether it was the real way back and whether Denise could sit on the bike again for two hours. The sun was setting fast, and a hot wind blew across my back.

"I'm riding back fast, I must get home," said Ramón, and he hopped on his scooter and was gone. Jaime vaporized into the jungle.

THE TWO-HOUR RIDE BACK FELT LIKE TWO DAYS—LONG, *long* days full of black asphalt, creepy jungle noises, and unsure turns on roads that were dark and unmarked. Denise and I didn't speak because we couldn't: I was locked to the scooter's hand grips and the search for any familiar sign on the road. She was locked to my waist.

After an interminable ride over a never-ending ribbon of blacktop, we pulled into our commune, dropped the scooter to the ground, and staggered to the cabana hut, flopping our bodies against the bar like a couple of half-dead fish. A beautiful, midnight blue woman was bartending, and before we could utter a word, she said, "Do you like piña coladas?" and placed two icy and creamy glasses in front of us. We grabbed them and sucked at the straws like our very lives depended entirely upon pineapple, rum, and the strength of that cane-made bar.

Maybe I should have reconsidered our trip then.

But we were past any midpoint, beyond turning back, and, besides, I'd never opted, never actually had the option of abandoning or running away. For better or worse, I marched to the beat of a no-choice, you-made-your-bed, tough-it-out mentality.

For these reasons, or elusive, Freudian others—really, who knows?—I wasn't ready to throw in any towel.

Yet.

CHAPTER FOURTEEN

Bay of
(Bleeding Like Stuck)
Pigs

Denise flipped on her sweet, conciliatory face for the customs officer, the face she relied upon to charm framing clients and men. She didn't have a visa to enter Cuba, so our plan was to snatch back her passport before the agent could slam a Cuban seal on it, thereby eliminating any evidence she'd ever dishonored the U.S. embargo.

I, on the other hand, did have the proper papers. The minute we'd considered the Cuban jaunt, I had contacted the State Department, who had no qualms about issuing me a journalist's visa. I tried to piggyback Denise on my paperwork by telling them that she was the photographer in our combined journalistic endeavor, but they couldn't get a visa-rejected letter back to us fast enough.

"It's okay?" Denise flashed her fun-and-flirty smile at the stern-faced official. He stared down at her passport for what seemed like an eternity, then he reached out to grab the ink-laden stamp. *"Por favor,"* she said sweetly. I didn't know she even knew that expression. She grabbed my passport and government-issue visa and signaled to him that he should stamp my passport only—not hers.

I thought we were headed to Cuban jail pronto when our agent called a pal over to commiserate. Then the two men smiled at us. Denise ratcheted up her Svengaliesque mojo, the voodoo she employed when she wanted things to move smoothly, when she wanted to hoodwink whomever without them catching so much as a whiff of her quick-draw, under-the-radar magic, and she and the customs agent exchanged knowing looks as he motioned us to move on.

Celia Lopez and I first set eyes upon each other doing exactly the same thing in the same place—hunting for a stranger amid chaos, customs agents, and Cuban-inflected Spanish. Celia grinned and held high her handcrafted sign, which read: KATEE Y DANEEZE. I did likewise, only mine said: CELIA LOPEZ? Denise had scratched it out minutes before with a lipstick pencil and a paper bag—while I held a barf bag to my mouth against the plane's lurching teeter-totter halt on the José Martí airport landing strip.

We ran toward each other's signs, and, though we couldn't understand a word they said and they didn't know English, we somehow came to understand that the stunning Cuban woman was our hostess and her *amigo cubano,* Fidel, our guide. I immediately felt their warmth, their hospitality; their faces were open and expectant, promising something like a buttery balm after our Jamaican mishaps.

In the midst of entering Cuba, of meeting Celia, I fought against my mounting sense of doom. I had more than a niggling worry about us being there. Despite Denise's organic breeziness in dealing with customs agents and ancient airplanes, I couldn't shake her meltdown in the jungle.

The tropical winds and the warm Cuban people worked to distract me, but even they barely mitigated the gut-churning feelings that begged for my attention. I knew I couldn't talk to her about what I was feeling; she'd have shrugged her shoulders and walked away. There was no one to blame but myself.

You can't tell an obstinate, take-charge businesswoman much. You can't correct her or advise her, let alone defy her. You can only snap to and keep up. There's something about that business instinct, that self-assuredness, that enviable arrogance. Call it the Donald Trump syndrome: he's got that awful hair, and even the press makes fun of him, and he's on his third marriage. He's got that ego as inflated as those garish buildings New Yorkers love to hate, but all that pales because, at the end of the day, he can *buy* New York.

Denise was much the same, large and in charge with that sense of not just destiny but predestiny. It seemed that I was supposed to be there, at that time, no matter the mysterious and escalating, whacked-out mix of events. While, on the one hand, I felt a sort of entrapment, once again, in circumstances beyond my control, on the other, I wasn't an unwilling participant.

Then a weird thing happened. Perhaps it was Celia's warmth, perhaps it was the magic of Cuba, but in the thick of my angst, a tidal wave of profound gratitude washed over me. Even as this happened, I knew that any shrink on earth would, probably rightfully so, diagnose my sentiment with all the jargon: codependent, martyr syndrome, whatever.

But I knew better. I knew I was being handed something extraordinary, though I would have been unable to name it, at that moment.

WE VENTURED OUT INTO THE HEADY HAVANA CLIMATE OF moisture and flowers and traffic and climbed into a half-orange, half-cobalt-blue 1957 Cadillac with Chrysler fenders and Chevy headlights, a car that you could tell Fidel was proud to have arranged. A ten-minute ride later, through streets of pastel buildings and dark, pretty children, we were standing on a rooftop looking at what was to be our home for the next seven days—a cobbled-together hut atop an Old Havana apartment building—complete with a bird's-eye view of the rolling waves of the Straits of Florida.

Fidel was warm and welcoming, built sturdy, and chocolate-skinned. He was chivalrous, insisting on lugging our bags up the six flights of stairs by himself. I didn't know if Denise could make six flights of stairs, and this dampened my excitement at seeing the city. What were we going to do in that building with no elevator? The staircase was old, crumbling, and scary. Denise heaved herself onto the bottom step. There was no handrail.

For a moment she didn't look up, she just sat there, catching her breath. Then she put her elbows behind her, one stair higher than the one she sat on, and lifted her body with her elbows, a sort of crawl-lift. She did it again. I had a hard time watching, a hard time hearing her labored breathing. I knew her body language well and knew she'd likely physically block me if I tried to reach out to help. I plodded slowly up the stairs and felt my heart race as I listened to her struggle for breath.

That was the worst shape that I'd witnessed yet; she looked as bedraggled, as exhausted as she had the afternoon in the Jamaican jungle, and I figured that it was all over with, that Fidel was going to have to find us a ground-floor place to camp.

Twenty-eight minutes later, Denise pulled off the last of her crawl-lift maneuvers up the six flights to the rooftop, where she slouched her entire body against the door to Celia's apartment and fell, rather than walked, in.

"GRACIAS, GRACIAS," I SAID, EXHAUSTING MY SPANISH vocabulary as Fidel fretted over Denise, grabbing her at the top step and leading her through the apartment door. Fidel was electric in his enthusiasm for our being there and let Denise lean on his elbow, jovially walking us into the house: a tiny combo living-bedroom, plastic chairs against one corner, a double bed in the other, with barely enough space to slide between the furniture and into the middle room—which served as combined shrine to the Blessed Virgin Mary, dressing area, and what appeared to be a closet.

But it turned out not to be a closet at all. It was a squared-off corner of the midroom, holding a toilet and a makeshift shower. The shower water fell directly onto the toilet before hitting the drain in the floor, allowing one to pee and shampoo simultaneously, making the toilet sort of unnecessary—at least some of the time.

We wandered to the very back, where a jerry-rigged kitchen housed a Formica-topped table and a tiny fridge pressed to the wall. A wood-burning stove crowded against the opposite wall, leaving no walking space, the appliances all jumbled together.

"*¡Bienvenidas!*" said Celia. She flashed us a movie star's radiant smile.

"*Descansen, descansen, suban sus pies, relájense,*" Fidel chimed and motioned us to sit down, but we didn't rest long. Fidel was so eager to entertain us, he insisted we head outside, and so we ended up across the street from their building at the Malecón—*the* Havana waterfront promenade, where lovers and rich summer breezes and the vast and sparkling Straits of Florida lapped against miles of oceanfront concrete walkway. Looking toward the city from the waterfront, you could sense the glamour of decades gone by, of posh hotels and exclusive nightclubs, of well-heeled Americans and mob money, of all the vices that hung in the tropical air, keeping Havana history alive, present, undeniably real, like a woman's lingering perfume.

"I'm going to take a walk by myself," said Denise. She and I hadn't entirely recovered from our squabble over Flip-Flop Fred or the scooter fiasco. She said she had the money thing all worked out, but I wasn't so sure. We had to pass back through our Jamaica resort for one last night before returning to the States. Would Fred present us with a ten-thousand-dollar tab?

"Why go by yourself?" I said. But in my heart, I knew. She was tired of being the cripple, she was sick to death of being a burden, and she was outraged that she was not the Denise she'd always been—someone to be reckoned with. Still, having her head off into this unknown city made my chest clench with worry.

"Why don't we take the day and walk the city tomorrow?" I asked.

"I just want to look around." With that she turned and walked away, shaking out the fold-up walking cane she'd brought along just in case.

I watched Fidel and Celia watch Denise depart. *"Es no problemo,"* I said to their worried faces. I felt ridiculous. My lack of Spanish-language skills had reduced me to Lisa Simpson–speak. *"No problemo,"* I repeated, like a dope.

I YEARNED TO TOSS OFF MY DISTRESS, WANTED TO SIMPLY stand on the Havana streets and gape at everything. Pre-1959 Chevys and Chryslers and Fords, renovated in a kaleidoscopic car-parts mishmash, and painted red, purple, orange, and black, often in two-toned mixes.

So I was thankful for the distraction when Fidel led Celia and me to a *paladar,* which looked like the back-door entrance to an underground apartment.

"A comer, a comer," said Celia, and then we were in a tiny room with chickens that pecked at our feet.

"Bienvenidas, siéntense, siéntense," said a chubby brown woman, and I sat down. Then I was eating from a table loaded with beans and tomatoes and beer and what I thought was chicken in a spicy sauce. I had to keep kicking away the

chattering chickens from my feet, and, when we were done eating, I pulled dollar bills from my bag, and the chubby lady took three of them.

It was getting dark, so we headed back to the apartment; I was worried sick that Denise was lost forever to La Habana Vieja. We sat in Celia's tiny living room, and Fidel left for a few minutes, then returned with another man.

"English," said Fidel, grinning.

"Hello, I am Roberto," the man said in the deep, milky way only the Robertos of this world can.

"You can translate?" I asked.

"With pleasure," he answered.

The door to information exchange was finally thrown so wide open that Celia and Fidel and I all started talking at once, and we ended up laughing at our colliding dissonance of words just as the world went completely dark.

"It is a blackout," Roberto said. "It is normal."

For the next three hours, the four of us sat cross-legged, facing each other on the bed, highlighting our faces with the flashlight Fidel had dug up when it was our turn to talk. I learned that Celia had a nine-year-old daughter, fathered by an American who had once passed through Havana (he was now long gone), who was staying with Celia's mother while Denise and I visited.

I didn't feel so great about her daughter's being displaced. When my kids were her daughter's age, I loved knowing they were home and sleeping safe and sound in their beds. I liked making their beds with fresh sheets, a Raggedy Ann doll or E.T.-themed bed pillows to curl up in. It was a sweet ritual, bath time, then a little TV, then the rhythm of crawling into bed. It felt safe and warm. It felt like love. So even though Celia's mother had her daughter, the absence, our taking a kid's bed, bugged me a little.

I learned that the apartment-shack, hand-built by Fidel, actually belonged to him, but Celia and he were longtime platonic childhood chums, and so he lived across the city with his father, allowing Celia and her daughter to take the apartment.

Just when I was ready to call in Castro's army to launch a full-island search for Denise, we heard the familiar step-clomp-wait of her gait, only now it was step-clomp-wait-slam because she was using that cane. I was happy to hear her managing the six flights of stairs without scooching up them on her butt, and for the first time in hours took a deep breath.

"Christ, Denise, where've you been?" I asked when she opened the apartment door. I was relieved and pissed off at the same time. "I found this incredible hotel out on the boulevard," she said and fell down next to me on the bed. "I sat out on this gorgeous patio and ate ice cream like I've never had."

Fidel rattled at Denise in Spanish, his face stern, and Roberto jumped in. "He said it is very dangerous for Denise to be alone on the streets," said Roberto. "Especially after dark—and he is right."

"Roberto's a neighbor, and he speaks English and Spanish." I stated the obvious to Denise.

"I was fine," Denise said.

"How'd you get back in the dark?" I said to her. "There are no streetlights out there, right?"

"Nope," she said. "I have no idea," she added just as the lights flickered back on.

In the startling moment of sudden light, we all blinked and looked at each other.

"Ah," said Fidel. *"Lo que necesitamos es música,"* and though we didn't understand a word, he headed to the kitchen and came back with a tape player pouring deep, sweet, Caribbean music—violins and trumpets and men's voices—out into the room and through the open windows, grinding rhythms that insisted we get up and move and dance and laugh.

"Vamos," he said, and in one movement he pulled Denise up and they rumba-rumba-rrrrummmbaed out the door and onto the rooftop, Fidel's hands on her hips and Denise's teeter-totter hobble gone for the moment, the two of them slipping into a syncopated beat, maracas and bongos under-scoring pure sex-in-music, which made Roberto grab my and Celia's hands, and we all danced and hip-thrusted and twirled and cha-chaed and sweated, transporting that roof and the tropical breezes and the star-clustered sky to a time when ca-sinos and Chryslers were common Cuban comforts.

"NO DEBEN HECHAR PAPEL EN EL INODORO," FIDEL SAID first thing the next morning when we were all up and sipping bad coffee.

Denise and I looked at each other.

"Well, Señorita Español Spitfire," I said to Denise. "Want to provide me with *la translación*?"

She grabbed the Spanish-English dictionary. "I know he said 'toilet,'" she told me, quickly flipping through the book.

"*No hay papel en el inodoro,*" Fidel repeated, and I snatched the book from her and flipped to the English word *paper,* scanning for its Spanish translation.

"Oh, *papel, papel,*" I said, having not one clue about what he was trying to tell us.

Fidel took my hand and led me to the corner toilet-closet. Denise and Celia followed, Celia grinning that brilliant, white-teeth smile again. I could tell that she was enjoying everything and that something was up. Fidel held up a tampon, pointed to the toilet, shook a finger at the toilet, and said, "No."

"We can't flush tampons," Denise said.

"*Sí,*" said Fidel. "*Y no.*" He pointed to toilet paper and a box of super maxi-pads with wings that Denise and I were soaking up faster than a dry sponge dropped into a full bathtub.

This was bad news, delivered to us at, perhaps, the worst point in both of our menstruating lives. We were, as we'd realized before leaving the States, in the throes of full-blown perimenopause. It was God's whimsical joke, both of us simultaneously gushing through one of those midlife final flows, if you will, in a third world place without accoutrements: no tampons, no Kotex, no Midol.

"*Sí, sí,*" I said to Fidel. "*No problemo*—okay." To Denise I said, "This is great. We are having the Niagara Falls of periods, and there's nowhere to put all the paper we're bloodying up."

I don't know how Fidel understood, but he touched my arm and showed me a paper bag. "*Aquí,*" he said, and Denise and I got that we were to use the bag for gathering up some of the most private and messiest aspects of our current selves so that a relative stranger, a man we'd met less than twenty-four hours previously—who was handsome and dark like licorice and cognac swirling together—so that that man could pick up and bundle and then transport our blood-soaked paper products away.

AFTER A FEW DAYS OF WALKING THE CITY, FIDEL PLANNED a day trip to the beach, to Playa Santa María del Mar, he told us, a resort of sorts—a boundless, white-sand-covered beach that snuggled against aqua blue water so glittery, the sparkle of it hurt your eyes.

We took a cobbled-together Ford-Cadillac cab and found ourselves under sun and palm trees, stretched out fully on a picnic blanket and gorging on Fidel's bounty of fruit and juice and rice and beans.

Everyone took pictures of each other. I was struck again, squinting through the viewfinder, by Celia's exquisite beauty. Denise had carried a black, strapless bikini all the way from the States through Jamaica and into Cuba for our then-unmet hostess. There could not have been a more perfect gift for her. *How did Denise know?* I wondered, looking at the bikinied Celia. How could she know Celia wasn't chubby or simply not suited to an itsy-bitsy swimsuit? The bikini was a perfect metaphor, slight and stunning, just like its wearer, fitting Celia as if it was made for her long and well-toned body, a suit that suited Celia's openness, her expansiveness, a titillating sample of the heart of the Cuban spirit.

I saw a horse walk into the camera's viewfinder and stopped before snapping the picture; all four of us turned to watch a man leading the huge and majestic-looking animal along the water's edge.

Before we knew it, Fidel had arranged for us all to have a ride on the horse's bare back. At first, we were to take turns, but the animal was massive, absolutely mountainous, and after Fidel hoisted me up and on, he saw that I was nervous, the horse's broad back intimidating, so in one graceful mount, Celia swung up onto the animal, confidently settling in front of me.

It was the devil in Fidel's eye that told me something was about to happen. He got down on his hands and knees in the sand next to the horse. The horse's owner had Denise's hands in his. Tentatively she stepped onto Fidel's back, using him like a footstool, and then the horse's owner put his hands under Denise's butt and hoisted her up and on behind me.

Celia took the rope lead and gave the horse a kick, and Denise grabbed my waist and I grabbed Celia's and we started out trotting, then galloping, then we were flying down the beach, the brilliant water and sand whipping by us like a sped-up movie.

Denise laughed hard and lost her hold for a second and I screamed in a primal glee and we were sailing, sailing high above the water and sand and time into the clouds and against a marine-blue sky—time stopped and no one was sick and men didn't leave and there was plenty of everything you could ever want or need: money, love, life, laughter, time, health, and energy—and you didn't need any of that stuff anyway.

We were speeding forward and free, the horse command-ing a rhythm, glad to bear our trio, his back slapping against our inner thighs, and we rode till we couldn't hear our screams any longer, our tears blinding us and wetting our cheeks, forcing Celia finally to turn and lead us back because we'd arrived at the pinnacle and we all knew there was something richer and you and everyone you care about was there and it could and it would last forever and ever and ever.

CHAPTER FIFTEEN

Illegals

At the airport Fidel insisted, again, on lugging our bags by himself, easing us through Cuban customs, making sure we had the bag of candy he'd bought, then insisted we pack for the flight.

It was time to board. I reached to hug Fidel and was caught short, shocked. His warm, always smiling face was shiny. Tears ran down his cheeks, and he made no effort to wipe them away.

"No quiero que te vayas," he said to me, and I glanced at Denise with a look that said *What's this?* She shrugged back, *Got me.*

"It's okay," I said, awkwardly. "We'll come back."

"Regresaremos," Denise insisted. *"Gracias, Fidel y Celia. Regresaremos."*

I looked at her. *Now* you recall your Spanish?

Fidel wiped his face with the back of his hand as we hugged. He knew he'd never see us again. He knew this was Denise's final trip. Fidel operated from a seventh sense, readily apparent in spite of our language barrier. He displayed it when he took us to the backs of old apartments to score cigars. He demonstrated it when, as Denise hobbled in during the blackout, he snatched her up and made her into a *rrrumba* dancer—purposely not asking her, making sure she couldn't say no.

He took us to a beach where magic could happen, where no Coca-Cola or Holiday Inn signs existed, where there were no real buildings and even fewer people. He absconded with us in a rickety mobster car to a place of electric blue water with wickedly handsome men and horses as huge as Clydesdales.

He didn't see us coming, Americans stealing his heart and not his wallet. He particularly didn't see a tender yet tenacious woman living with him for a week, a woman obviously ill, to whom he must say good-bye forever.

I glanced back through the plane's open door at his stricken face.

Regresaremos, I mouthed to him. He turned for a final time, wiped his hand across his cheek, and walked away.

THE FIRST THING WE DID EACH MORNING IN CUBA WAS carefully count, then recount, and then recount *again* every single dollar bill we had. We did this every day without fail, struggling as we were to make it in Cuba's cash-only commerce. Each morning, we tallied up the remaining dollar bills, the all-day-long, only-thing-that-worked currency, and noted how swiftly our stack diminished.

We wanted to see what a credit card or check could do, so one day Fidel led us to the Hotel Nacionale and presented the clerk with an array of credit cards to see if we could get some cash. "No, no," the clerk said before we even opened our mouths.

Denise held up a traveler's check. "No," the clerk said again.

I pulled out a personal check and held that up. She just shrugged. We concluded she'd never seen one before.

The next day I knew we were cash-strapped as we walked into the Montego Bay airport. It was a steely, gray, and scorching hot structure, and we grappled with our bags and the oppressive heat, working to traverse the airstrip and get to the customs agents. I retrieved the fifteen-dollar reentry fee I knew I had saved, the last of my cash. We were hoping against hope that Flip-Flop Fred would cash a check for us.

Denise held up a five-dollar bill.

"That's all the cash you've got?" I asked.

She nodded.

"How can that be?" I said. "We figured all of this out. Where's the thirty dollars you had yesterday afternoon?"

"Well," she started, "I found this wonderful art plaza. There were these Cuban dancers, dressed in some kind of native costume, so I stopped to watch. The next thing you know, I'm having a huge banana split. The largest banana split I've ever seen, by the way."

"A twenty-five-dollar banana split?" I said. "*Now* what the fuck are we going to do? They won't let you go find an ATM at customs. You've got to have the money in your hand to even get through the gate." I was mad. Fed-fucking-up. On the flight back to Jamaica, Denise had let on that she'd had to agree to frame an obscene amount of art and posters—100 pieces, or something, more than a year's worth of work—for Flip-Flop Fred's resort in order for us to check out owing him no money. I was suddenly very tired, tired that I had to be the grown-up while Denise enjoyed the luxury of being blithely unaware, the one who got to live for the moment.

"You've got that fifty-dollar bill John gave you before we left," she said to me.

"You're counting on that to get us back into Jamaica?" I couldn't believe it. "That's gone—how do you think I paid Celia for our stay?" Denise wasn't supposed to know about that money; John had slipped it to me as we were leaving Boulder, telling me to stash it for an emergency. I was furious that she had been counting on that money as her backup plan. Plus, I *did* give half of it to Celia; it was extra—staying in her place at fifteen dollars a night, plus putting her daughter out of her own home, felt crappy.

Too wiped out to argue, I pulled the twenty-five dollars from the back of the paperback I was reading and handed it to her.

THE LINE TO REENTER THE STATES WAS LONG AND WINDING and full of people who looked just like us: haggard, weary, impatient. I lugged a suitcase full of Cohibas and Montecristos I had absolutely no intention of paying duty on—let alone the embargo-breaking fines I'd have to pay if caught.

We had a plan for the non-duty-paying part: I'd be the psychotic distraction. When I was handed the paperwork to reenter the United States, I'd purposely screw it all up, fill it out incorrectly, become confused. I'd be exactly what the agents didn't want, a ditz holding up the line.

Our plan worked flawlessly. I handed the agent my form, swearing that I'd brought no contraband into the country and that I didn't owe a nickel for duty and, yes, I was, indeed, a U.S. citizen. Except, of course, I had filled out the wrong part of the form.

"Here, you need to fill *this* out," the agent said, pissy and pointing to the section I'd left blank.

"Oh," I said, puzzled. I mock-studied the form and noted that my cigar-laden suitcase was being pushed along the conveyor belt. The agents cared about one thing: getting the idiot woman to complete the form correctly, then getting her the hell out of there.

The line coiled out the doors with no end in sight. People shifted their feet, got fed up, and headed to other lines.

"I don't have the keys to the car," Denise said. I was still working the fake out, watching my suitcase enter the United States uninspected.

"What?" I was hurrying to fill out the form correctly and get going. We were almost home free—literally and figuratively. Just the flight from Miami to Denver and I'd be sleeping in my own, God bless it, three-hundred-count-sheet-covered bed. But it was Denise's car that waited for us in long-term parking back in Denver.

"I don't think I've got my passport either," she said. "I think I left my fanny pack in the bathroom in Jamaica. It's got my car keys and my passport in it." Denise searched her bags, pulling stuff out and opening zippered pockets. Every person had left our line, making the other two lines a block long.

I stooped down and pretended to help her search. "Are you fucking kidding me? Jesus-God-almighty. Think. *Think* when you last saw it," I whispered hard at her. "We're clear, my bags already made it."

"No," she said loud enough for the agent and anyone else who wanted to hear. "I'm not kidding. I don't have either."

"Sweet Jesus." I wanted to cry. I felt like we were Dorothy and Toto, and we were a hairsbreadth away from Kansas. "What can she do if she doesn't have her passport?" I asked the agent. I was all efficiency and clarity then, and he gave me a look that said I was full of shit and the very last thing he needed on his shift.

"She'll be detained," he said.

"What? We've got a connecting flight," I told him.

"She can't return to the U.S. without a passport," the agent said. "She'll be sent over to—"

"*I found it!*" Denise pulled her passport from her backpack. "I must have kept it separate from my fanny pack," she said, handing it to the agent. "But we still don't have keys."

I called John from the airplane on one of those phones that cost thirty-nine dollars a minute or something, and he had to drive a good hour in the dead of night to bring Denise's extra set of car keys to the airport. By then, Denise and I weren't speaking at all. Her fanny pack with her car keys was, evidently, back in the Jamaica airport restroom or on a Cuban street or God knows where—but not with us.

John met us as we walked off the plane. He eyed me empathetically, then handed off Denise's extra car keys without a word. I snatched them up and marched past them both, leaving the Jamaican jungle and Flip-Flop Fred and Denise's solitary Cuban walks and running out of cash behind me, steering her car at eighty miles an hour along the pitch-black highway, racing to my house with the big fluffy bed.

CHAPTER SIXTEEN

28 Days

Time turned topsy-turvy, like when you're hanging upside down on a carnival ride. Neither of us knew it then, but it would be a full month post-Jamaica-Havana before we would utter so much as a word to each other.

Oh, she tried calling me. She rang me at exactly 6:30 in the evening, when *Seinfeld* was on and she knew I was curled up on the couch, glued fast to the tube.

Me: Hello.

Her: Hello. This is Denise.

Like I didn't know.

Me: Let's talk in a few weeks. I need to decompress.

Click.

CHAPTER SEVENTEEN

Faulkner, Fidel, and the Feds

On a deliciously cool New Orleans afternoon in 1985, I stood on the bottom steps of the fifty-story One Shell Square building with then Louisiana governor Edwin Edwards, interviewing him about his recent indictments for conspiracy, particularly those charges concerning a little under-the-table $2 million fee paid to his law firm.

Edwin Edwards—long before he was ultimately shipped to a federal minimum-security prison in Oakdale, Louisiana, and when he still might have gotten away with gambling payoffs, racketeering, and the like—was a full-blown carousing Cajun, a caricature of the Good Ol' Boy. He was a handsome, silver-haired gent, lauded by men, blue bloods, blacks, and debutantes alike for his quick Southern charm, his dashing presence, and his world-famous ways with the ladies.

He could not have been more William Faulkneresque.

That cool New Orleans afternoon, I was working to get off the typewriter treadmill and into a journalist's job of any sort, that particular time as a television reporter. I cannot recall the exact question I posed to Edwards, but I do recall that all of the competing television stations were filming the interview, and I also recall exactly what I was wearing: super-tight short blue skirt, superpermed and ratted-up big hair, and 1980s-style, rising-star television-reporter stilettos.

I asked Edwards something like "How can you account for the magnitude of the sums paid you, personally, during your administration?"

Edwards, in the way only Edwards could, went into over-drive, smiling all those whites at me and delivering some evasive nonanswer while slipping his hand to the small of my back.

The camera composition was tight. I could not step away. We fledgling TV reporters were taught in Reporting 101 to make sure everybody's heads were close together. So I stayed rigid. I had no choice but to let that hand sit at the bottom of my back.

I shot the next question at him, pointed the microphone to his mouth, and gave him my sternest serious-journalist grimace. He chuckled at whatever question I'd lobbed and delivered a breezy Edwards answer just as he slipped his hand full on to my ass and rested it there.

The TV cameras hummed, my face froze, my body arrested all vital functions. I was twenty-nine years old, a single mother of two kids under twelve, and I was tired of typing. I wanted the job.

There are few times I've had an out-of-body experience, that textbook disassociation where the psyche exits the body because it sure as hell can't stay there. It can't stay there as a man arrogantly slips his fingertips to the bottom of your skirt and tickles your ass because he *can, sugah*. The psyche can't stay put knowing that 200,000 people are in their living rooms watching you get groped on the *CBS Evening News*. Live.

But after Jamaica and then Cuba, after two and a half weeks of struggle that escalated to fear that escalated to what felt, in the end, like trauma, that's where I was again.

Dead.

Frozen.

I didn't know what to do next. I knew dark times were drawing near, yet my heart played tricks on me. One day I was devastated and couldn't stand the anticipatory pain. The next day, I felt hollow. The next, I was overcome in a primal wash of love and gratefulness—all immediately replaced by sorrow.

Since it was such a kaleidoscope of emotion, often laced with terror, I stayed immobilized.

Very much like that day at the bottom of the steps of One Shell Square.

FOR THE FIRST TIME, I REVIEWED RESTAURANTS WITHout Denise. I took people with whom I'd just as soon not spend fifteen minutes, let alone a whole meal. But how could I size up a restaurant based on one plate of pasta and two glasses of wine? Besides, the newspaper covered all expenses, so I felt compelled to bring another eager eater along.

That's how I stooped to taking Judd, the sometimes boyfriend. A descendant of Volsk or Vologda or some Siberian region, he was eager to "eat Russian," so we hit the Little

Russian Inn. Judd the Dud, who was at least an hour late for everything, a habit he boasted was part of his Russian-Jewish ancestry.

"I'm on Moscow time," he told me by way of explanation. "Nothing starts there before noon."

"*Vee hahve beef in specsheel sauce,*" our waiter informed us in a fake Russian accent.

"Uggggh," Judd groaned with a vegetarian shudder. You could pretty much see the bile rising up his throat at the word: *beef.*

"*Vee also have many vohdkahs,*" the waiter offered.

My teetotaling companion grimaced, and I rested my head in my hand, feeling every fine point of the slamming inside my temples, as if a pile driver had gone awry. I looked across the table at that non-meat-eating, organic-juice-drinking fellow, a loner who'd made it well into his sixth decade without ever having taken a wife or having had a child, who was prissy and pompous when he wasn't full throttle into self-righteousness—and I wondered what I had found so appealing in him. Why had I ever thought him smart? How had I managed to confuse his chronic condescension with careful discrimination? How could I have confused his cheapness with frugality, his self-involvement with sexy mysteriousness? I thought about the five decades he'd already burned up and knew, with the same certainty that I knew I'd never be described as tall and thin, that he'd spend his *next* decades as alone and narcissistic and boring as he'd always been.

Which forced me to rethink Denise and John's relationship. At first I had considered their situation cool and progressive, the answer to all cerebral folk who found it hard to live for decades with their spouses, half of whom, as divorce rates illustrate, ultimately don't. But really—was it hip and happening, or was the arrangement flawed and ultimately fatal?

I didn't know.

I'd searched my entire life for a guy with whom I might link my fate, a cosmic-dictated, delicious destiny. Just two people gaga for each other.

Through my youth and then midadulthood, I felt certain that the rest of the population enjoyed the blissful unions Hollywood portrayed, while I was left on the sidelines, struggling with an often unmanageable and overwhelming life, all of which left me feeling despairing, aching, alone, and out of the game, though I'd tried. On the heels of my children's father leaving, I desperately, briefly married and divorced twice more. Fifteen years of therapy later, I'd come to know that being driven by fear pretty much guarantees failure. Marriage, it now seemed, guarantees nothing.

Free from the strife-filled life, sitting at that dinner table, I felt it dawn on me that no one had it easy, that it was a messy world for everyone: for Judd, for John, for Denise, and for me.

The waiter finally gave up, dropped the dopey accent, and offered Judd potatoes and salad. Judd jumped at the opportunity to eat "true" Russian, openly salivating over his plate of arugula and organic cherry tomatoes that had nothing to do with the former Soviet Union and everything to do with the glitzy Whole Foods Market down the street.

"Oh, this is wonderful, very authentic," Judd said knowingly, pouring balsamic raspberry vinaigrette onto the vegetables.

"Yeah," I said and looked out the window at the sun dipping behind the Flatirons. I thought hard about a lot of things: Fidel, Ricky Ricardo, Denise, and St. Petersburg, Russia. How, when I lived there, I trudged for months through the brutal winter, under the steeliest, grayest skies on the planet, in ice and wind that laughed at my wool coat, how I went for nearly a year without seeing (let alone eating) one fresh vegetable. Months of yearning, aching for something green, anything fresh and crunchy, and finally—in August, after a three-hour train ride into the Russian woods to a friend's dacha—I reached to the ground and ripped a ripe tomato from its vine, eating it raw and dripping, I was so starved for it.

Some tender part of me softened toward Judd. My irritation dissipated. I glanced over at the fussy, lonely man across from me, and, suddenly, my soul traded places with him. I thought of the pizza nights years ago, when my kids were little, when we curled up on whatever cheap rental living room floor we had for the moment, and watched *Happy Days* and *Little House on the Prairie,* content to be there with full bellies and just each other. I looked at Judd and knew that he'd never have those moments to fall back on.

"Yeah." I sighed. "Must take you right back to Murmansk." Which ended up being the very last words I ever spoke to him.

CHAPTER EIGHTEEN

Lined Up Like Soldiers

My conscience got the best of me. I couldn't hold a grudge to save my life, so I decided to ease off my moratorium. But I didn't tell Denise that. Instead, I waited for her to call. She was good at dealing with moodiness. She knew that the one who ignored it, who treated snits like they were nonexistent, won. It was something I admired and normally could not do. But I was learning at her knee.

I also caved because I knew that each day was like a golden nickel, in short supply, a day that I was frittering away. The day would come, I knew, when I would automatically pick up the phone to call a person no longer there.

As was our rhythm, there wasn't a big scene or long, heartfelt makeup discussion. We communicated and acted in declarative-sentence style. Clipped, direct, forgetting whatever hiccup, whatever bruise, the one had caused the other.

It was sweetly simple. It made for efficiency. Our style often made for fun.

"I need to do a Costco run," Denise said over the phone, all full of her matter-of-fact voice, surprising me (which she fully planned) by ringing me up at the crack of dawn.

"Yeah. Me, too," I said in our fourth week of not speaking to each other. "Drive out here to Longmont. We'll go to Wild Bill's Diner and get some breakfast first. I've got a review due."

SHE ALREADY HAD US SET UP ALL COZY WHEN I ARRIVED: window table, pot of coffee, tall glass pitcher of orange juice all aglow. We sat on opposite sides of the table and looked at each other, awkward, like a couple of reconciling lovers.

It was ridiculous.

"I don't get why you had us going to Jamaica without a plan for paying for it," I started. "And now you've got a year's worth of work to do—and I can't even help you because I don't know how to frame." As an afterthought I added, "I guess you could teach me."

She rolled her eyes dramatically, like the thought of trying to teach me to frame art was her very worst fucking nightmare.

"It feels wrong," I went on, cutting into a stack of three blueberry pancakes dripping with flown-in-from-Vermont maple syrup. I was thinking three and a half forks. Forks were my signature rating system. Stars were so *yesterday.* "It's awful you've got to work like a slave now," I said, licking syrup off the side of my hand. "Especially for that pig Fred."

"I'm not worried about it," she said, slathering a bagel with cream cheese and biting into it.

"It's good?" I said.

She dropped the bread ring with a heavy clatter onto her plate.

"It's *not* good," she said. "But we're in Boulder; they don't know a bagel from a barn door."

"I can quote you?" I said.

"If you pay me," she answered.

"Speaking of pay . . . Why did you blow every last dollar you had before you left Cuba? What if I'd also spent everything? What if I'd expected *you* to have stashed some extra money away?" The coffee had me good and hyped.

"Cathie, it's not like I set out—"

"You *never plan* to get us deep in shit," I said. "Why do you always think that's a great excuse? We could have really been in a jam. We're lucky we didn't get killed in Jamaica—"

"There's a reason I—"

"Oh, save it, Denise. I've about had it. How many times—" I didn't finish. I got wound up just thinking about the jungle, the heat, those two assholes who'd set us up. "It pisses me the fuck off that we went through the money-counting ordeal in Havana every day. Why'd you go through the motions if you were just going to spend willy-nilly anyway?"

"Because I decided at the last minute to get you these." She opened an oversize shopping bag that she'd been hiding under the table. One at a time she lifted a first, then a second, painting—luminous renditions of an artist's Dalí-like impressions of the Cuban car culture. The whole presentation reverberated drama—wiggly bumpers, exaggerated headlights, haunting paintings executed in motley, many-splendored colors—all wrapped in sleek, black frames. I'd admired, lusted after, the two works in Old Havana.

I was ripped in two: thrilled and mad at the same time. Tears came to my eyes, and I blinked hard. In Old Havana, we'd wandered one afternoon into an outdoor art show. In a third world country without tourism, the local artists' displays were all the more compelling. There was an edge, a trumped-up liberation, in the works that felt distinctly Cuban, certainly not of America. Wild-colored paintings of exotic, sexy rumba dance scenes and renditions of eighteen-piece orchestras grandly playing on the sidewalks. One photographer devoted her exhibition to schoolchildren, laughing, dressed in Catholic uniforms, hanging from ornate balconies.

It took Denise and me an entire afternoon to drag ourselves away, we were so charmed.

"Still," I started to say, reaching out for one of the paintings. It was so alive, I wanted to stroke it. "We could have been thrown in jail. *When* did you get these?" I asked lamely, all my fury dissolving, realizing she must have taken one of her isolated walks back deep into the heart of Old Havana— not easy to get to from Celia's apartment—to buy the art I'd so badly wanted.

"God, this is incredible" was all I could say. "How'd you sneak these back into the U.S. without me seeing you?"

She said nothing, giving me the look I was sure was the look of Denise of yesteryear: self-satisfied, happy to make me look like a jerk, capable of pulling off anything and everything she damn well wanted to.

"This is nothing but a doorstop," she said, affecting profound disgust and tossing the bagel to her plate. "I can't finish it."

"YOU DRIVE," SHE SAID. "THERE'S ROOM FOR THE ART IN your car. John can bring me to get my car later." Everything was back to normal, our spat all mended. I had to admit I was glad.

"Let's get some spareribs at Costco," I said. "In those huge packs. We'll make John do that Jack Daniel's, smoked-barbecue thing to them."

"He'll do it if you ask him," she said. "He likes that you appreciate his cooking."

"What do you need at the Big Store?" I asked.

"Oh," she said. "Nothing really."

I took my eyes off Longmont's presentation of the all-American Main Street—a village cow town lined with antiques stores, a few restaurants, an Ace hardware—to glance sideways at her.

"Then why'd you tell me you needed a Costco run?" I said.

"Stop here." Denise pointed at a sign hanging from a storefront that read: ARROW GUNS AND COLLECTIBLES. The window out front was lit up with 30% OFF SELECTED STOCK in neon orange paint.

A glass counter ran the length of the narrow shop, a place that smelled of men and leather, like something had happened a long time ago but lingered, like when you put out a cigarette and the smell's still there. An invisible resonance hung in the store.

"I know you," Denise said. I turned to see her talking to a fat lady behind the counter. The woman's ash-colored hair was swept straight up into bulbous tiers of shiny sculpture, and she wore a ring on each finger. "I framed those," Denise told the ringed lady and pointed to a wall above our heads. We all looked up at poster-size, heavily framed pictures of ducks and Labrador retrievers.

"Oh, that's *you!*" the woman squealed. We were the only ones in the shop. "My husband got those framed for me."

Because I was Denise's friend, Ring Lady let me try on any ring I wanted. She was glad to humor me, though she could tell I wouldn't buy a thing. The jewelry, locked under the glass counter, was bedazzling and artificially glitzy, hundreds of baubles trapped beneath warm lights that transformed the tiniest chips into the Hope diamond. I pointed to one, and when Ring Lady pulled it out for me, I was disappointed in its lost luster under regular lighting.

"Those are the heaviest frames I've ever done," Denise told Ring Lady. She said it proudly, and I grew bored and slightly annoyed that she was trying to impress the woman. They kept talking, ignoring me, and I stopped playing the try-on-jewelry game, mainly because the pieces now looked tawdry.

"Well, I'm thinking we're going to put up some more art," Ring Lady informed Denise. "We got some prints at an auction last month, and Otto thinks they'd look good over there."

She pointed at the opposite wall, where pistols and handguns shone from glass cabinets. Above the locked gun display cases, old and intricate rifles were lined up like soldiers, hanging one beneath another, all the way to the fourteen-foot ceiling. A grid-like group of worn and weathered armory. I studied the guns' chambers, the large stocks, the triggers, all oversize, it seemed, too big to hold with one hand. Vaguely feeling their power, I imagined blood and innards. I thought about cocking a hammer back, holding it taut with my thumb. Then irrevocably, irretrievably squeezing the trigger.

I stood stupefied, lost in grisly thoughts: *What's it feel like to have a bullet pierce your heart? How long does it hurt? If you pull one of these triggers and shoot a person's head at close range, does blood and brain splatter on you?*

"What are you doing?" Denise said, impatient and ready to go.

"You're ready?" I said, my mind jerked back to the store.

"As I'm going to get." She was already halfway out the door.

I followed her out onto the sidewalk and opened my mouth to ask why we'd even stopped at the dumb store. It wasn't a place Denise would normally frequent. It was rednecky, and the owner, who looked like Will Ferrell in drag, was as sleep-inducing as Excedrin PM. I hurried along the sidewalk to ask her why we'd stopped, but her long legs worked well that day.

She was long gone, already a half a block ahead of me.

IT WAS A QUICKIE COSTCO TRIP, ALMOST POINTLESS. Denise's demeanor had turned listless, and it infected me. I didn't even bother getting the spareribs. She was silent, saying nothing while I drove back. I was confused, maybe even a bit worried, but I looked west at the mountains and thought my regular mountain thoughts: that "purple mountain majesties" was Katherine Lee Bates's perfect phrase for the crimson-coated peaks in front of me; that John Denver knew what he was talking about with "Rocky Mountain High." That's what I did with the vast vista in front of my moving car—recalled song lyrics in order to process a scene almost too stunning to absorb.

"Did you just enjoy a nice, big fart?" I said, pulling up to the curb in front of her house. I gave Denise an accusatory wrinkle-nose. I was sort of joking, trying to rouse her from her funk, but it smelled foul in the car, so I unrolled my window and let the car idle.

She was having a hard time opening her door; her hand couldn't get purchase on the handle, so I reached across her to do it and had to not breathe because of the stench.

I knew before she told me but waited to hear her say it anyway.

"I shit my pants," she said, falling out of the car and grabbing the door handle, trying to get her balance.

"Wait, I'm going to come in." I leaned over to grab the door so I could shut it and park.

"*No.* Don't," she said, and meant it. I didn't know what to do, so I sat there in the middle of the street, the car running, watching her as she missed when she tried to step up to the curb, as she had to try it again and finally, almost falling back down, made it.

It was excruciating to watch, and I almost couldn't. I was enfeebled by her efforts, and the strength left my hands.

When I tried to put the car in Park, I had to work at it. I had to watch her not make the curb, to take in that she might not make the stairs looming in front of her, that she might have to sit and rest, in her shitty pants, on each step, and that she needed to get to the bathroom and to the privacy of her bedroom—way at the back of her house, through the living room, the dining room, the kitchen—that it must have felt the length of a dozen football fields to her at that moment. I grabbed the steering wheel with both hands. I didn't know what I was holding on to, but I was holding hard nonetheless.

She wouldn't let me help her. I couldn't help her. I also couldn't drive. I couldn't do anything, which is not my way or hers. We are take-action types. We figure things out.

We were crushed and knew the worst was yet to come, but who can take all that in?

Not the girl using every ounce of strength she might have left just to scale a few steps, stay standing upright.

Not me. My love for her felt impotent, laughable, and I silently screamed at the universe to take us both anywhere but there.

Tears plunked—*plunked*—to my lap as an avalanche of heartache crushed me, Denise, her house, the car I sat in. I knew I was at some sort of cruel crossroad, some shaky bridge that I needed either to walk completely across or to leap from. My body literally trembled at all that had come before that moment, and what I knew lay ahead.

A tiny whimper escaped my throat, and I put my hand to my mouth to stifle myself.

I didn't want Denise to think I was watching her, pitying her, so I looked over at Longs Peak and saw it silhouetted in front of an orange half sun. Then I stretched across the seat and unrolled her window so the air could circulate. A spring wind picked up and brushed my chin, flurrying through the car, the mountain air clearing everything out. I used two hands to click the transmission into Drive. I worked to not look back.

CHAPTER NINETEEN

You May Find Somebody Kind
to Help and Understand You

Denise wouldn't take a smell of beer. She turned up her nose at a margarita, said merlot gave her headaches, and dismissed anything labeled "chardonnay" as vinegar. She enjoyed the fruit of the vine only if it was red and a cabernet and really, really cheap—read: thick, sweet, and suck-ass—though God knows I did my very best to get her to sip something above the five-dollar-a-bottle range. The woman had a sweet tooth.

So when, days after the pointless Costco run, she fondled a jug of Mud Slide—a brown-gray substance that looked like moldy chocolate milk—I offered to treat her, ignoring the fact that something called Mud Slide was to serve as forget-juice for her having shat her pants.

"Here, I'll get this," I said and grabbed the jug from the shelf at Quicker Likkor. "This shit looks disgusting," I added, immediately regretting the "shit" part. "We'll get some rum," I told her, "and use one of those tractor-size blenders of yours to mix it up with ice. It'll be yummy." I looked to see if the idea raised any interest, maybe even provoked her to let go of her funky mood.

Each day had become an emotional crapshoot with Denise. Though mood swings are typical MS symptoms (symptoms of anyone in a health crisis, for that matter), they were still hard to reckon with, hard, if not impossible, to address. It was a pins-and-needles game that left me worried, exhausted, often frightened. I needed some sort of salvation amid this calamity of ours, which left me running toward—helped to open me up to—what I was coming to think of as the rest of my life.

A bowling magazine wasn't exactly a writer's dream job, but it *was*, fortunately, a brain-cell-burning distraction, and doors were beginning to open. The restaurant review gig had, as I'd hoped, brought offers to write for larger publications. That meant more space, more readers, more money. And though my kids were gone, their regular phone calls, their need to connect with me, didn't stop, thank God. Our phone conversations kept me grounded. It didn't matter what we talked about—their day or mine, the weather, the news, their boss. The point was that those calls pulled me out of the day-to-day minefield called Denise.

And while it was true that I'd kissed Judd good-bye for good, I was glad to have had the experience. Judd showed me that I had decades of dating in front of me, if I wanted it, and that not having to factor in someone's potential stepfathering abilities was an entire new world of getting-to-know-you.

So I held up the jug of Mud Slide in front of Denise and made a let's-party! face, lifted eyebrows and all.

"Whaddaya say?" I asked, trying to gauge if she was easing out of her depression, even just a smidgen, or not.

"Okay," she said, which gave me no clue.

I GRABBED AN ICE TRAY FROM HER FREEZER AND CHECKED inside one of her blenders for paper dye or newspaper slivers. When I didn't see any foreign gunk, I tossed in the cubes and some rum, then tipped up the jug of Mud Slide. A good-size glop of the chocolate stuff flopped into the blender, and I pressed High.

"That blender's for my papermaking," she called over the whir. "Don't break it."

"You've got all those," I yelled and pointed to the row of machines along the countertop, as critical to her artwork as any painter's palette. I realized, suddenly—my mind strained to reject the realization—that I hadn't seen a new piece of work from her in months. Dust coated the blenders.

She waved her hand at me in a you're-not-worth-my-energy gesture. Dismissed.

"What's that?" John yelled as he walked into the kitchen. I hit the Off button.

"Chocolate glop." I filled a frosted goblet and handed it to him. Then I filled a second. "Here, give this to Denise."

Our impromptu party suggested that we were at least still alive, and the gloom that had hung about Denise since we returned from the Caribbean seemed to lift slightly. John plugged *Mars Attacks!* into the VCR, and Denise finished her first shake and signaled she wanted a refill.

I reached to take her glass and then looked to see if John wanted more, but before I uttered a syllable, he gripped his stomach and fell to the floor.

"What's—?" I sprang to where he lay in a full fetal curl, moaning, holding his gut, and turning gray-white.

I thought I'd killed him with our alcohol shakes, but Denise gave him a look that said: *faker.* Then, suddenly, she got that he wasn't joking, and she started to stand up, only to lose her balance and fall back onto the couch.

"Call 911!" was all I could I manage, my panic mounting in direct proportion to the purple cords straining through his neck.

"That'll take too lon——" John couldn't finish.

I was terrified, his face so white, his arms locked around his stomach.

"You drive to the hospital," Denise said to me. "Can you walk, can you move at all?" she asked him.

Denise and I worked to pull up all two hundred pounds of him, and he leaned into both of us, still bent over. I thought my shoulder was going to break as we limped down the front steps. The fleeting question of how Denise was handling this left me the moment John gasped with pain. Somehow we got the car door open and poured him into the backseat. I was sure we couldn't get to the hospital before he died, and so I watched him in the rearview mirror as he collapsed forward into the back of the driver's seat. He rested his head against the back of my headrest, and I saw sweat bead up on his temple as I careened around corners and ran traffic lights as fast as I possibly could. I prayed a cop would see my erratic driving and help us.

"PANCREATITIS?" WE SAID IN STEREO BACK AT THE woman in the flowered nurse's outfit, a pajama-looking getup. "He's just going into surgery soon," she said. "You can come see him now if you'd like."

We both stepped forward to follow her, but the nurse snagged my arm with one hooked finger. "Just family," she told me, and she and Denise left me looking at the doors that flapped in their wake.

At 4:00 A.M., as the night lingered like a black and impenetrable cloak, the birds started chirping. We sat on Denise's couch and studied the art on the walls. I was wiped. What day was it? Did I need to go to work?

John had made it through surgery, we'd learned before leaving the hospital. Actually, we got the news while sprawled on plastic furniture in the green waiting room, eating peanut-butter-and-cheese crackers with those little hospital milks.

"I could spend the night," I said, halfheartedly, counting on her to say no because neither of us, given the chance, slept anywhere but her own bed.

She pulled herself up from the couch and hobbled toward her bedroom.

"Night," she said.

I CALLED IN SICK TO WORK. MY REPUBLICAN PUBLISHER and all his "sooner" cronies were just too much to think about. I didn't hear a thing from Denise or anyone else the whole day, which seemed normal, given the events. But by dinnertime I couldn't take it. I wanted to know how John was recovering and how Denise was managing with all the hulla-baloo, so when the phone rang, I pounced on it.

"It's not just pancreatitis," she said without a hello. "Some-thing's infected. He's in pain; he's really, really sick."

"Well, are they letting him out?" I said.

She said, "No," delayed-like. She wasn't talking right, and I didn't think she was listening at all. "They don't know when he's getting out." Then she hesitated. "Edith's there. She's feeding him and . . . whatever."

"Denise, do you want—?" but before I could finish, I heard her crying. Bawling. Her giant, racking moans bel-lowed across the telephone wire. I felt them in the receiver at my ear. We sat for a few seconds, and I listened to her sob.

"I'll come over," I said.

"Don't," she said, more emphatically than she'd said any-thing in days.

"It's stupid for you to be there alone," I told her.

"Everything's stupid," she said, the words all full of fluid and mucus. "I can't do this anymore."

No! No! No!

I would not let her give up. As long as I didn't quit, damn it, neither could she. I wouldn't let her.

But I could not think of one magic word to say to her.

"You can't do *what* anymore?"

"Any of it. All of it."

"John's not going to be in the hospital forever," I said. "Plus, you just said, he's got his mom to take care of him."

"I don't mean just him being in the hospital," she said. Then she blew her nose. "Edith let me live here without paying rent when I was first diagnosed with MS."

I waited for her to continue. "But she never stops telling me how much she could get for this place."

"It's your home, Denise," I said. "You're John's wife. You don't owe anyone anything."

"I can't take the fatigue," she said. "I can't take any of it . . . any of this. I tried to write down a phone number a few minutes ago, and I forgot the number just when the operator said it. Then I couldn't hold a pen to write it anyway. My right hand's numb."

"It's not always going to be like this," I said. "You and I both know the MS goes back into remission."

"I can't get out of bed," she went on like I'd not said anything. "I can't do my art." Then she sat quiet for a really long time. I almost didn't hear her, her voice was so low and soft. "I shit my pants," she whispered.

"Have you been in bed all day?" I said.

"Yes." She was crying again. Then: "I've got lesions on my brain. That's not going to get any better." For a few seconds we waited again.

"It's too much," she murmured. "It's all too much."

I opened my mouth to reply, but she hung up first.

CHAPTER TWENTY

The Lights Are Much Brighter There

November 9, 1987. When my sister called that frigid fall morning to tell me that my brother was dead, that he'd asphyxiated himself in my dad's garage, in my dad's car, that he'd had a series of DUIs and that, as usual, my dad had threatened to throw him out on the street—this after a dozen years of abandonment followed by a shaky reconciliation between the two—when that phone call came, all time stopped.

Holding that phone to my ear, listening to my sister sobbing and saying over and over, "Henry is dead, Henry is dead, Henry is dead," my mind leapt back to a dozen instances where I might have, could have, certainly would have—changed the course of events.

I should have invited him out for Thanksgiving. I should have inquired more into his life, his work. *How's your music going, Henry?* And, *Are you still dating that adorable brunette— the chubby one from St. Louis?* I should have, could have— just back the fucking calendar up and give me one more chance—been a less-involved-with-my-own-life big sister, and helped him find a place to live outside of my father's verbal assaults, his loathing of his own kids.

I had eight years on him and, if we could just flip back to yesterday, to before that phone call, to before my hysterical sister screaming the news into the phone, if we could just go a few precious hours backward in time, I could help my handsome, Robert-Redford-look-alike, musically gifted brother see some light at the end of his tunnel.

If. If I just had one more chance. Just one more. I could.

"WELL, GET HER *OUT* OF HER MEETING," I TOLD THE twelve-year-old who answered the phone at the McKaiser. "This is an emergency."

"Hold please."

Pin prickles of panic crept down my neck, along my back and chest and into my legs like a creeping electric current. My fear leapt up and out of me. But I waited, listening to Petula Clark croon *Downtown*, thinking that maybe I shouldn't call Deborah—Denise and my "shared" therapist.

That she and I saw the same shrink didn't seem like a coincidence at all to us. After three years of comparing life notes, we'd learned we shared a number of coincidences. We both had loving, caring mothers who had a ditz factor that made us each, respectively, insane.

"When I was eighteen years old," Denise once revealed, "I was still living with my mother in the Bronx.

"I remember insisting she hire an exterminator. I couldn't take another day living with the cockroaches," Denise said.

"You can't believe how long she went on about how we didn't *have* roaches.

"That night one crawled across my face while I was sleeping," she said. "That was it. I packed my bags before the sun rose."

"*My* mother ran out of gas every single month of her life," I told her. "Her entire life. I can remember her, at different times, handing over her wristwatch, a set of earrings, and, one time, her wedding ring to gas station attendants so she could buy a dollar's worth of gas to get us home.

"Sometimes," I went on, "we'd have to walk home—we'd all have to climb out of the car on some road somewhere and walk a mile or three home. Once, my mom was about twelve months pregnant with my little brother. She had four kids under the age of eight, plus that big, pregnant belly. We walked all afternoon till it was dark. Who regularly puts a bunch of kids in a car with the tank on Empty?" I asked, incredulous, to Denise.

"Somebody with no money and a bunch of kids, that's who," Denise answered, pragmatism and a give-your-mother-a-break-for-crissakes attitude in her voice.

And then there's what we came to call our Twinsy Sisters. That is to say, we each had a sister who mirrored the other's.

Our juicy Sister Set took up entire conversations as we compared Twinsy Sister tales of terror, anecdotes heightened when Denise lugged out the DSM-IV. We diagnosed them on the spot as we read, studious, heads pressed together.

DSM-IV. Antisocial Personality Disorder: . . . a pervasive pattern of disregard for, and violation of, the rights of others that begins in childhood or early adolescence and continues into adulthood . . .

Mmm-hmmm, we murmured knowingly, and then kept on reading . . .

. . . tends to be callous, cynical, and contemptuous of the feelings, rights and sufferings of others . . . inflated and arrogant self-appraisal.

"Oh, *that*'s her," Denise pronounced. And then went on to detail all the wrongs and slights and slings and arrows that made *her* sister the worst. Denise sniffed in contempt. "She cares about herself and absolutely no one else."

"*Puhleeeeze!*" I countered. "You apparently don't truly understand this definition." I point to the page. "My sister's burned through so many people!

"Callous—check.

"Cynical—check.

"Contemptuous of feelings—check.

"I WIN!"

We slapped shut the big, fat DSM-IV, feeling vindicated. A word existed to encapsulate our narcissistic sisters, a diagnosis that summed up the psychological root behind siblings we couldn't believe were related to us.

Our shared therapist, Deborah, then, was just one more in a long list of common denominators.

. . . Listen to the music of the traffic in the city . . . linger on the sidewalks where the neon signs are pretty . . . Petula cranked it up. . . . *how can you looooooze . . .* Maybe, I thought, I should go over to Denise's and get her out of the house. Maybe I didn't know what to do.

"Hello," a woman finally said.

"It's me . . . Cathie. Deborah," I began. "I know you're not supposed to talk to me about another patient, but hear me out."

Deborah was slow. Denise and I bitched about her to each other whenever one of us came back from our appointment.

"I can't stand it," Denise had once commented. "Deborah is like the CNN international satellite feed. You know, where a reporter is at the scene of an earthquake or some other hell and you can hear the reporter's voice all right, but it takes the image a few seconds to catch up to the sound."

"I know. Or like watching a movie with the Slow-mo button held down," I'd added.

It was unnerving, waiting for her to process. We believed she sustained herself with quaaludes and were certain she had finished at the very bottom of her class. But it took months to switch to another therapist, and you could easily end up with someone worse.

"I'm calling about Denise Katz," I said.

I gave Deborah the several seconds I knew she needed for the information to percolate through her brain.

"You know her. I've mentioned her in our sessions. I know that she sees you too." Again I waited for Deborah to catch up.

"She and I are friends and I just got off the phone with her. I think . . . I feel that . . ." And then I stopped. I didn't know for sure what I thought or felt. "Would you call her? Right now? She's very depressed. We just got off the phone." I realized I was repeating myself.

"Well, normally we suggest that our clients," Deborah's stress was very much on the word *clients*, assuring me that we were *not* (oh, no *no!*) *patients*, "go to the emergency room of their local hospital, or—"

I considered driving to the woman's office and smacking the ever-lovin' shit out of her.

"I don't think I can help her. She's really depressed. She's *extremely* depressed," I said, then waited for a few seconds and listened to her nothingness.

Impatient, I played my trump card. "My brother committed suicide. This sounds like the same thing to me."

More silence. We both listened to Deborah doing nothing. Saying nothing. It was a whole bunch of white space, that conversation.

"Okay," she said, her voice heavy with resignation.

"You'll call her now?" I said, sure she'd head straight back to her meeting—if she even had a meeting—and make a note to call Denise next week, next month.

"Yes," she said and hung up.

But the phone line didn't go dead. Instead, Petula was still there. . . . *forget all your troubles, forget all your cares and go . . .*

I sat for a while with the phone pressed to my ear, watching the birds outside my window yell and flap at each other, watching them flutter and fight over the expensive sunflower seed I kept stocked in their feeder. . . . *downtown,* Petula belted the tune . . . *downtown* . . . *everything's waiting for yooooouuuu* . . . *DOWNtown.* . . . I watched the birds until they'd gotten a belly full of each other—screaming and arguing and pecking at one another, till they were satiated with seed, till they bolted away on the hunt for a bigger, better meal.

I HAD JUST ARRIVED AT THE OFFICE—I WAS ABOUT TO throw my purse on my desk—when the phone rang. Shit. I spilled my coffee as I reached for the ringing phone.

"Cathie?" Denise said to me on the phone. She said it like she was accusing me of something, like she was watching me lift cash from someone's wallet. It came out "Cath*EEE*?"

"Denise?" I said. "What are—?"

"Cathie," she said again, then waited a second. "I'm at the hospital."

"You are? Well, how's he doing?" I said.

"*Noooo,*" she said slowly and carefully. I could feel her jaw grinding with impatience and outrage through the phone. Then that hesitant wait again. "I'm *in* the hospital, in the psych ward. As in locked up."

"You're *what*?" was all I could manage.

"The police came to my house," she said. "They put me in handcuffs and committed me to a seventy-two-hour suicide watch. This is my one phone call."

"What in the hell? Do you want me to come get—"

"No," she ordered. "I want you to call my mother-in-law and tell her to come get me. Here's her number."

I took it down, quickly. "Why don't I come get—"

"No," she said. "They'll only release me into the care of a family member. Track Edith down. Track. Her. Down. Do you understand? I can't call you again. Make sure she comes."

"HOW *DEED* SHE GET THERE?" EDITH SCREAMED AT ME. "Oh, I don't know how *Jahhnn MahREE eeze* going to handle *zees! Zees eeze zee* last thing *Jahhnn MahREE* needs!" her accent accelerated in direct proportion to her hysteria.

How Jahhnn MahREE *is going to handle this?*

I was rage-filled in a way I hadn't been in years. I wanted to grab Edith and choke her—her precious middle-fucking-age *son's* reaction? The phone shook in my hand as I listened to Edith screech at me.

But, of course, it wasn't Edith I was outraged at. I wanted to shoot myself. I got Denise locked up. I took a dying woman searching for a grain of hope, a sign of life, anything that might give her one reason not to check out, and I got her hand-cuffed and sent to the pit, with straitjackets and drugs and indifferent doctors and beds that strangers have slept in, peed in, beat-off in.

And I wasn't even there to help her.

The doctors, the system wouldn't let me help. I could lock her up with a phone call, but since there wasn't blood or law binding us, I couldn't do one goddamn thing to get her out. I could race up to that hospital and scream myself silly, threaten lawsuits and anything else I could dream up. They'd ignore me or lock me up too.

My mind raced in a wild scramble, an agonizing terror: I didn't know what Denise was going through.

How did they get her there?

Was there an ambulance?

Did someone check her over or did they throw her into a padded room and lock the door?

Were there bars on the windows?

Was she even near a window?

I couldn't think of what an orderly might face with a raging, ambushed Denise being dragged into a hospital, handcuffed, taken away, committed, without her having an inkling it was coming.

Then I thought of Deborah. Correction. I thought of *murdering* Deborah. I thought of the fucking lawsuit I'd wage and of all the bullshit, half-ass therapy I'd wasted with her. I thought of getting her license yanked.

And then I was nauseous. I wondered if Denise knew that I'd called Deborah. Should I tell her? I couldn't imagine what Denise would do with herself while she waited for Edith. I couldn't imagine what she'd say to me. I wondered if I had any of the Ativan left that Deborah prescribed for my flying phobia.

I carried the cordless into the bathroom and rummaged for the bottle.

HOW WE WENT FROM RIDING IN CORVETTES AND SEEING too many movies and eating M&M's till we popped—to that moment—I had no idea. My brain struggled to patch it all together, to make sense of it. Plastic surgery, chandelier-buying, living large in overpriced restaurants, and stealing new-house money all seemed like it had happened to other people.

Now we'd catapulted into a black abyss. It was a familiar place, ethereal, like a recurring nightmare. And there was a certain comfort in its familiarity. It might be a hellish dream, but it was *my* hellish dream. They can't take *that* away from me.

Things fucked up beyond belief, me unable to do anything at all, save trying to explain to that French nutcase what she needed to do, scary details I couldn't get my psyche to digest—yeah, we're home now.

I was the six-year-old throwing herself between parents who were pitching knives at each other. I was like that terrified child who ran screaming to neighbors, slamming all of her forty-two pounds against their front door so they would come break up the parents who were killing each other.

I was too late then, too.

The neighbor lady carried me across the yard and into our living room where my mother lay prone and not breathing on the floor.

Then the ambulance took her away and when she came home a week later it was with a slash of stitches through her eyebrows, where my father had sliced her with the knife.

If I could get Edith to do what was necessary, Denise would get to come home soon, to her regular hell, but at least it was hell with cable television. She thought things were bad when she called me to say John's pancreatitis was worse, to say she had lesions on her brain and they weren't going to go away. She thought she knew hell. Ha! But then she called me and I took it *up* a notch. I *ramped it up* to a whole new brand of pandemonium even *she* couldn't have imagined.

That's what friends are for.

Rummaging under the bathroom sink for the Ativan bottle, my eyes locked on the toilet. Would they let her go to the bathroom when she needed to? Would she tell them she needed to go in time? If not, would they help her clean up? Could she endure that: the business of an orderly coming in and helping her strip down and then the washing and the shame and the stench of it all? Would she survive?

Holy Mother of God.

I snatched the dusty Ativan bottle from the dark recesses of the cabinet. It was empty.

"THEY CAME TO MY HOUSE AND WOULDN'T EVEN LET ME take a coat." Denise was red-hot mad. She'd been home just thirty minutes, sprung less than twenty-four hours after they'd picked her up. Her hair was a frizzy, wild mane. I suspected it hadn't seen a comb in a couple of days. She was a spectacle.

"How did they know to come and get you?" I ventured. "Who sent them?"

"Deborah," she answered.

"Deborah—Deborah our therapist? Called the psych ward?" I asked, my suspicions sickeningly confirmed. Deborah had made the easy call, the one that allowed for instant lock-up. The call that let her off the hook—an HMO-inspired legal move, no doubt—getting a depressed patient quickly into someone else's potentially liable hands.

I considered spilling the beans about my conversation with Deborah, but choked up. Denise's hands were shaking. Her eyes were dilated, her breath short with fury. I couldn't tell her. I just couldn't.

"My nose was running, they wouldn't even let me have a Kleenex. It was the most degrading thing I've ever been through."

I thought she was finished, but then she went on.

"And all because I was trying to get an appointment with my neurologist, because I insisted I needed to see somebody," she said.

"An appointment?" I asked.

"Yes, I can't see half the time, my vision's nearly gone," she said. "I needed to see my neurologist, so when they said it would be two months before I could get in . . ." She stopped to catch her breath. "When they told me that, I insisted, I told them I was depressed. They must have seen Deborah's name on my chart and called her. She set this shit in motion."

"Why don't I get us some dinner, bring it back here," I said. Relief trickled through me.

Denise kept on talking. "The next thing I know, I'm locked up! I'm alone in a room, I can't talk to anyone. I can't even go to the bathroom!"

"You need to eat something" was the only thing I could think of to say. I made benign, reassuring noises, coos that were stupid.

And then she fell apart. She flung her head forward and heaved up large, animal-like wails into my neck. I held her tight, absorbing her whole-body cries. The earth cracked open and a terror swirled around us. Her deep, consuming sobs shattered the two of us like glass. I lay my hand on her messy hair and patted it.

CHAPTER TWENTY-ONE

What You Need Is a Good Boost(ier)

We were at Puttin' on the Glitz, a boutique Denise had frequented for twenty-five years. It was a Good Day, one of the last, so precious I stood still in the realization.

"This used to be a head shop," she announced.

"I always thought head shops were weird," I said with a look that made sure she knew I was in the spirit of things.

"That's because you were born five years too late. You only saw seventies head shops," she explained with authority. "In 1969, this store's manager had the most beautiful marijuana crop in the state. Really—it was incredible. Then came the eighties and it all went to *pot*." She slapped me on my shoulder and laughed appreciatively at her own joke. "Jerry—that was his name. He looked just like Jerry Garcia, too. Anyway, Jerry also had the largest collection of bongs I've ever seen. He kept them in a room out back." She pointed a thumb toward the back of the store. "Twenty years later he was into cocaine. How do you think he paid for this place?" She swept her arm around to indicate a spacious store filled with strappy dresses, feathered boas, and platform shoes. She gave me a look and poked my chest with her index finger for emphasis. "*Not* by selling earrings."

Twenty minutes later we were in a dressing room built for one 110-pound woman, making us, collectively, 250 percent over its mass-per-cubic-square-inch limit. If it were an elevator car, we would've been hurtling to our deaths.

"Hold your breath—*in*, not out," I said through clenched teeth.

"I *am*," she said, pissy.

I burst out laughing when the zipper slipped from my pinched fingers. My fingertips were way too sweaty to try again, so the garish number she'd insisted she had to have—a black-sequined corset with a silver-sequin star stitched across the front—slipped from both our grips and let loose her boobs in a wide splash, like the Hoover Dam broken wide open.

She bent over at the waist to catch her breasts in the corset, but she was laughing too hard to pack them back in. The bend-over made her butt slam me against the closet's mirror so hard, I was certain it cracked.

"I can't take this." I tried to sound fed up, but her giggling was contagious, and I ended up laughing, too. "I'm getting out of here."

"Don't you dare," she warned.

"I can't get a good grip on this thing," I said. "Denise, let's go get a larger size—you are *not* going to wear this thing in public."

"Shut up," she said. "It's very French; it's a *bustier*." She clenched the glittery harness closed with both hands and gave me her back. "Here," she ordered. "Zip."

"Stand still," I told her and watched my fingertips turn a pained red against the strain. "Suck in."

She did, and the metal teeth hesitantly, reluctantly, came together.

"I am *so* out of here," I said and slapped the door open. She stepped out, too, and glanced about the shop, moving in front of a three-way mirror. Flesh poured from the top of the sequins, from her armpits, from her back. I thought the thing was going to snap wide open and we'd be smothered in Denise tits and flesh.

"What do you think?" she asked and turned side to side, admiring herself in the mirror. "Do you think Ricky will like it?"

"I don't get this Ricky thing," I said. "He's a drunk, he's brain-dead. Why are you bothering with this loser? At least Merle's a businessman. Ricky hibernates in a shack. The whole fixation makes no sense to me."

"You don't understand," she said and worked to push her boobs down into the sequins. The breasts, however, were having none of it, instead rising like two yeast-laden bread loaves. "Twenty years ago he was so handsome, he was one of the best-known singers in Colorado. When I ran into him on the street, I recognized him right away."

"Running into a has-been is one thing," I said. "Delivering vodka, cigarettes, and yourself is something else entirely. *Whyyyy* are you sleeping with this guy?" I whined. "He sounds icky."

"Just go with me tonight," she said. "You'll see."

For that one night, we were pretending that John was not laid up in the hospital leaving Denise struggling to hold together their framing business. We were pretending that we weren't middle-aged women with too much bulk for corsets and tight dresses.

Our charade and the Ricky guy's comeback performance was taking place at something called the Horse Shoe Inn. But first I had to attend the company open house, an obligatory event the Publishing Republicans had crowed about for months. The New Office amounted to plush digs built alone in the midst of sage and brush, a spot best suited to shoot a John Wayne movie. The private offices reserved for the Oklahomans were against the perimeter, with lovely glass walls, privacy blinds, and wooden doors. The rest of the space paid tribute to Jack Lemmon's workplace in *The Apartment*—rows of worker-bee tables pressed so tightly together it was hard to spot your own area in the morass.

"All right. I'll go to this dive," I said, "but only on one condition."

"This is perfect," she said to the mirror. "I'll wear a black jacket over it with black jeans and boots."

She pulled in a roll of stomach pouring from the gap between *le bustier* and her Levi's. "What's the condition?" she asked absentmindedly.

"Help me get dressed for that stupid open house," I said. "We've been ordered to wear 'evening attire.' I'm sure that's supposed to mean Barbara Bush clothes, but I'm wearing a tiny black dress cut down to here. The only way I can get into it is if you come over and help me pull on my new Jaws. It's got a padded push-up bra built in."

"Pull on *what?*" she said and turned her back to the three-way, shaking her butt back and forth for effect.

The monstrous, garish silver-sequin star began near her belly button, then rolled up and over—like scaling the Rockies—her ample bosom.

"The stars at NIGHT," I broke out singing at the top of my voice, *"are BIG and BRIGHT."* Clap! Clap! Clap! Clap! *"Deep in the heart of TexASS!"*

She made like I wasn't there, but the rest of the shop patrons—mostly überhip, bone-skinny coeds—stopped shopping long enough to get a load of Denise's full back-and-armpit spillage.

"You're helping me with my new Jaws," I told her. "At this point you pretty much owe me. I may make you go to Little Office on the Prairie's company party, too."

"Uh-huh," she said, admiring herself and paying no attention to me. She began doing a little Denise dance at the mirror. I was afraid to look, but from the corner of my eye, I could tell other customers were starting to look at us. Then she began humming, which never failed to make me laugh. She was perfectly tone deaf. She ignored my giggling, as usual, and, in fact, improved upon her little show. "The stars at night, hmm, hmm, hmm, hmm," she half-sang, half-hummed because she didn't know the words. With each beat of the hum, she'd shake her ass at the mirror. "Let's go get a couple of chocolate-and-peanut-butter smoothies," she said—just as the metal zipper teeth groaned and strained and snapped wide open, flinging her boobs everywhere.

With the store's population already jaw-dropped, Denise calmly gathered her nipples and sequins, then checked her ass once more in the mirror. Chin raised and buck-naked from the waist up, she passed the bustier off to a salesgirl who stood by, stunned by the spectacle.

"Wrap it up," she said.

"THIS IS IT." I HELD UP A BLACK SPANDEX TUBE THE SIZE of a loaf of bread. A loaf of bread with two puffy bra cups on top.

"This is what?" Denise asked, preoccupied. She was arranging tiny paint jars in a drawer.

"My new body smoother," I said. "You hold this open with both hands." I demonstrated by pulling the spandex apart at one end. "And I step into it."

"What in the hell is 'Hydrowire Maxihold'?" She read the garment tag. "*You're* going to try to get into *this*?" She grinned and tossed the tag at my face, then slapped a fistful of paintbrushes into a drawer.

"I'm not going to *try*. I *am*," I said, irritated. "*You* question *me*, Texas Tits?"

"Did you try this on in the store?" Denise asked, eyeing the tube. She swiped a shelf of paint containers into a bin. "Someone else help you?"

"No."

"Well then, how?"

"I did it myself. I stepped into it and shimmied," I said and stepped into the tube to show her. "Then, when it was pulled over my hips, I hooked the back on a doorknob. When I squatted down, the doorknob pulled it up." Then I added: "But I couldn't get it pulled all the way up. Hence: you."

"That sounds like a sex act," she said, her brow furrowed as she worked to shut a drawer too full of brushes.

"No, that would be your department."

Her studio—the passageway between the living room and kitchen—was more organized than I'd ever seen it. It was pristine. No brushes or paints in sight. She'd even wiped down the cabinets she stored art junk in. I was beginning to think a fling with this Ricky guy might not be such a bad thing after all.

"I don't know," I said and flopped onto the couch. The very thought of working into the tube tired me. "Why are we going to this dive again?"

"Because," she said. "He's a good musician."

"Right," I said. "Are you kidding? You think Waylon Jennings is Wagner. Now you insist we be groupies at a redneck bar. It makes no sense."

"Exactly," she said, clapping dust from her hands. "Nothing does."

WE SAT ON BAR STOOLS, AND I FELT A VAGUE SADNESS AT the fact that the back end of my butt hung over the edge. Then I remembered my dad, Grand Barfly of Them All, had once admonished me, when he dragged us little girls into one of his favorite Saturday-afternoon watering holes, that only whores sat on the bar stools. Ladies sat at tables. Which, of course, left me a regular bar-stool sitter.

I made the company party visit as short as was possible to be able to say I'd attended. First to arrive, I found myself all dressed up and alone in empty office space, so I shot back a glass of wine, then waited for the company president to show up. A quick hello and an even quicker "This-place-is-just-toooo-wonderful, Mr. President!" I figured—and I'd be gone.

I decided to wander around and open a few of those office doors, view the plush where *la familia* would be conducting their so-called publishing work. My empty plastic wineglass in hand, I meandered about the ghostly sea of empty desks. I eyed my reflection in the glass walls of the Big Shots' offices and noted how good I looked.

I wanted another glass of wine, and a publisher I vaguely knew had a reputation for keeping a decent stock in his office. But lots of offices had moved the previous week in anticipation of the party, so I wasn't sure which was his. I opened one door and peeked in to see copy machines. I opened a second that sat empty.

Door Number Three looked promising, but I pushed it open too hard and stepped swiftly, almost falling, into the room. I stopped short because I nearly knocked an editor's well-ensconced penis out from a not-so-young female publisher's open mouth. She was a woman I was pretty friendly with, whose good ol' gal Southern persona lent color to long days spent writing about bowling.

Her eyes connected instantly with mine, though I must say she never lost her grip on the editor's dick. She and I held glances for a split second. I don't know what mine said, but hers appeared to say, *Can I help you?* I stepped twice backward and, like a cartoon in reverse, started to reshut the office door behind me, but not before she removed his little pink penis head from her mouth and said, "Nice dress, sugah."

I was itching to tell Denise the story. It was funny, and I giggled thinking about how I'd embellish it a bit, maybe have the publisher bite down in her surprise at me discovering them—but the band was so damn loud, I could feel the bar shaking beneath my arms. "Isn't he good?" Denise yelled at my ear. I looked around at a thick smoke film I knew was sure to latch on to my hair for the next two days. The stage in front of us was really only a corner of the bar, a barely visible mirage beyond the gray cloud.

"Which one is he?" I yelled.

"In front, singing."

I saw a skinny guy, a ruffian, unshaven. He was caterwauling into a microphone, but I couldn't hear a note. Two pool tables behind us clacked with pool balls poked at by baseball-capped men who talked and yelled at each other like the band wasn't there. Fat women squeezed into booths at the stage's sidelines. They lit up slender cigarettes midsentence, expertly shaking their matches out and dropping them into tin ashtrays, making me ache for my smoking days.

"Care to dance?" A cowboy tapped Denise on the shoulder. She almost fell to the floor trying to navigate his big, rough hand and the high bar stool, but once in front of the band, she moved around the barroom floor with only a hint of a falter.

WE ENDED UP CLOSING THE HORSE SHOE, FINALLY HEAD-ing to the car at 3:00 A.M. and leaving then only because, when the cowboy who'd plied us with Bloody Marys yelled " 'nother round!" at 1:49 A.M., the barkeep said wearily, "Closed, pard-ner." Denise tried to introduce me to Ricky between sets, but he had spent his fifteen minutes of not very much fame lean-ing against the bar, eyes closed, head down.

"Are you still going to see that guy?" I asked, driving home slowly so as not to attract hidden-patrol-car attention.

"Yes," she said.

"I don't get it," I said.

"You don't have to," she replied.

"WE'RE NO LONGER A GOOD FIT," THE PRESIDENT SAID. He called me into his office, and from his sour face I already knew he didn't have good news. I saw then why he was ex-cited to get into his New Space. Mountain views to the west and north. More space than my living and dining rooms combined.

"What?" For a second, it didn't truly register what Mr. President was plainly telling me. I thought the "no longer a good fit" referred to the new offices, like a piece of furniture wasn't quite fitting the New Space. At some gut level, there was a stab of surprise, the pang of rejection.

"We've come to the end of our road," he tried again. "We're giving you two weeks pay, and your benefits will terminate."

"If I get in a car wreck, I can't go to the hospital?" He had my attention then. I was scared of no medical insurance. Once, years ago, when I was in a fender bender in New Orleans, the police sent me to Charity Hospital to get checked out. Charity's ER doors swung open to a ghastly scene from a 1950s B movie: black people chained to welded-together plastic chairs, screaming and peeing right there on the linoleum floor. I got ushered into an exam room right away—clearly because I was white and wore a size seven denim miniskirt—all in rhythm with the Deep South's racial caste system. The med students doing time at Charity's ER were visibly thrilled I was their patient for the next hour, gathering around me and avoiding, with all the lack of power a free hospital residency program affords, that waiting room behind the curtain they'd drawn around us.

I worshipped at the altar of blue-crossed-and-shielded white plastic cards.

When I'd grabbed my coffee that morning, when I'd raced out the door and sped to work so Jack wouldn't give me the you're-late eyeball, I didn't imagine I might be tossed right back into that uninsured pool.

"*Uh hghm.*" Mr. President cleared his throat. "I, uh, think we'll let Jack and HR take over from here," he said and moved to his door.

"No need." I held up my hand and stopped him. "I get it. Mind if I use your phone?"

He was painfully solicitous. "Oh, oooh—of course," he said, nearly handing me the receiver. Then he backed out of the room and shut the door.

I moved around his desk and sank into his big leather chair and pressed buttons on a sleek black instrument that looked like it belonged in a science fiction movie.

"What are you up to?" I said to Denise.

"Cathie?" she said, surprised to hear from me at 8:45 on a Monday morning.

"I just got fired," I said, scanning the mountain view that rolled for miles.

"Perfect!" she said with no beats missed. "Edith's on her way. They're letting John out and she's getting his house ready. Get over here, quick."

I TRIED TO CRY ALL THE WAY FROM LITTLE OFFICE ON the Prairie to Denise's house, but no tears came. Even when, at a stoplight, I put my head down on the steering wheel, thinking about my checkbook and my new big mortgage, nothing came out. I considered, for a few moments, all the stories due for the next issue of *BowlingBiz*. Then I had the sweet sense of having dropped thirty pounds with no effort.

I was able to swap grief for relief because I felt a vague confidence and optimism about my work. I had a career. I'd negotiated the highest salary and benefits package ever at that publishing house and I'd been able to do that because Denise had taught me that that's how real businesspeople, particularly cum laudes with master's degrees for good measure, can and should operate.

She'd somehow convinced me that the same world that had launched me as a desperate welfare mother was finally rolling out a bit of the red carpet.

When I pulled up in front of Denise's house, she and Edith were unloading Alfalfa's Organic Grocery bags from Edith's car.

"Oh!" Edith exclaimed. *"Zee hospeetahl says Jaahhn-MahREE must have zee very healthiest diet."* I didn't know who she was talking to—or what she was talking about.

I walked to Edith's trunk and lifted a grocery sack. Denise rested against the fender. "I barely made it home in time," she whispered to my ear.

"What are you two jabbering about?" I said. "I feel like I've walked into a *Twilight Zone* episode—that I just left one loony bin only to walk into another." While I was packing up my desk to leave, a couple of brave co-workers, including the ding-dong-sucking publisher, had come over and helped me gather desk clutter and throw it into a cardboard box that Jack the publisher was only too glad to supply.

"I spent the night at Ricky's," Denise said, leaning next to me and pretending to reach into the trunk for a bag of groceries. "I just got home before you called."

"Pleeeze!" Edith called from John's front door. "You must help me prepare *Jaahhn-MahREE's* bed."

"You must be relieved John's coming home," I said, probing her, wanting to know how she was registering all the chaos around us.

Denise looked across the street to the empty school yard and waited a few seconds before she answered.

"They still haven't figured out what's wrong with him," she said. "They've given up." She waited again before finishing. "He'll be bedridden indefinitely, so Edith's more or less moving in. I have no idea what we'll do for money."

"How are you going to manage all this?" I said.

Denise shot a glance at Edith, who was carrying in a stack of clean sheets from the car. "You're kidding, right? It's all *already* managed," she said low to my ear. "You don't see that?"

"SO WHY'D THEY FIRE YOU?" DENISE ASKED, STUMBLING in her front door with the largest box of Spic and Span I'd ever seen. She'd gone off on a cleaning-supply errand for Edith, who was bent on scouring her son's house from top to bottom. We could hear her through Denise's wall, throwing open John's cabinets, turning the kitchen sink on, then off, then on again, cleaning with a rabid French vengeance.

"I don't know," I said wearily, remembering the unpaid bills in my desk drawer at home. "I don't know. I guess because they didn't like me . . . or maybe because I saw that editor's frozen-Armour-hot-dog penis."

"Or maybe he wanted you and his own teeny-weeny *en fellatio*?" she said, smiling.

"You sure are in a good mood lately," I said, thinking that Denise and I had switched mood swings. She wasn't exactly singing, but she was doing things. Like getting dressed and running errands for her mother-in-law.

"Don't leave me alone with your mother-in-law ever again," I said. "When you went to the store, she made me mop John's floor. I don't even mop my *own* floor. By the way, since when does it take an hour to go get some Spic and Span?"

Then I knew.

"His place is on the way," she said. "I just dropped off some cigarettes and said hello."

"You're going to get caught," I said halfheartedly.

"Not unless you tell," she said, then noticed my hangdog face and switched gears. "You hated that place. It's good you got fired."

"My checkbook doesn't think so."

"You'll find something better," she said. "You always do. Plus you've still got the restaurant column—and you've also got this."

She pulled a bottle from the nook next to the couch where she kept her purse and presented it to me like it was the Holy Grail, which it was. She surprised me with—no, it couldn't be—a red wine, from Spain. An incredible Vega Sicilia Valbuena, a lightly dust-covered bottle that was impossible to find in the States, that, if you could find it, went for no less than ninety-five dollars.

"My *God*" was all I could say. I stroked the bottle like a pet, and she headed to the kitchen for glasses. "You can't afford this."

"Let's open it," she said. "It's a congratulations-you-got-fired-from-a-stupid-job gift."

"It's not even noon," I said, not really caring a hoot about the time.

She hobbled back into the kitchen to get a corkscrew. When she returned, her left foot dragged and caught on a warped floorboard. She lost her balance for a second, then righted herself with a chair back.

"We've got all day and night," she said. "You got something better to do?"

"Vee hahve to preeepare." Edith slammed through Denise's front door, a mop in one hand and window cleaner in the other. *"Vee must hahve his house cleeen, cleeen. Eeet is so he can heal properly."* She marched by us, heading back to Denise's kitchen.

"No, actually," I said and jammed the metal screw into the cork, "I don't."

CHAPTER TWENTY-TWO

Mo' Bile

Jaahhn-MahREE came home to a great deal of fanfare, complaining in Archie Bunker–like fashion about his pain, about wanting everyone to leave him completely alone, about how his mother and wife were particular irritants who wouldn't let him rest. I walked to the back of his house to say "hello, I hope you feel better," and found him lying on a bunk bed built five feet off the floor, a platform high as the top of my head. Despite his alleged near-death incapacitation, John Marie had managed to crawl up the ladder onto his pedestal-bed contraption. At me he barked: *"Get out!"*

Denise quit answering her phone. I knew this because I rang several times a day for two days straight. Since I was then the master of my schedule, an itinerary packed tight with Oprah Winfrey and a twenty-four-hour *Bonanza* marathon, I was keenly aware of the silence. Except for the nonringing phone, Michael Landon and Dan Blocker were my focus.

I imagined Michael and Dan to be old friends. I had met them, or more accurately, they had met my backside during the 1966 Indianapolis 500 Parade, the parade that forms part of the 500 race hoopla held at the Indianapolis Motor Speedway each spring.

I was in the fifth grade, had been twirling a baton for three years, and felt I'd invented the art. It was a thing you could take up if you lived in scary neighborhoods with no money for lessons of any real value. I wanted to take piano lessons. I wanted to sing. I wanted fantasy parents who lived in California and wrote poems. I got, instead, three years of baton lessons because a high schooler who wore turquoise eye shadow, white frosted lipstick, and shorts cut so high her butt hung out taught them for ten cents a session. Even I could scrape that together.

After taking some fourth-tier trophy in the 1966 Indianapolis 500 Baton Twirling championship, I marched and twirled in the Indy 500 parade, positioned twenty-five feet in front of the *Bonanza* cast—all of whom pranced directly behind my ten-year-old ass. Ben Cartwright couldn't control his horse; it kept dancing in circles and pooping and whinnying. When my mother got her Brownie Hawkeye black-and-whites developed, one was of Ben on a blurred brown object, the remaining eleven were of Michael. Glued to *Bonanza,* I studied Michael's face and thought of my mother's blatant lasciviousness.

Except for our four-week, post-Havana hiatus, Denise and I didn't go twenty-four hours without speaking. After two days I couldn't stand the silence or one more *Bonanza* plot. (Horses are lost. Bad man has them. Michael woos dame. Wrap it up.) So I drove over.

"I *hahve* not seen her," Edith said. She was on the *Jaahhn-MahREE* side of the porch, lugging a tureen the size of a large baby. Broccoli soup infused with real cream splashed across her chest as she huffed and puffed beneath her burden.

I pushed at Denise's front doorknob. It was locked. My heart did a little race.

"When did you see her last?" I asked, eyeing Denise's car in her handicapped parking spot at the curb.

Edith, striving to get the soup to Le Convalescing Bébé, gave me a once-over and sniffed, "I do not know. *I hahve not seeen her all day.*" It was clear that I had interrupted her mission.

I jumped off the front porch and raced around the side of the house. Panicky, I shoved the side door open with my full weight and fell headfirst into Denise's pitch-black kitchen—the shades over the sink were drawn tight against the world.

A weird click-click-clicking noise came from her bedroom, something I heard but couldn't see. I reached my hand out in the dark to feel for the door frame, to guide myself toward the clicking noise, which I recognized as a tape stuck in her Books for the Blind tape player.

Moving into her bedroom, I stomped on the cat, which shrieked and shot like a bolt from beneath my foot. "Denise?" I said tentatively to the dark.

Nothing.

"*DENISE?*" I scrambled to locate the bedside lamp—her turn-of-the-century house didn't have updated wall switches— and felt my arm swipe her huge, heavy-as-hell porcelain lamp from the nightstand. It slammed to the floor and shattered into what sounded like a thousand pieces.

"That was really helpful" came a voice in the dark. Like a caged animal let loose, my heart slowed its slamming, and my shaking hands groped, trying to locate the bathroom, to at least turn that light on. But I didn't really give one rat's ass about the goddamn light anymore since I'd heard her voice, since her sarcasm had leapt out to soothe my nervous system.

"God damn you," I said, my voice weak with relief.

"Tell me a story about your mom's wooden leg," she said quietly.

I found the edge of the mattress with my fingertips and eased myself onto it, ignoring the cat smell.

"I'D JUST LANDED AT MY MOM'S APARTMENT. MY HUS- band had been missing for a week after skulking away in the middle of the night," I started. Then I stopped. "You sure you want to hear this?" I had no idea what I was about to tell her, but I didn't care. Blabbing whatever came to mind would, I hoped, hold her attention.

"No one knew where he was," I began again, "though we pretty much figured out that his parents were hiding him two states away. I was pretty lost. Everyone else I went to school with had just graduated from college. It was the late seven- ties, and I'd had to leave our house after he left us in Colo- rado and go back to the Midwest, where I never wanted to be. I didn't have a job. I didn't have a car. I had no idea what to do next.

"My mom was newly separated from my dad," I told Denise. "She had a four-thirty-five-an-hour receptionist job that she hated, in a dying little insurance office in a strip mall. One of my teenage sisters was pregnant. The others would be pregnant in a year or so.

"Oh," I added. "My mom drank a fifth of vodka and a six-pack of Stroh's a day. My kids and I slept on a foldout cot in her second bedroom with two of my sisters."

Denise stayed silent.

"One afternoon, the whole lot of us walked to the park: my pregnant sister, my brother, me, my kids, and my mom. One of my kids was cranky and started screaming, so my mom grabbed her and marched to the far side of the play-ground. She plopped them both down in one of those leather swings, the kind that make a U at the bottom, and she took the baby, who by then was red-onion-faced, kicking and scream-ing, and she forced her clenched fingers around the chains, which made the baby screech louder. But my mom calmly pushed the ground away with her foot, the real one—not the wooden one—and started swinging.

"Are you awake?" I said to the dark.

"Yes," Denise said.

"Soon she and the baby were swinging pretty high," I picked up. "It quieted the baby, and it was sort of fun to watch them. You didn't know why you watched it, but you did. You couldn't help it. My mom had thick reddish brown hair, and it flapped against her face, blinding her for a sec-ond, then it spread up and out like a crown behind her head. It sort of hypnotized the baby.

"In the meantime, everyone else, including the pregnant sister, was playing kickball."

I took a break from the story and listened to Denise breathing. My eyes had adjusted to the dark just enough to see her lying with her eyes closed. The mattress was stripped.

"So I was sitting there watching my mom and baby swinging higher and higher—and I was holding my other kid on my lap, and there was this bloodcurdling, 'YEEEAAAgh!' screech behind my back," I told her. "The kid I was holding and I both looked away from my mom, and we saw this cream-colored thing. It was a wooden half leg. My mom's leg. Actually, it was her leg with a bobby sock and a penny loafer on the end. We watched it sail over our heads, then crash into a bush at the curb."

In the near dark I saw Denise's cheeks move slightly with a tiny smile.

"But that's not the story," I said.

"My mom was screaming, 'Somebody get my damn leg!' And 'One of you kids help me!' The baby was gripping the swing. My mom couldn't get out of the swing; she had this one flaccid pant leg hanging down in front of her.

"A little black boy had been trying to balance himself in the middle of a teeter-totter. He saw the leg, but you could tell it wasn't computing for him. His jaw was all hanging loose, and his eyes were bugged out like saucers.

"My sister wrapped herself around one of the swing-set poles, bent double from laughter. She had a weak bladder anyway, and then she cramped her hand over her pee-pee to keep from wetting her pants—about ten feet from this little boy."

I reached over Denise's head to the shelf in her headboard and grabbed her glass of water and gulped.

"That water's from last night," she told me, a fact I could have gone without knowing.

"Want some?" I offered her the glass. She shook her head no, and I put it back on the shelf.

"*Any*way, the little boy fell off of the teeter-totter and righted himself, and the whole time his mouth hung open in a big O. He looked from my mom's empty pant leg to the curb where her leg landed and then he let out this little *ooooh,* like he was going to throw up, and this sent my sister, who was heading over to get the leg from the bush, into hysterics.

"I had to go pull that leg from the bush and slip it up my mother's slacks."

"Mm-hmm," Denise mumbled. Then: "So. Did your mom have a handicapped parking sticker?" She rolled onto her back and laid an arm across her eyes.

"What?" I said. "She didn't even own a car most of her life."

"Did she ever have to use a cane?"

"No." I hated where she was going with this. I was trying to tell her a funny wooden leg story. "Let's get out of here."

"Did she ever use a wheelchair? Did she ever even *consider* it?"

"Denise. It was a different time. She came from a farm with big, crazy thrashing machines and shit. Limbs got chopped off."

We sat for a few seconds, and I added, "They didn't even *have* handicapped stickers back then." I felt tricked into the conversation. "Get dressed," I ordered.

"How old was she when she died?"

"Christ. I don't know. I can't remember." Which was a lie.

"Mmm," Denise murmured in the dark. "So she never saw fifty either."

"DAH-NEEZE?" EDITH CALLED OUT FROM DENISE'S LIVING room, jangling both our nerves. "I'm leaving now!"

"Come on," I said to Denise. "We'll drive her home." To Edith I called, "Want a ride? We were just heading out."

"She hasn't left here since he came home from the hospital," Denise said. She lay still, the arm still flung across her face. "Except to run errands for him."

"That's no reason to ignore my phone calls," I said, reverting to let's-buck-up mode. "So he'll get better, and then everything'll be back to normal."

She moved her arm, opened her eyes a sliver, peeked at me, and closed them again.

"Right," she said. "Do you know what it's like to not be able to read one fucking page of a book? I can't see anything."

I heard the low drone of John's TV on the other side of the wall.

"So we'll go to Kaiser and get you some glasses," I said. I clicked on the bathroom light, and we both blinked against it. Pieces of the orange nightstand lamp were strewn all over the bedroom floor.

Denise rolled over on her side, her back to the light. She didn't answer. I looked around at the clothes piled on the floor, at the dusty earrings hanging on their dusty bars. The bustier was bunched up in a ball in the corner, the sequins dulled from her cat sleeping on it.

"You know. Maybe a wheelchair's not a bad idea." I stooped and picked up lamp pieces, threw them in the bathroom trash can. "We can get you one of those motorized ones."

She squinted her eyes open, her look all disdain and despair. "What's this *we* bullshit?" she said. "A wheelchair's the end. It means the end."

"*That's* bullshit," I said, though I wasn't half as certain as I was trying to sound. "Social Security or Medicaid or something like that will pay for it. It won't cost you a dime. They make them light these days, in cool colors like metallic turquoise or something. We'll get one with a horn." I hated the words falling from my mouth. I hated that I was making like a chirpy nurse selling happy medicine that's sure to crush your soul.

"What's new with Ricky?" I said, angling to switch topics, to penetrate the impenetrable gloom of the room.

When she didn't answer, I walked to the kitchen and opened the refrigerator. It held only the nearly empty Mud Slide bottle and half a dried orange.

"Ricky's history," I heard her say from the bedroom. When I turned and went back, she was curled sideways. I saw the sheets a knot at her feet; her hair greasy on the pillow.

"What happened?" I asked. "You just started seeing him."

"Nothing," she said. "I just quit going over there. John's really sick." She rolled onto her back and looked at the ceiling. "It's too much, both of them in bed, complaining."

"Shit," I said. "I forgot about Edith. Let's get out of here."

Denise groaned, leaned onto an elbow, and lifted herself to a sitting position. She lost her balance when she tried to stand and fell back onto the bed. I reached to steady her.

"Don't!" she snarled, grabbing her arm away from my outreached hand. She lurched the three feet to her bathroom, righted herself on the dresser corner when she wobbled, then slammed the bathroom door. I was relieved to hear her pee.

"Edith," I called out. "We're getting ready—give us a sec," but she wasn't there, popping back in to say *au revoir,* I figured, to *Jaahhn-MahREE.*

I picked up the cassette case from Books for the Blind on Denise's headboard shelf and held it against a strip of light coming through the blind. It read: NATIONAL LIBRARY SERVICE FOR THE BLIND AND PHYSICALLY HANDICAPPED. On the last line, the title: *Death Be Not Proud.*

EDITH CLIMBED INTO THE PASSENGER SEAT, AND DENISE heaved herself into the back, letting her head rest against the window and shutting her swollen eyelids.

"*Eet is a meeestery,*" Edith said. "*Heee's always been so helllthee.*"

"When did he start getting sick?" I said. "I don't remember anything before that night with the Mud Slide drinks. Do you, Denise?"

"I don't know," she said. "I remember him saying he didn't feel well . . . about the time I closed the shop those couple of days, when I couldn't keep up."

We were quiet for a few minutes, navigating traffic, waiting for the lights to change, for other cars to get out of our way. Springtime in Boulder is usually brilliant and promising. Iris farms nestle up against entire blocks devoted to tulip gardens. But the flowers had already bloomed and were past their prime, their heads hanging in weariness, like they were already regretting the approaching summer heat. The blooms looked tired of trying to look good.

"I never heard him say a word about stomach pains—or any other pains for that matter," I said. "He hikes and bikes every day."

"When I was getting too confused and mixing up orders . . . ," Denise said. I saw her put her head back on the seat. "I don't know. He hates dealing with customers."

"I think John resented having to pick up the work Denise couldn't do," I said. I realized, as my trap flapped, that I was directing my verbiage at no one and nothing in particular—at the windshield, the gearshift, the ashtray full of gummy, neglected pennies. "I think he didn't want to do more work in the frame shop than he absolutely had to."

I heard Edith make a little snort and felt her look toward me, but I didn't look at her. I knew I'd just drawn a steel mesh curtain firmly down the middle of the front seat, between her and me, but I didn't give a shit.

In a low voice Denise said, "He can't stand customers. He wanted me to shut the shop down for good." Then she was quiet. "When I couldn't run it anymore."

I pretty much fell over some edge, some emotional em-

bankment where I'd been perched, watching Denise deterio-
rate daily. A ledge where I'd witnessed Edith prepare tender,
special-made meals for John, taxi them over and serve them,
yet I never saw her leave a morsel for Denise. I was at some
precipice that I knew, once I toppled over, I couldn't climb
back up.

"Sometimes," I said, "people *will* themselves to get sick."

The silence in the car riveted us. Denise sat up straight in
the backseat, watching my face in the rearview mirror.

"Like my mom," I said. "She supposedly died of cancer
when she was forty-nine. But that was just a symptom. She
really died of resentment."

I didn't know if they were listening to me, but I was driving, I was telling the story. "She had a wooden leg, and she
had a rotten husband." I took a corner a little too close, and
the tire jammed against the curb. I righted the car and
kept on.

"She was a big joker, a big oh-don't-worry-about-me person about that leg. She'd knock on that leg in front of a little
kid for the fun of it, and the kid's eyes would pop wide,
not believing such a loud, wooden, knockety-knock-knock
noise could come from her shin. When she got drunk, she'd
turn the foot part—the foot was screwed into the wooden
shin—backward so that all the other drunks around her
would think they'd had one too many and they were seeing
things."

I glanced in the rearview mirror, and Denise's eyes locked
straight into mine. I'd never told her that part.

"My mom's father ran over her foot with a weed mower when she was three years old," I said. "Chopped it off."

"Vee should turn here." Edith said. She turned her face, her entire upper body so far toward the passenger window that she was nearly outside the car, trying hard to get as far away from me as possible.

"She married a man who impregnated her eight times, then left her for a slutty bookkeeper," I continued. "She was alone with a house full of teenagers. She'd never held a job in her life. After he left, my dad hid out. He never supported anyone or anything after that but his partying habit."

Denise was bent forward with her head near mine and Edith's.

"She got cancer because she wanted out," I said. "She died because she hated every single thing in her life."

We were pulling up Edith's street, part of a desirable sub-urb in its heyday: long, multilevel ranch homes with elon-gated glass walls to take in the mountain views. It was a mature neighborhood with yards blanketed in the rich green of spring. We wound through streets with wide driveways lined with cars and RVs. Most of the homes had hiking trailheads that lead from the backyards straight out into open space where deer and fox wandered regularly.

"When I was raising my kids alone, I didn't get sick for twelve years straight." I couldn't stop. I couldn't stop anything I was saying any more than I could jump from the moving car and stop it with my bare hands. "I *couldn't* get sick."

I turned and looked directly at Edith and shot my words at her like bullets. "Can you imagine? Never a sick day in *twelve* years? Who'd take care of everything? I *willed* myself to stay healthy. I had to."

You could see a hiking trail lift out and up from Edith's wide-open backyard. The trail disappeared into an embankment covered in deep blue-green pine trees.

"When my kids were teenagers and I knew they could fend for themselves, I fell flat on my back with strep throat so bad I was bedridden for two weeks," I kept on. "I was delirious with fever. It was like I'd stored it all up for those years."

We pulled into Edith's driveway. She couldn't gather herself together quickly enough. "I think John *willed* some of this on," I said to them both. "I think he didn't want the responsibility of taking over the frame shop and all the work that entailed. He didn't want to pick up where Denise's MS left off." Lordy, the air was thick in the car then. "I think that grunt work"—I wrapped it up and looked squarely at them both—"gives *Monsieur Jaahhn-MahREE* gas."

Edith didn't slam the car door with flaming fury. Her umbrage came a week later, in a seething missive sent by mail. "Jean-Marie never, never made himself sick!" she wrote. "How can you say such a thing!" In my head I heard: *"Jaahhn-MahREE nehvar, nehvar made heeemself sick! How cahn you say such a theeeng!"*

Later, Denise told me that, when she got home, Edith called her and went berserk, screaming into the phone about how horrid I was and what Edith thought concerning me: *"Sheeee should be locked up! She eeze insane! She's more than a leeetle crazy!"*

I said to Denise, "Her point?"

THE PAPERWORK TO SECURE A WHEELCHAIR WAS MORE painful than the wheelchair shopping itself. It took days and days and more days to fill out the forms exactly right, gather doctors' notes—including copies of *all* of her CAT scans and MRIs—before finally, *finally* the Social Security Administration of the United States of America reluctantly said yes, we will pick up two thousand dollars of the cost of a three-thousand-dollar wheelchair.

I held open a door that had HORACE BROS. PROSTHETICS AND AMBULATORIES painted in gold on the glass. Denise struggled to walk up the tiny step into the store, leaning heavily on a cane. I thought she was going to topple any second.

Her hair, pulled into an oily, unkempt ponytail at her neck, was shocking to look at. Her high of little more than a few weeks back, of bustier wearing and cowboy flirting and dancing in redneck bars, seemed like a notion only I had, like a long-ago breeze that flew off as quickly as it came.

Inside were wheelchairs with engines, wheelchairs with brakes, scooters with extra-big seats for particularly wide asses, and more chairs with horns to honk people out of the way. There were aluminum and metallic red and green and blue models with names like cars: the Blazer, the Champion. I thought of a *Seinfeld* episode that Denise and I screamed with laughter over, where George Costanza—the resident putz, the loser—faked a disability in order to score a motorized cart, riding it all over the place like he was disabled. I tried to remember why it was funny.

Denise fell into a recliner chair that stood the sitter up via a motorized lift. "I don't know what I want," she said to a sales guy who'd seen it all before. "Here." She thrust her paperwork at him.

"I think one of these carts," I told him and pointed to a shiny, copper-glitter-painted machine. "See, you only have to push a button to move," I said, and I showed her the Forward button on the cart's little black handle.

"I'm hardly going to use whatever I get," she said, and I saw she was sweating with the effort it had taken to get in the door and into the showroom. "I'll just take something that's light and folds up."

"Why not get a motor?" I said and realized as I was saying it that I'd admitted defeat, that she was, indeed, at the end of her walking days, that she needed the machine, the apparatus that required no coordination, no visual capability, and no strength in order to be mobile again. The fancy copper cart with the high-tech, pseudo-bicycle handgrips practically screamed, *You're hosed!*

"I'm just going to throw the thing into the back of my car. I'm never going to use it." She said this to me directly, looking straight at me. She said it in a tone and with a glaring stare that conveyed: *Why don't you mind your own fucking business?*

The sales guy moved off, hovering somewhere outside our sphere. "How does someone get to be a wheelchair salesman anyway?" I asked Denise. "Do you want to look around? See what they have?"

"No." She wasn't leaving the chair. Her face was set, red and speckled from the effort of getting into the place.

"Why don't I see what the possibilities are?" I said. "I'll come back and tell you." I looked around for our salesman. He'd know what to do, what was the right buy. He'd make it all quick and painless. We'd order up the right thing. I'd convince him to help me get Denise back out the door and into the car. Next week, she'd be mobile again, scooting around like it was nothing, and we'd review restaurants and take in a movie.

It would all be fine, very fine.

Yes, oh yes, I was full of my vision: I'd push her everywhere and she'd be happy and grateful. I swam into and through my little mental movie—What, *can't move? What's a little immobility? Look at Stephen Hawking.* She'd paint with her hands and mouth *together,* she'd get glasses, good glasses with extra-strong lenses, and we'd get Deborah to dispense little Valium-steroid cocktails to help keep it all running smoothly.

"Fuck you," she said.

I didn't think I'd heard right. I looked at her, at her mean-set face.

"What's up with you?" I said back.

"You had me committed to a mental hospital, to that fucking psych ward," she said. She was laid deep into the cushy chair, but her eyes were aflame, repudiating.

"I did not have anyone committed," I said. My head was spinning; my ears and eyes rung with the knowledge that she knew I'd telephoned Our Deborah behind her back. "I called Deborah because you wouldn't get out of bed—because you were so depressed I was scared—"

"Who *the fuck are you* to call my shrink?" She was savage in her indignation. "Do you know what I went through in that place?"

"Denise, in a million years I never thought Deborah would call the mental hospital." The tears started welling, and I blinked hard. "She was supposed to call *you*. That's the only reason I called her, to get her to telephone and talk to—"

"To the police? That's what she ended up doing—calling the police on me." I saw the hand on her cane tremble. Suddenly, almost in a spasm, I felt our lives switch places. My family, my history, and much of my young adulthood was fueled by anger. More times than I care to count, I was the girl who could explode, unannounced, like a rocket, bawling my eyes out and yelling.

Denise, on the other hand, came from domestic sturdiness, an assurance bred by family, a sense of place. Her personality might be abrasive at times, and no one would argue that she couldn't be overbearing. But those were most often playful traits, exhibited for fun and usually cloaked in mirth.

She came with built-in reason, with logic and rational thinking wired into her brain. I came from the lowest-rent, inner-city white trash, with unchained emotion, screeching, frequently laced with alcohol.

We were trapped in some horror movie, and we'd switched roles, circumstances dictating one person adopt the other's persona and vice versa. The room started to spin.

"I'm getting the fuck out of here." She pushed the button that lifted her up. She would have stormed out, but her body wouldn't let her. My heart broke a little, watching the let-down display of her anger. She was getting shortchanged again, unable, even, to stomp out when necessary.

When the chair finally cranked her all the way upright, she tilted into the cane and it slipped and she nearly landed facedown, but the sales guy was there and he caught her arm.

"Get your goddamn hands off me," she growled and yanked her arm away and shuffled slowly toward the door.

"What would *you* do?" I said, holding the HORACE BROS. PROSTHETICS AND AMBULATORIES door open for her. Her face was grim, sweaty. The ponytail had loosened from her neck, and her hair stuck out in wild knots, in her eyes, plastered along her greasy forehead.

"I know what I *wouldn't* do," she said, and I froze in horror as she hobbled toward the street traffic. She'd forgotten that our car was in front of the store and was trying to walk away—to get away—from me. Then she stepped into three lanes of fast-moving cars and trucks, and I ran toward her and she stepped backward.

She raised her cane over her head. I stepped out into the traffic with her and instinctively reached to grab her back, but she had her arms up, holding that cane as if to hit me with it. Cars swerved to miss us, and I heard the nerve-racking squeal of tires against the asphalt.

"I'd know that calling someone's therapist is stupid!" she shrieked, shaking the cane over her head. I held my breath. She wobbled backward, and it looked like she was going to fall even farther out into the street, in front of the cars rushing around her.

I stepped toward the traffic and held both of my hands up to divert, to at least slow the cars and trucks barreling down upon us.

"*You're* the reason they locked me up!"

She pitched her cane into an oncoming car, and I heard it snap and crunch beneath the wheels. The driver laid on his horn and screeched around us, shouting profanities at Denise, who was bent over at the waist, like she'd been sucker punched, heaving huge sobs at the ground.

Somehow we got back to the car.

"I never meant for all that to happen, and you know it," I said, trying to drive and look at her evenly at the same time. "Denise, you *know* that."

"You should never have called Deborah. Never!" she said. Though my eyes were on the road, I saw her turn straight toward me. "I'll never, ever trust you again," she added, then lowered her voice to a snarl. "I mean *never.*"

Her words seared me somewhere deep in my stomach. I strained to deflect them, make them false.

Never?

I knew that word. It's what inevitably happens. The leaving. The now you see him, now you don't.

But *come on.*

This was Denise and me. My mind rejected her claim, *never,* the finality of it. I almost expected, just for a second, that we'd both burst out laughing.

Wasn't that how we worked?

I didn't know how or when she'd figured out that I'd phoned Deborah. I didn't know how or when she'd put two and two together, but I couldn't think of that right then. At my core, I knew that it had somehow dawned on her that I was the one who'd made the call.

My palms were thick with sweat, and they stuck to the steering wheel. It was hard to drive. My brain felt like it was splintering, like it was blinding outside. I maneuvered the streets in a fog.

"You went behind my back," she said; her voice turned self-righteous and affected calm. "I don't want you near me or my house again."

This, I sort of thought, is the MS out of control. This, I sort of thought, will not last, because as soon as she's home, in air-conditioning, and not in a store to buy a wheelchair, realizing the magnitude of knowing she'll probably never really walk again, that, at the age of forty-seven years, her business is gone, her husband's checked out, and her body has finally, irretrievably given up—as soon as all that gets digested, well, she'll cope, she'll feel better, and everything will be back to normal.

"I've called an old friend of mine," she said, evenly, through tight lips. With finality, with resolution, with unwavering conviction. "*She's* going to help me get a wheelchair."

She opened the door at the curb, slammed it shut, and was gone.

CHAPTER TWENTY-THREE

Clairol Loving Care

My peg-legged mother gardened every year of her life. She was a farmer's daughter.

In the summer of 1972, she would garden wearing nothing from the waist up but a ratty old brassiere, at the back of the lot of one of the almost a dozen rented houses we lived in, the last one, the one in which I conceived my first child when I was seventeen. She was thirty-six years old that summer, getting fleshy around the middle, struggling to stay afloat under a boatload of midlife bitterness.

My father left every week to sell plastic signs from the trunk of his Plymouth Fury to little businesses, mostly one-man whiskey joints set in farm towns. He was gone pretty much all the time. It was the year he began his barefaced affairs, my mom finding his love letters in a drawer, the beginning of all the girls eventually getting pregnant as teenagers. It was not too long before my brother's suicide and before her descent into terminal lung cancer. It was the time Mom aged ten years in two.

But before all that, my mother would kill the interminable time in that old farmhouse by gardening. Ninety-six-degree heat coupled with 98 percent humidity spelled tomatoes as big as grapefruits, fourteen-foot-tall cornstalks, cucumbers embarrassingly huge.

She spent those long, devastatingly hot afternoons out behind the shed, beyond the overgrown rosebushes, hidden away from us kids, escaping the house, with its shabby furniture and cockroaches. She'd take a stained Tupperware glass full of iced tea and a fresh pack of Kool menthols to the edge of the two acres, where the railroad tracks separated the yard from untamed farm fields lined with old cornstalks and mosquito-laden weeds.

She'd yank off her blouse and snap the straps off the grayish bra, her skin worn and leathery as old shoes. She'd wear thin cotton slacks and keep her tennis shoes and socks on because all that clothing hid a lot: the seam where the foot screwed into the ankle, the sobering metal hinges that allowed the leg to bend at the knee, like a real one. Leather grips wrapped and laced at her thigh, keeping the hollowed-out wood against her stump, which ended in a point at mid-shin. Military-strength cord tied in double knots gave it purchase to her thigh. The flat shoes, the socks, the long pants, worn every day of her life—even in hundred-degree midwestern heat—were a clothing prison that hid her fake limb.

But from the waist up, she'd free herself.

She would rub Johnson & Johnson's baby oil up and down her arms, across her chest and bare belly, over her shoulders.

Then, cigarette hanging from her lips, she'd bend over and weed and plant and move vegetables about the plot she'd turned over with a shovel and that leg, the rows she'd dug easily because her wooden leg gave extra push to the shovel, digging the blade deeper than a mere flesh foot ever could.

And the trains would roar by next to the garden, regularly, twice a day, morning and late afternoon. If you walked back there, which you knew you weren't supposed to do—you knew even as a teenager, in some quiet, unspoken way, that the garden plot hidden from everyone except the train hoboes and the engineer was her spot, her time—but if you did walk back there and she didn't hear you, you'd see a brown-skinned woman with disheveled, Clairol Loving Care auburn hair who'd stop her weeding and digging to watch the train roar down upon her and within but a few feet of her radishes and onions.

You'd see her take the smoke from her lips and hold it between two fingers and with the smoke there in between her fingers, she'd wave at the engineer and the hoboes, all of whom would be gathered at the train's open doors. They'd come upon the garden waving and catcalling to her like mad, like thunderous politicians on a cross-country campaign, waving like they'd all been waiting for her, like they'd organized the group on her behalf.

She'd give them a show, her glistening sweat-and-oil skin, her hair billowing back against the blast of the train, her unwavering stance, even as the ground shook with the train's power. She'd wave at them coming, wave at their arrival, then turn and wave them off as the caboose screamed away down the tracks. Like they'd all had a little party, like they all had an agreement that she'd flash them her shiny upper body, bare but for the bra, that it was all in passing and that she wasn't going to be there much longer anyway, which she wasn't, the cancer already creeping about her lymphatic system.

And then, in the late summer and early fall, came the tomatoes. Endless tomatoes, tomatoes till you wanted to retch, tomatoes sliced and fried and given away and thrown at each other and smashed against your butt when you turned away.

DECADES LATER I WAS IN MY OWN GARDEN, MY COLORADO garden with its pathetic cucumber vines, laboring to produce fruit in sandy soil too dry to grow much. I was pulling weeds and it was ninety-eight degrees and I had on a swimsuit top and a pair of cutoff shorts and a bandanna on my head. There were more weeds than vines, and I questioned the point of my effort.

When the answering machine beeped through my kitchen window, my immediate reaction was frustration that I hadn't brought the cordless phone to the garden with me, but I wasn't used to cordless yet. Denise and I had bought them together a few months back at the Big Store, and carrying a phone to the garden hadn't really occurred to me.

The machine screeched an ear-piercing beep. Then: *Well. I know you're there, so pick up.*

We hadn't spoken since she nearly threw her cane at me, since the afternoon she about got us both killed in rush-hour traffic. Three months was a long time. I heard her waiting for me to answer her.

This is Denise.

Christ. Her insistence on identifying herself.

Listen. Gladys is in town.

Gladys, her half of our matching sisters. I listened to the window as Denise waited for me to take in the news. I was struck that she knew to wait. That she knew to allow me to register that she was calling me after all the silence, and she was telling me what to do.

Business as usual.

What she didn't know was that I'd spent a hell of a lot of myself coming to terms with our fight. I stewed. I cried. Then I stooped to calling the WOW members—those Denise and I had immediately and permanently dissed after disassembling WOW—seeking sympathy. Or at least a little empathy.

I called a bunch of them, and all of the conversations more or less went like this:

"Sandy?"

Size-Five Sandy, to whom I'd not spoken in a year, said, "Who is this?"

"Cathie. Cathie Beck. Listen to what Denise Katz did. She quit talking to me! After all that—"

"So? You remember when she told me my hair looked like a football?"

"Well, I don't remember, I guess so, but listen—"

"Good riddance—that's what I say," Size-Five Sandy said, her voice riddled in comeuppance.

"Wait, you don't understand—"

"Gotta go."

I'd also left Denise plenty of reasonable, logic-laden voice messages.

"You *know* you're not making sense. Call me."

And "When are you going to get over this?"

And "Enough already. Dr. Lutz says he'll give me a full-body liposuction for free if I write a story about him. You *have* to go with me."

Silence.

Ceaseless silence.

Nearly three months, and things changed. I got a puppy, what she'd always called "shit machines." I knew then that the shift was happening, that we were done. I did everything alone, out of preference, not wanting to break in anyone new: movies, plays, the Big Store. I took myself to swanky restaurants with linen tablecloths and wine lists. When her birthday-dinner restaurant reopened under new management, changing its name from Apéritif to Delicioso's, I made a reservation for one, dined on veal smothered in mushrooms and a red-wine sauce, drank an Australian pinot noir by myself.

I did all of those things calmly, steadily, yet my heart was heavy, aware of its profound loss. I felt that not only had a chapter finished in both of our lives but a mammoth work of exquisite literature had ended. Our paths had crossed when we both least expected it, finding people we never dreamt we'd come to know, let alone surrender our very lives to.

I didn't have all of that philosophical perspective then, but somehow my soul did. My soul knew.

Yet even my soul refused to completely loosen its grip. When, eleven weeks after the wheelchair shopping, I heard her voice through the phone, through my kitchen window, wafting out onto the sad cucumbers, when I heard her say *Listen,* that she was right there for the taking, damn it, I couldn't react, couldn't propel myself backward, like the last three silent, vacuous months hadn't happened. But my soul was tempted.

My soul was a wild animal ricocheting inside my body. It wanted to step right back into our rhythm.

Do you want to meet her?

I started to the kitchen, to the phone. I could tell she needed me to meet Gladys.

The part I didn't allow myself to understand—I shut it down the second it reared its revolting head—was that Denise needed me to meet her sister before she died. After all, Denise had hopped on a plane with me two Thanksgivings earlier, flying eight hundred miles to meet one of my sisters. Then she wrote her an eloquent letter telling her how glad she was to meet her, a letter that made my eyes water over its sincerity. Meeting hers was only fair.

She wanted to present living proof of what she'd been telling me for four years. And time was up.

I realized—in hearing her voice, its Bronx-inflected familiarity, its warmth, its humor, all its inherent comfort—I realized right then that she'd picked a fight with me to get me out of the way, so she could leave and not worry about me preventing her exit. She could do a whole hell of a fucking lot—put up with MS, travel, run a business as her life caved in around her—but, by God, she couldn't worry about me *and* figure out how she'd escape this hell as well.

Many people were afraid of Denise, but not me. Many people mistook her ballsiness for bitchiness, her inquisitiveness for nosiness, her brevity for rudeness. They missed the boat and she let them, because she knew she'd never be able to put up with their sluggish pace.

They never saw her wild generosity and how it stacked up against her scathing ability to strike deals that made Warren Buffett look lame. They missed the opportunity to watch her, transfixed, in the midst of an art project—one that she'd sell for ten times its value. They weren't privy to her unparalleled ability to charm complete strangers even as she made them hand over whatever thing they had that she wanted.

I'd won the lottery. She took me to the mountain and showed me the view. It took my breath away.

But then Gladys came and Denise needed to put me in front of Gladys and put Gladys in front of me. Here, now. Never mind that she'd need to push me out of the picture yet again at some point. That part would have to wait.

The realization, the knowing that she'd soon leave and that she'd make me leave her first, again, evaporated even as it was being formed.

I sat down in the dirt between the cucumber vines and the tomato plants. I stared at the window and considered changing my mind, driving over. I should meet Gladys.

But I didn't. I looked up toward the answering machine that sat inside the window, and I listened.

Hello? Are you there? Well, just stop whatever you're doing and come over when you get this message.

I turned and lay on my stomach, a patch of cool vines jumbled beneath my belly. I hid my eyes from the harsh sun and rested my forehead on crossed arms. I let tears drip into the sandy loam beneath me. The reasonable part of my soul struggled to assure me: *Time to let go, time to let both of you loose.*

CHAPTER TWENTY-FOUR

When Vintners Weep

*H*ere.

John handed me a zipper-lock bag. An inch of dull, gray powder hung at the bottom. I didn't know what it was, and I didn't know why he was giving it to me. I did notice that it was not one of the pricey Ziplocs with the new easy zipper, but a knockoff, a pinch-it-with-your-fingers baggie.

"I thought you might want one of these," he said. "I gave one to her sister and her mother."

I looked at the bag hanging from my fingers.

"Potassium cyanide and juice. It didn't take long. They took her away pretty quickly and cremated her. I wish you would have come to her service. It was nice." He hesitated. "Her college roommate said something. We had it out front in her garden. I think she would have liked it."

I looked at Denise—or one-third of her—in the plastic. Then I sat down on one of the few remaining items left in her living room, one of her Salvation Army chairs. They were high-backed, orange-and-green geometric print, startling in their garishness. The second we saw them at the thrift store—ludicrously arranged, showroom-fashion, amid a hi-fi, a tree lamp, and a fake wood coffee table with an oversize turquoise ashtray in the middle of it—she insisted they be hers. No one else would ever have paid money for them.

He continued. "You know, she left a shitload of framing undone. She wasn't worried about all the framing she owed for that Jamaican trip because she knew she wouldn't be around long enough to do it." There was more. "Did she tell you that she shoplifted a gun that day you two went to the gun shop? While you were trying on jewelry or something. She said she walked over and slipped a gun down her jeans. But she couldn't go through with it."

I stood up and walked into the middle room, her studio. It was empty. Just her painting supply cabinet. I pulled open a drawer: paint tubes neat as canned sardines, brushes clean and straight. She'd distracted me with Jaws-of-Death talk, with stupid, how-you-gonna-get-that-girdle-on gibberish. So she could prepare. I slammed the drawer closed.

I walked through the kitchen, then into her bedroom. A bed frame held a naked mattress. Her earring ladder sat absurdly alone on the floor.

"Do you want anything here?" he asked. "I've taken what I want, moved some of her art to my house. Her sister and mother took a few things. I'm getting a bid on the Zoa Ace piece in the front room. I'll probably sell it before I rent the place out."

Explosions of devastation lit about my face, in my brain, my chest; little pinpricks of anguish shot along my arms.

Could she—would she—have held on longer or happier with a doting husband? A family close by? If I'd been a better friend? More patient?

I looked past his shoulder and into the kitchen and saw her blenders lined up on the cabinet, like art-making soldiers, the machines she used to swirl paper and plaster of Paris and color into. They were beyond dusty, their lids gummed to the pitchers. I understood that, had I blown the engines in all six of them at the Mud Slide party, it would not have mattered. She was finished with them.

"Well, if you see anything you want—"

JOHN AND I STOOD A FOOT APART AND FACED EACH OTHER in what used to be her bedroom. He was sexy, handsome, and smart. I was edgy at the niggling attraction I felt toward my best friend's husband. Denise's absence created the vacuum for the draw. With her gone, we were a triangle missing a side.

I wanted to slug him, but I walked past him, my steps echoing against the empty house. I stopped in a corner of the living room. Her wine rack at my feet was a piece of art. She'd ordered it from some goofy Art Deco catalog that I made fun of at the time: swirly steel circles piled on top of each other, like a pyramid. Metal curlicues, interesting to look at all by itself.

One lone bottle rested in the rack, and I pulled it out, rubbed light dust off the label.

VEGA SICILIA UNICO. I read it again: VEGA SICILIA UNICO. Where did this come from? I started to ask John but stopped before uttering a sound. The bottle had cost $250. It couldn't be found outside of Spain. It was the Valbuena's—Denise's get-fired-gift's—big brother. It made vintners weep.

Like a blind person, I ran and reran my fingers across the label, feeling raised print.

"Maybe you can get an urn for her ashes," John offered. "Sure you don't want to take—?"

Before he could finish, I lifted the rack and swung it over my arm. I pressed the ash-filled bag to my chest, held it fast with the Vega Sicilia Unico.

I looked around not knowing what I was looking for, what it was I wanted to see. I imagined the furniture back in its place, the plants lush and green and tucked between pedestals that held a lifetime's collection of sculpture. Art covered every available spot on the walls, and the late-afternoon sun glimmered into the room through the front window. We were together, watching *Seinfeld,* ordering takeout so we could spend the evening sipping and supping and sassing anyone who got in our way.

At her front door I saw the school yard across the street, framed in clouds hanging like pillows around the church steeple.

Denise and I and the wine rack and the Vega Sicilia Unico reached the sidewalk to see her creeping clitoris out of control, bold, purple blooms big as softballs, black-eyed Susans bursting across her front yard, hollyhocks jutting everywhere like wild, red-and-orange arrows.

It was time to drive away. I knew that because the church bells clanged, bang-alanging playfully, even joyfully against each other, a cacophony of notes, of bells, of music signaling to everyone for miles, the hour.

WHEN I GOT HOME, I PUT THE WINE RACK ON THE FLOOR inside the door, slipped the wine into it. I lay down on the couch, placed the baggie on the coffee table and stared at it. The puppy loped up and sniffed the hell out of it. Knowing how Denise would react to that choked me, and I wrapped my arms around my stomach, curled my knees to my chest.

I thought of 1968 and Ash Wednesday and little gray crosses painted on our foreheads by priests dipping their thumbs in ash. I knew I'd never do that again because I quit the Catholic Church as a girl, which made me think of other things that would never happen again.

Done, finito. Never. Never coming home. Gone for good. Never gonna see you again.

She'll never lose her grip on a pen or get us lost in Wyoming or blindside me with gifts of Cuban art and a house down payment. Her brutal wit, the kind that made my chest convulse in front of the rabbi at Rosh Hashanah, is forever silent. I'm sure I'll never laugh like that again.

The puppy rested her head on my cheek. I swallowed hard and looked at the bag, then wrapped my arms tight around my waist, rolled over onto my back, and held on.

I forgot to tell you, I said out loud, *that I'll never think Meryl Streep a good actress.*

I also forgot to tell you that you gave me chutzpah to say this aloud and not give a shit that the rest of the world loves her.

My mind left my living room and took her with me. We were at Zabar's in Manhattan and she was ordering Norwegian lox in her know-it-all voice, and then she was leading us to that incredible art exhibit in the West Village where the entire room was built of glass beads.

We were hurtling skyward on the elevator to the top of the World Trade Center, and vertigo and anxiety had me near fainting. To distract me from my terror, she pointed to my nose, and, because I'd repeatedly discouraged her from getting a nose job, said to the crowd, "Will you all *look* at this perfect nose? Look how it turns up."

It was my fortieth birthday and she was giving me underpants for every day of the week as a gift; next, it was my forty-first and she was handing me a breathtaking rose-paper, copper-framed sculpture she'd worked on for months.

She was there, right in front of me, with a patient face and ready glass of wine as I complained about one of my kids, and then she turned to me with that look, the one she wore all day long after the Realtor handed me the keys to my new house.

I shut my eyes and let the dog lick wildly at my wet face.

THE RED LIGHT WAS BLINKING ON THE TELEPHONE answering machine when I moved her to my office desk because I didn't know what else to do with Denise in a sandwich bag.

I reached over and pressed the Play button. A hang-up. But a saved message played back.

I know you're there, her voice ordered me.

Pick up.

And I nearly did.

EPILOGUE

It's been over ten years since Denise has been gone, but I don't count the years. I work to ignore those kinds of anniversaries. I schedule loads of distractions: appointments with eye doctors, dentists, exterminators, *whatever*. If I can't get professional services lined up, I catch up on *Seinfeld* reruns or clean the refrigerator to a state so sparkling I don't want to put food in it.

Maybe too many anniversaries pile up over time.

A few years back, on the tenth anniversary that wasn't an anniversary, I met with an ophthalmologist who would perform the oh-so-expensive surgery that would restore my eyesight to that of a sixteen-year-old. I was sick to death of glasses and losing glasses and of how unattractive and old glasses made me feel. Dr. Gould (who had an Elliot Gould thing going on) was my third ophthalmologist "estimator," because if I'm going to blow money I don't have, I like to shop for it wisely. Twenty minutes into chatting about the magic of correcting my vision I developed a crush, though he sported a thick gold wedding band and was probably fifteen years older than me.

Like I cared. He was lively, funny, cute, and smart as hell. I assumed he was rich, which made him even better.

Dr. Gould put that little eye-test thingy to my face and, in the midst of the exam, we bantered and laughed. We chatted about traveling and food and art. Turns out we both had pieces done by several local artists whom we mutually admired. Plus, he was happy my bad eyes were going to pay for his Tibetan vacation.

Damn, he was cute.

I walked to the reception area to leave, but everything in my body shut down.

Showcased on his waiting room wall was a four-by-six-foot blue-paper sculpture, chrome-framed-and-boxed artwork. A duplicate of the rose and copper paper sculpture Denise had made for me for my forty-first birthday. An exact duplicate: size, shape, everything but the colors.

My heart stopped. *My* paper sculpture is showcased exactly as Dr. Gould's was. One wall, one oversize spotlight, one resplendent, compelling architecture of sculpture.

"Where did you get that?" was all I could manage.

"That?" He looked at the piece, then back at me. "You know . . . ," he began, then stopped, rubbed his chin, and looked thoughtfully toward me. "That's by Denise Katz, a wonderful Boulder artist. I discovered her at the Open Studios Art Walk, and she was auctioning off this piece. I bid on it—for some charitable cause about breast cancer or breast implants or something—I can't remember. I *do* remember that I couldn't get out of her studio. We talked for over an hour. My wife had to drag me away.

"I've been trying to find her for years. She said that this piece is one part of a two-part work. She'd just begun the second part when I met her. I'd like to buy the other, but I tried to call her and her number's no good. I even drove by her studio, and it's boarded up.

"Come here," he said, and he took me to another room, where an oil painting of brilliant blues and shadows and creams was displayed, a painting of a garden of opium plants. "What?" he said, because he saw my face.

It was a painting Denise did of her opium garden, a tiny plot of opium that she pretended no one else knew about, even though she showed it off to anyone who'd walk to the far corner of her backyard.

"I'd like to get more of her work," Dr. Gould said. He stopped for a second, hesitated, then went on. "She's really a scream. I think my wife was jealous, to tell you the truth. I mean, we couldn't stop talking. I still can't find her. You'd love her. She's great. I should find her and show you her studio."

I just stared at him.

"You'd appreciate Denise Katz."

I WENT HOME AND SAT IN THE QUIET OF MY LIVING ROOM and stared at Denise's paper sculpture. The phone rang.

"This is Millicent. From the women's group," the voice said. I'd not heard from her in over four years. Millicent.

"I can't stop thinking about that woman in our group who died, Denise," she said. "It's bugging me I forget her last name. I should remember because she hand-painted those two graduation cards for my sons and put a hundred-dollar bill in each one. I still can't believe she did that. She never even met them."

Then Millicent talked about Denise introducing her to the laboratory chief who is now Millicent's longtime boss. And the time Denise had uncultured pearl necklaces handmade for everyone in the group and gave them to all seven of us, unceremoniously, as if she had some trust fund just sitting around so she could spend it on jewelry for people she professed she didn't even like.

I didn't want that conversation. I wanted distraction.

I got off the phone to work, but I didn't work. That was a record-breaking, scorching Colorado summer's day that could have been filled with any manner of things having nothing to do with anniversaries and loss and beginnings and ends. But it wasn't. I didn't go swimming or lay out in the sun or try to get a real job in an air-conditioned office, something that would have increased my net worth. I thought about how John long ago had rented out Denise's side of his and Denise's duplex and it's now a dilapidated, scary shack–looking thing with a junkyard where Denise's garden used to be. I thought about how there's no more women's group, and really who gives a good goddamn about it all

anyway? But mostly I thought about Denise and our friendship, about all the crazy things she did with me, for me,
to me . . .

I hit Callback on caller ID.

"What are you doing tonight, Millicent?"

"Nothing."

I retrieved the Vega Sicilia Unico from the cool basement,
the $250 cabernet I'd never had the heart to pop. I telephoned
the publisher from *BowlingBiz* magazine and a handful of
other women.

We waited till dark, then slid the cover off the hot tub
Denise scavenged from a construction site, the one with the
built-in stereo CD player and sixty-three jets. I wiped the dust
from the Vega Sicilia Unico, and we all slipped into the tub,
most of us buck-naked. We found spots and oohed and aahed
as the jets smacked our backs and butts. Millicent reached
over to the CD player, and guitars heated up the dark, strum-
ming into the night. The bass beat, and, on the downbeat, the
rough-edged voice of Jerry Jeff Walker crooned, *I like my women
just a tad on the trashy side.*

I opened the zipper-lock bag, and we took turns reaching
in for pinches of ashes; we sprinkled them over the outside of the tub, where the clematis climbed. Then, what the
hell, we grabbed more ashes and sprinkled some in the water.
The ashes spread out and around us in the steam, bouncing in
the jet-bubbling rhythm, and it was good. Millicent climbed
out with ashes in her palm and pushed them into a pot, fertil-
izing an opium plant she'd brought. She's got her own opium

garden now, from seedlings Denise gave her long ago. She brought me a starter.

Everyone held out her wineglass, and I poured a bit in each.

I gulped my wine, happy for the little buzz it gave me, and I wiggled my toes and thought about Denise, and then I got misty-eyed; I never could drink and remain unsentimental. I thought of how low I was, how wanting I was when I first met her. How decades of strife and heartbreak and outright fear of life had beaten me to a pulp by the time I'd reached my mid-thirties, how, until that day I met Denise, life had felt like one long tractor pull and I'd been the tractor. I thought of how tired I was, how insecure, how over it all I was that fall of 1994.

A rush of memories washed over me and I gazed into the hot tub's bubbles and I saw Denise lecturing me on negotiating a salary, and stroking my hand when I was terrified at the dentist, and fixing me up on a blind date with a local radio DJ—who actually was blind—and how she laughed hysterically for months at the joke on me, a fix-up she'd arranged because I'd once mentioned to her that I'd never been on a blind date.

I thought of what I knew then and of what I know now. I thought of the woman who helped bring me from *there* to *here*.

I didn't know, pre-Denise, that you could be a girl—a smart one who asked a lot of life and who was willing to work for it—and that it was just fine, just fine to expect to get it all, get it all and maybe even then some. I didn't realize the endless possibilities, that virtually anything imaginable was possible.

I didn't know that people come into our lives, and sometimes, if we're terribly lucky, we get the chance to love them, that sometimes they stay, that sometimes you can, truly, depend on them.

I thought of how I never knew that crossing paths with one person, if only for a relatively short time, could so powerfully change one's life, redefine it. And I thought of how there was a time in my life when I actually didn't know that people routinely watch each other's backs, that people can be utterly, completely loyal, that giving can and does return ten thousandfold.

That someone could give so much, expect nothing in return.

And then the coup de grâce: a woman could, even as life ate her alive, find fun and joy and adventure in each day. Even if she was falling apart at the seams, even if life let her down on an almost hourly basis, extracting, at an excruciatingly slow but methodical pace everything she'd hung her heart on—hell, even if she couldn't make it to the bathroom in time—there was always the sidesplitting joke. She could still live large, drum money up and give it to those worse off, blindside best friends with gifts, rub another's back when her heart got smashed to smithereens.

Once, I knew none of that.

I laid my head back on the edge of the tub, tried to drink in the entire twinkly, Rocky Mountain, starlit night. I poured a little wine into the water and watched the red spread and then disappear into the warm little waves.

Then I sipped the most expensive wine I've ever had in my life. Such a huge wine. It was magnificent.

It was not cheap cabernet.

Finally, I was fully distracted, swimming in inexhaustible net worth.

Cuba, 1996: Denise, Celia, and me.

Me as a Queen and
Denise as an Angel,
circa 1995.
(Who are we kidding?)

In all my Baton-Twirling Glory, circa 1968.

Denise and me flanking Ann Rule,
the Queen of God-Awful Gore.

Multiple Sclerosis:
Hope and Help

No one should have to face multiple sclerosis alone, including the family members and loved ones of someone who has been diagnosed with MS.

Approximately 400,000 Americans have MS, and every week about 200 people are diagnosed. Worldwide, MS affects about 2.5 million people. Because the Center for Disease Control and Prevention (CDC) does not require U.S. physicians to report new cases, and because symptoms can be completely invisible, these numbers can only be estimated.

Since the early to mid-1990s, the time at which this book is set, there have been many advances made in treatment possibilities for those diagnosed with MS. Though there is no cure yet, there are new, FDA-approved medications that have been shown to "modify" or slow down the underlying course of the disease. In addition, many therapeutic and technological advances are helping people manage symptoms. Advances in treating and understanding MS are made every year, and progress in research to find a cure is very encouraging.

For example, the FDA recently approved the marketing

Ampyra (formerly known as Fampridine SR, Acorda Thera-peutics) to improve walking in people with all types of MS. This is the first therapy specifically approved to treat a symptom of MS, and this oral therapy represents a big step forward for the many people who may benefit.

Clinical trials also hold promise, and research in MS is progressing at a remarkable rate, with more potential thera-pies in the pipeline than at any other time in history. Progress continues to be made in MS research in genetics, molecular biology, and MRI. Palliative care—a holistic philosophy of care that brings a team of providers together to develop a plan of care for the physical, psychological, social, and spiri-tual well-being of the affected person and her family—is also gaining attention in the treatment of MS.

Furthermore, chapters of the National Multiple Sclerosis Society offer those diagnosed with MS and their families many options for emotional and psychological support. In this day of Internet access (in its infancy and mostly unavail-able during the time at which this book is set), a plethora of online forums and support groups await those wanting to know more about living well after being diagnosed with MS.

Visit www.nationalmssociety.org or call 1-800-344-4867 to learn more about resources available to you and your fam-ily concerning MS.

Note: A portion of all proceeds from the sale of *Cheap Cabernet: A Friendship* will go directly to the National Multiple Sclerosis Society. A link at www.cathiebeck.com also directs visitors to a contribution page on the National Multiple Scle-rosis Society's Web site.

Reading Group Guide

1. Why does Cathie feel the need to start a women's group? What crossroads has she arrived at in her life? How does her children living away from home change the way she feels about her place in society?

2. Cathie and Denise become fast friends, but their relationship is far from smooth, even at the beginning. In what ways do their personalities clash? In what ways do they complement one another? Why do you think their complex relationship ends up being so special?

3. Why does Cathie retell the story of applying for food stamps when her children are young? What does that story tell the reader about Cathie's life as a young mother? What do we learn about her background, and how does it inform the woman we meet in the memoir?

4. Denise and John have a unique and unconventional marriage. How does Cathie feel about their relationship? Do you think she envies them, or is she confused by them? What about the marriage works for Denise, and in what ways does the arrangement fail her? Do you think John and Denise are in love? Why or why not?

5. Cathie had very complicated, mixed feelings about Denise's illness. In what ways does Cathie let Denise's MS affect their

friendship? Would you say that Cathie takes care of Denise when she is ill? In what ways does Denise's MS frustrate and disappoint Cathie?

6. Discuss Cathie and Denise's trip to Jamaica and Cuba. In what ways is the trip a turning point for both women? What do they each discover about themselves on the trip, and what do they discover about one another?

7. Why does Cathie include the story of her visit to New York to see where Denise grew up? What does visiting Denise's home, and meeting the women she grew up with, tell us about Denise and her upbringing? Why does meeting these women have such a profound effect on Cathie?

8. Toward the end of the memoir, Cathie writes about her own mother, and the struggles she faced raising Cathie and her siblings. Is Cathie anything like her mother? In what ways does Cathie escape her family's legacy? In what ways does she continue where her mother left off? How does her family and her childhood haunt her into her adult life?

9. In the end, Cathie and Denise have a falling out and Cathie does not attend her friend's memorial service. Do you think Denise orchestrated their rift to protect Cathie? Do you think Cathie can really find closure?

10. *Cheap Cabernet* follows in a tradition of many great memoirs, novels, and movies about women's friendships. How does this book fit into that tradition? How is Cathie and Denise's friendship unique from others you have read about or seen?

A Conversation with Cathie Beck

Q: This is your first book. What's it about?
A: It's a story of an unlikely friendship that ultimately became the most powerful I've ever had. I met Denise Katz when I was as lonely as a woman can get. I was thirty-nine, too young to be the "empty nester" I was. My kids were newly out of the house, my boyfriend had just dumped me, and since I'd been an adult graduate student—ten years older than my fellow students—my grad school friends had all moved away. I'm a social person who suddenly found herself alone. So I placed an ad in a newspaper for $1.75 stating that I was forming a group called WOW: Women on the Way—to an insane asylum, rehab, whatever. It was nuts, but I wanted to meet people. The week after I placed my ad, my phone was ringing off the hook, so clearly I wasn't the only one. Based on our phone conversations, I invited eight of the women to meet in my living room one Wednesday night. In walked Denise, an award-winning artist and savvy, beautiful businesswoman who, through luck and life, ended up being some cosmically chosen best friend to me.

Cheap Cabernet is about how life is much wilder, much more unpredictable, and—ultimately—much greater than we ever imagine it could be. Really, it's about not giving up, because no matter your age, no matter how much you *think* you've got it all figured out, you don't know what's around the next corner—or who might be there waiting for you.

Q: You've been published in Glimmer Train, Poets & Writers, *and* Zoetrope, *and you've written a memoir about a joyous female friendship. Why do you think the literary world so often views these accomplishments as mutually exclusive?*

A: I don't have a clue. So many writers, if you look at their early bibliographies, published in different genres at different times in their lives before their "big public break" came. I've had short stories published in literary anthologies and academic publications for years. I've also written longer feature stories that read like literary short stories for newspapers and magazines. *Cheap Cabernet* is a natural outgrowth of all of that previous work. In fact, when I first drafted it, I honestly said to myself, "Okay, let's write a short story, but a longer one." And then I created a first draft of ninety pages.

Q: Why did you title the book Cheap Cabernet: A Friendship?

A: It's a metaphor that came from the process of telling this story. So much of my childhood and young adulthood felt cheap. But humor always prevailed. Something about humor plus low-rent circumstances makes me laugh and want to write country western songs. *Cheap Cabernet*—the title—honestly fell from some crazy, heavenly place into my lap. To me, the title *and* the metaphor have all the mirth and fun and humor and "low-brow" feel of a sassy, funny country western song.

Denise had a profound affect on my life. On the surface, we might at times have appeared—and, ahem, behaved—in something of a "low-brow" fashion. We certainly had sass, fun, and a big-hearted "low-rent" vibe in our friendship. As it turns out, our story is anything but cheap. It's profoundly priceless—just like the extraordinary Spanish wine divinely bequeathed to me at the end of the book.

Q: What drew you and Denise to each other? Why was her friendship so crucial for you at the time you met?

A: This is a fact: When Denise came into my living room that first night at the WOW meeting, something happened. There was a palpable energy between us. You might think I'm making that up. I'm not. The only thing I can compare it to is the "love at first sight" experience. But I don't believe even *that* adequately captures the joie de vivre, the silly, delicious humor, the innate understanding the two of us felt throughout that evening. We were cerebral girls and we shared a wicked sense of humor. It was a glue that worked.

As with any intense and profound relationship, a number of factors ultimately fed our relationship, and timing was everything. For the first time I didn't have children at home and Denise was childless. My life-long sense of vulnerability was starting to lift, and I believe she was feeling a profound vulnerability due to her illness that she had not felt in her youth. One person who read the book said, "It's like you two were on the same staircase, you going up, and Denise going down. And you met on the same step." Bingo.

Q: You open and close the book with lyrics from a Jerry Jeff Walker song: "I like my women just a tad on the trashy side." How is this refrain emblematic of you and Denise?

A: It's about humor and not taking yourself too seriously. Jerry Jeff Walker sang those lyrics because they reflected *him*, even though he wasn't trashy—he was a successful recording artist. But Jerry Jeff knew the soul of the "trashy women" he sang about.

Denise sang those lyrics for the same "opposite" reasons: she wasn't trashy and she wasn't from any rural or country western culture. But she was a woman with a sense of humor and she fully appreciated where Jerry Jeff was coming from. Sing those lyrics in your head to any melody you'd like. Don't they make you grin?

Q: On a roadtrip with Denise, the two of you talked a lot about the perfect moment. What did "perfect" mean to the two of you?
A: We both somehow knew this secret of life: "Perfect" is when things look rotten.

"Rotten circumstances" offer a fountain of opportunity. I know that sounds all New-Agey and Wayne Dyer–like. But the two of us somehow knew, and knew the *other* was also well aware, that when circumstances are upside down and despair is your middle name, have a party. If we didn't know that before we met each other, we learned that throughout the life of our four-year friendship. It was an extraordinary, life-changing gift to us both, and we never saw it coming.

It liberated us, this knowledge. And we both delighted in finding another person who thought this way. It liberated us to laugh at just about every single thing that happened. It also allowed us to cry our eyes out, unashamedly, to fight—with others and with each other—because aren't emotions supposed to be used and experienced? And really, what the hell good comes from suppressing emotions anyway? Isn't that how addicts and serial killers are born?

Q: Denise was a vibrant, beautiful, fun-loving woman, and yet when you met her husband, he seemed to warn you that you were about the only other person around. Why was that and what was he telling you?
A: Aren't smart, independent women often alone by choice? Isn't it their way? Don't they often live in their heads—and therefore

spend, out of choice, a lot of time alone? I know I did, and I believe Denise did, too.

She owned a business, she was an artist, and she was married. That's a full life, and Denise didn't court frivolous relationships. Her family lived out of state. For these reasons, she might not have had a gaggle of friends or companions circling about as other women might. And she had MS. Having a chronic, debilitating illness encroach upon a strong woman's life, I believe, contributes to isolation. I think all of these circumstances led to me meeting Denise at a time when there were not a lot of other people occupying her life.

It was in hindsight, recalling my first meeting her husband, that I remembered his benign remark about "nobody left but us chickens." The truth is that I may have read more than intended into the comment, but it stuck with me and I've recalled it, more than once, over time.

Q: Is there a scene in Cheap Cabernet that captures your friendship with Denise?
A: Honestly, so many, many moments are emblazoned upon my heart; it's nearly impossible to choose one. The two of us watching Seinfeld, the ease with which she completely ignored me, illustrates the comfort of our relationship. Reviewing restaurants for my column, especially the ridiculous, hip-thrusting belly dancer restaurant, was so typical of our many, many escapades. We laughed a lot together.

Perhaps the "Urethra's Got Two" escapade best captures our rhythm, our in-tandem unity, our luscious, shared laughter at what can often be this crazy thing called life. We made up names to sneak into the beauty school (with the really nasty title). We paid pennies to have our nails painted. Denise gave me a moniker only *she* could produce off-the-cuff.

And it made us both so damn happy, that day, I can't even put it into words. All for $12.

Q: How long after Denise passed away did you begin to write this book?
A: My soul wrote a little of this book every single day for the ten years following her death. But you can't write about things on paper right away. You need time and distance so all the parts can settle and sort themselves out.

My grief at the loss of Denise exhibited itself in odd ways over the years. Sometimes, I'd hear a Jerry Jeff Walker song, and forget it—the rest of the day was spent on the couch with a five-pound bag of Peanut M&Ms. Once, I couldn't find the coffeepot for days and then discovered it in the back of the refrigerator. Another time, I pulled over to the side of the road because I couldn't remember why I was driving or where I was headed.

Eleven years after Denise's death, the tragedy at Columbine happened. I was paralyzed by the surrealness of the scene: kids jumping from windows, policemen running alongside the kids, the fact that it was a few miles from my house. Watching those kids run from a school building, terror in their bodies, their hands above their heads, it opened up something in me that allowed me to sit down with the notion: *I want to tell you a story about an extraordinary friendship.*

I can't explain why the two events—Columbine and Denise's death—converged for me. Sometimes a catalyst is just that. It's a catalyst and you act.

Q: What do you miss most about Denise? Do you approach new friendships differently now than you did before you met her?

A: I miss the "psychic connection," the knowing we understand each other even before we've spoken. I'm very lucky in that I've managed to accumulate decades-old friendships and more recently made new friends. But Denise and I could, truly, glance at each other across the wide expanse of a Costco warehouse—and know, in detail, exactly what the other was thinking. And then burst out laughing at the same time. I've never had that exact, symbiotic, unexplainable connection with any friend before or after her.

I don't approach new friendships any differently as a result of Denise. Each friendship is its own entity. I do, however, try to be open to new relationships and remember how much delight and potentially devilish fun there is in them. You can't force stuff, you know?

Q: *Did any authors influence the way you wrote* Cheap Cabernet?
A: Absolutely: Raymond Carver, Sherwood Anderson, Anne Lamott, Dorothy Parker, Chekhov, Barbara Kingsolver, Augusten Burroughs, David Sedaris, John Updike, Tolstoy. These writers and others make my heart stop when I read them.

Q: *The search for home is a powerful theme in this book. Could you talk about that?*
A: My parents never owned a home and we moved often. This one fact—throughout my childhood and into my young adulthood—unrelentingly unsettled me. While I was raising my own children it tortured me that I was unable to buy a house for them, no matter how hard I worked.

It caught me off guard that Denise struggled with the same fear: that someone else had control of the roof over her head. We were united in the fact that we couldn't relax because we didn't feel like we had a safe haven. People who live in houses they own have an extra self-confidence in a way they don't usually realize. They have a solid shore upon which to look at the rest of the world. Unlike decades-long renters, they can relax.

It was a strange adhesive that Denise and I shared: a visceral "Dorothy and The Wizard of Oz" anxiety. There's no place like home, there's no place like home. What if there is no home? What if you come home and find it's disappeared?

Q: One last, important question: Can you recommend a bottle of cabernet under $10 that doesn't leave you with a headache?
A: Spain makes great red wines in the $10 range. The 2007 Juan Gil Jumilla and the 2007 Las Rocas Garnacha are a couple of *great* wine secrets. I've seen them listed on restaurant wine lists at $40, but you can find them at liquor stores for about $10.

Spain was late getting on board with international marketing strategies. Just walk straight to the "Spain" aisle at your liquor store. Grab several in the $10 range. It's like drinking $25 Italian wine. Trust me.

Alternatively: Take a $7 Italian table wine. Fill a glass to the top with ice. Fill half the glass with the Italian table wine and the remainder of the glass with ice-cold Diet 7Up. Stir it with your finger. Trashy Women Sangria!

PERMISSIONS

ESCAPE (THE PINA COLADA SONG)
Words and Music by RUPERT HOLMES
© 1979 WB MUSIC CORP. and THE HOLMES LINE OF MUSIC, INC.
All Rights Administered by WB MUSIC CORP.
All Rights Reserved
Used by Permission of ALFRED PUBLISHING CO., INC.

IT SHOULD HAVE BEEN ME
Words and Music by EDDIE CURTIS
© 1959 (Renewed) UNICHAPPELL MUSIC, INC.
All Rights Reserved
Used by Permission of ALFRED PUBLISHING CO., INC.

PLASTIC
Words and Music by Shel Silverstein
TRO-© Copyright 1965 (Renewed) and 1968 (Renewed) Hollis Music,
    Inc.,
New York, NY
Used by Permission

TRASHY WOMEN
by Chris Wall
Copyright 1991 by Groper Music
Copyright Renewed.
International Copyright Secured.
All Rights Reserved.
Used by Permission of Groper Music.